Everyday Life in Tudor London

Everyday Life in Tudor London

STEPHEN PORTER

AMBERLEY

First published 2016

Amberley Publishing
The Hill, Stroud
Gloucestershire, GL5 4EP

www.amberley-books.com

British Library Cataloguing in Publication Data.
A catalogue record for this book is available from the British Library.

ISBN 978 1 4456 4586 5 (hardback)
ISBN 978 1 4456 4591 9 (ebook)

Map design by Thomas Bohm, User design.
Typesetting and Origination by Amberley Publishing.
Printed in the UK.

Contents

Acknowledgements 7

1 A Large and Magnificent City 9

2 An Organised Society 26

3 Continental Connections 46

4 In Sickness and in Poverty 64

5 Churches, Cloisters and Heretics 83

6 Dissolutions and New Foundations 99

7 Troubled Times 116

8 Prices and Trade 132

9 Cheerful Givers 152

10 Growing Pains 169

11 Recreation and Show 188

12 London around 1600 207

Notes 225

Bibliography 244

Index 251

Acknowledgements

I am very grateful to Jonathan Reeve at Amberley, for suggesting the idea for the book and supporting it thereafter, and to the staff there for producing it so efficiently and with such little fuss. For permission to reproduce images in their collections, I would like to thank the Royal Shakespeare Company, the Society of Antiquaries of London and the National Gallery of Art in Washington.

Once again, my wife Carolyn's uncanny ability to winkle out material from obscure and sometimes all-too-dark corners has stood me in very good stead. And when modern technology threatened to fail me, she stepped decisively into the breach and put both me and the technology to rights. What more can an author ask?

1

A Large and Magnificent City

'This is a powerful and busy city, carrying on a great trade with all countries. In the city are many people and many artisans, mostly goldsmiths and cloth-workers, also very beautiful women, but food is dear.' This impression of London was written by a German traveller, Gabriel Tetzel, in 1466. He was in the retinue of Leo of Rozmital, in Bohemia, together with a Bohemian squire known only as Schaseck, who summarised it more succinctly as a 'large and magnificent city'. The two men drew attention to the city's salient points: its size, populousness, bustle, overseas trade, the skilled artisans and beautiful women who lived there, and how expensive it was.[1] Their impressions were broadly correct, for London held an unrivalled position within England as by far its largest and wealthiest city, the centre of government and the law, the focus of power and patronage, with a diverse economy and many overseas connections.

Leo's journey through the Rhineland to the cloth-making cities of the Low Countries and then to the coast at Calais had provided Schaseck and Tetzel with a context in which to judge London. Tetzel described Brussels as 'a great city' and Mechelen as 'fine, large and well-built', and he was especially fascinated by Ghent, which he found to be 'a powerful city ... with a vast number of people living there'. Schaseck was impressed by Bruges and wrote that it was 'a large and beautiful city rich in merchandise, for there is access to it by land and sea from all the countries of the Christian world'. They did not visit Antwerp, which was then beginning to prosper and expand; it was the largest of the Flemish cities, with a population of 45,000, a little larger than Ghent and Brussels, and outstripping Bruges, which had 30,000 inhabitants. Antwerp was to be a significant trading connection for London in the coming century.[2]

By the end of the fifteenth century London's population was roughly 50,000, within a national figure of 2.6 million. In the context of northern Europe it was much more populous than Cologne, the largest city in the Holy Roman Empire, which was home to some 30,000 people, although it was only a quarter of the size of Paris in terms of number of inhabitants. Paris was one of five European cities with a population of over 100,000, the others being Naples, Milan, Constantinople, which was recovering after its capture by the Ottomans fifty years earlier, and Venice, the greatest trading city of Renaissance Europe.

Other visitors were prompted by London's size, wealth and the range of its functions to give positive reactions to the city. The Parisian scholar Domenico Mancini spent several months in London in 1482–3, leaving in early July 1483. He wrote an account of his stay at the request of his patron, Angelo Cato, archbishop of Vienne, and dated it 1 December 1483. Despite coming from a much larger city, Mancini was fascinated by London, which he described as 'the royal city and capital of the whole kingdom both in size and wealth' which was 'so famous throughout the world'. In 1497 Andreas Franciscius, a Venetian, commented on the advantages that the tidal flow of the Thames gave the city, which, he thought, had a position that was 'so pleasant and delightful that it would be hard to find one more convenient and attractive'. Around 1500 another Venetian, Andrea Trevisano, wrote that London was 'truly the metropolis of England' and that 'Londoners live comfortably, and, it appears to me, that there are not fewer inhabitants than at Florence or Rome'. He, too, noted the significance of the tides, which gave London 'all the advantages to be desired in a maritime town', with vessels of 100 tons able to reach the city.[3]

Verses by a Scottish poet composed around the time of Trevisano's visit extolled this 'Sovereign of cities', which was 'the flour of Cities all', for its beauty, as 'semeliest in sight', wealth and trade, with 'merchauntis full of substaunce and myght', and its river, which was busy with 'many a barge ... many a ship'. Also to be admired were the bridge, the Tower with its artillery, and the churches and their 'wele sowynyng' bells; while on its streets were the nobility and their 'most delectable lusty ladies bright', knights dressed in velvet gowns wearing chains of fine gold, and the clergy, 'famous prelatis in habitis clericall'. Finally, he praised the city's 'pryncely governaunce', under its mayor, for 'No Lord of Parys, Venyce, or Floraunce In dignytie or honoure goeth to hym nye'. A generation later John Major, or Mair, the author of the first authoritative history of Scotland, described it as 'the largest and the fairest in its situation' of all the cities in the British Isles. Major attributed its wealth chiefly to three things: the law courts, the almost constant presence of the monarch, 'who at his own expense provides for a great household and supplies to them all their food', and, most importantly, 'a great concurrence of merchants'. According to Major 'merchant vessels from every part of Europe' could be seen there, and 'ships (which they call "barges") in great numbers' plied between the city and the sea.[4]

London's domestic dominance in terms of size was such that at the opening of the sixteenth century it was four times larger than Norwich, the largest provincial city, and far bigger than the other regional centres of York, Bristol, Salisbury, Exeter, Newcastle and Coventry, whose populations ranged from 6,000 to 10,000. The disparity between London and England's other cities was even greater in terms of wealth. The tax yield from the city in the national taxation levied in 1523–7 was £16,675, while from Norwich it was £1,704 and from Bristol £1,072. No other city yielded as much as £1,000, and of the provincial capitals Coventry paid £974, Exeter £855, Salisbury £852 and York only £379. Newcastle, Chester, Carlisle and Durham were exempt – it is likely that Newcastle would have been fourth in the list of cities in terms of yield had it been taxed. But even when allowance is made for the four cities which were not assessed, London paid more tax than the total received from the next twenty-nine cities.[5]

Its population had recovered only slowly from the death toll during the Black Death in 1348–9, which had killed at least a third and possibly more than a half of its pre-plague population of approximately 80,000. The plague recurred intermittently thereafter. Another outbreak in 1361 killed roughly one third of the depleted population and was followed by a third epidemic in 1368, and in 1375 'a large number of Londoners, from among the wealthier and more eminent citizens, died in the pestilence'.[6] The burial ground at Smithfield, acquired especially for the emergency caused by the Black Death, was used in 1361 and again in the mid-fifteenth century. Not until the mid-sixteenth century did London's population return to its pre-Black Death level. Yet during the period of the Tudor dynasty, from 1485 until 1603, despite economic vicissitudes, intermittent outbreaks of the sweating sickness, influenza and, most destructive of all, recurrent visitations of the plague, it forged ahead, especially during the later sixteenth century, and by 1600 its population had increased to around 200,000 people.

The Tudor era began on 22 August 1485, when Henry Tudor defeated Richard III at the Battle of Bosworth; Richard was killed during the battle and the victor took the throne as Henry VII. To make his position absolutely certain Henry needed to placate London, for no ruler could govern successfully without its consent and financial support. During the Wars of the Roses over the previous thirty years Londoners and their rulers had been inclined to favour the Yorkists. They endured a bombardment from a Lancastrian force in 1460, and after they heard of Edward IV's victory at the Battle of Tewkesbury in 1471 they resisted a Lancastrian army of 5,000 men complete with a train of artillery, which attacked the defences at London Bridge, burning some houses on the bridge, and 'at Allgate and Bysshoppis gate, where they set howsis a fyre; but the Cite Issued owte vpon theym and slewe many of theym at these forsaid Gates; and anoon they fled'. When Edward reached London he was 'very joyfully received by the whole city'. Those events had taken place only fourteen years before the arrival of Henry and his army, which included sizeable contingents of French and Breton troops and contained, according to the chronicler Philippe de Commynes, 'three thousand of the most unruly men that could be found and enlisted in Normandy'.[7] Londoners perhaps feared the sack of their city, with unrestrained troops running amok, assaulting them and plundering their houses, or a compulsory levy to pay the troops, backed by the threat of force. The fear of disorder was conveyed in a peremptory order issued by the Mayor four days after the battle, instructing soldiers and 'idle people which have no masters to wait upon' to leave the city within just three hours of his proclamation, and imposing a nine-to-five curfew.[8] So it may have been with some apprehension that the Mayor and his fellow aldermen, the city's rulers, and the senior figures of its livery companies greeted the new Lancastrian king at Shoreditch. He had been out of England for twenty-five years and so was not in touch with the Londoners' mood.

In fact, it was not the conduct of his troops which marred the beginning of the king's reign but the sudden onset of 'a disease then new, which by the accidents and manner thereof they called the sweating-sickness'.[9] The disease 'swept the whole country; it was a baleful affliction and one which no previous age had experienced' and its impact was all the greater because most of its victims died within twenty-four hours of displaying the symptoms.[10] The outbreak began around 21 September, and by 23 September the Mayor, Thomas Hill, died. On the following day a Common Council was held, at which Sir William Stokker was chosen to serve the remainder of the mayoral year, who took the oath on 26 September. But two days later he, too, died, and so another Common Council was called and John Warde chosen. He survived the short period until the end of the term, but 'besyde the ij mayrs ... John Stokker, Thomas Breten, Richard Rawson, Thomas Norland, Aldermen, and many worshipfull comoners' also died.[11] Six of the twenty-four aldermen were carried off within the space of a few days, which must have been disruptive.

An alderman was the senior official each representing one of the twenty-four wards into which the City was divided for administrative purposes, and a quarter of this figure were carried off within the space of a few days, which must have been disruptive. The Court of Aldermen was the city's ruling body, providing the agenda for the much larger Common Council, the legislative body. In 1485, because of the number of deaths, thirty-three men served as aldermen: eight mercers, seven drapers, four grocers, three goldsmiths, two fishmongers, two skinners, two salters, two tailors, an ironmonger, a haberdasher and the prior of Holy Trinity, Aldgate. Clearly, a range of trades produced men successful enough to hold the office, with the time and cost involved, and no one trade was dominant. The Mayor was chosen annually from among the aldermen, as were the two men who served in the junior office of sheriff. In the fifteenth century an alderman held the office of Mayor once, or at most twice. Nor did dynasties emerge among the civic elite, for the second or third generations of a successful family typically chose to invest in land and become country landowners rather than continue a civic dynasty. And so London did not have over-mighty families that vied with each other for power and influence within the city.

The sweating-sickness subsided by late October, upon which the king returned. His coronation took place in Westminster Abbey on 30 October, after the customary procession through the city. It was a magnificent event. Purchases made by the steward of the king's household included cloth of gold at £8 per yard, white cloth of gold at between £1 13s 4d and £2 per yard, blue cloth of gold at £3 16s 8d per yard and green cloth of gold at £3 per yard. Among his other procurements was scarlet cloth of gold at between 7s and 14s per yard, bought from several 'citezyns and taillors'.[12] Lavish expenditure on ceremonies did much to foster good relations between court and city. The royal household and the courtiers were important customers for the merchants and artisans, buying not only fine fabrics but furnishings, plate, gems, a range of luxury goods and food and drink; visitors commented on the scale and duration of the banquets. As for the general cost of living, the concentration of people and wealth created a high level of demand, and London drew its supplies from a large hinterland – transport costs were a significant factor. But prices were thought to be high not only in London but in England generally. In 1497 the Milanese ambassador grumbled that 'everything costs incomparably more in this kingdom than in any other place'.[13]

England's capital city was described by Mancini as 'stretched out lengthwise beside the river, and lies partly on a level and partly on a slope. Beginning to rise from the banks of the Thames with a gentle and easy incline as much as half of the town is slanting towards the river'; that is, on the rising ground of the two low hills of Ludgate Hill and Cornhill. Along the river were 'enormous warehouses for imported goods: also numerous cranes of remarkable size to unload merchandise from ships'.[14] As well as overseas trade, London was busy handling vessels bringing cargoes from around the coast and river traffic on the Thames. Among the wharves along the Thames were two docks, Billingsgate below the bridge and Queenhithe upstream from it. Billingsgate had developed during the ninth century as a landing place, and a jetty was erected *c.*1000. Queenhithe was given to the citizens of London in the thirteenth century and was enlarged in 1471. Its position made it unsuitable for the transhipment of goods to and from sea-going vessels, which were restricted to the Thames below the bridge, but it was an important dock for river vessels from ports upstream, handling grain, malt and other produce.

The core of the city was enclosed within defensive walls, but the buildings had long ago spilled beyond them in the west, outside Ludgate and Newgate, and, according to Mancini, to its north were 'open fields stretching out towards other suburbs'. On the east side was a lesser, but expanding, development at Whitechapel, beyond Aldgate. From that gate the walls ran south to what Mancini described as 'a very strong citadel overlooking the river, they call it the Tower of London. From the Tower to Westminster, which is on the western side and also overlooking the river, is a journey of two thousand paces.' He added that 'the intervening space is not all included in the city, as, save for a thousand paces, the rest is a suburb continuing uninterruptedly from the metropolis and differing in appearance very slightly from it'. This stretch was along the line of the Strand, connecting the City with Westminster. Straddling the City's boundary between the Thames and Holborn was the developing legal quarter, with the four Inns of Court and the nine or ten Inns of Chancery that were attached to them. Across the bridge 'on flat and low land' was Southwark, which consisted of a ribbon development running south from the bridge and a built-up strip alongside the river. It impressed Mancini as 'a suburb remarkable for its streets and buildings, which, if it were surrounded by walls, might be called a second city'.[15] Indeed, it was larger than all but half a dozen of the provincial cities, with a population of roughly 8,000; because it was outside the City's jurisdiction until 1550, it was one of the districts where the 'strangers' lived, especially the Flemish. Southwark was home to perhaps 400 of the 3,400 aliens in the city around 1485. It was known for its many alehouses and brothels; in 1504 eighteen brothels there were closed down, but they soon reopened. Because of those living in the Bishop of Winchester's Clink Liberty, the prostitutes were known as 'Winchester Geese'; an alternative name was 'Flemish Frows'. St Katherine's, east of the Tower, was another suburb beyond the City where the Flemish congregated. Andreas Franciscius wrote that London's suburbs 'are so large that they greatly increase its circuit'; he estimated the city's circumference to be three miles.[16]

Mancini described the city in terms of three paved streets running westwards from Tower Hill, which were 'the busiest in the whole city and almost straight'. The lowest of the three was Thames Street, which ran parallel to the river from Tower Hill to a point close to where the River Fleet entered the Thames. It connected the wharves and was 'occupied by liquid and weighty commodities: there are to be found all manner of minerals, wines, honey, pitch, wax, flax, ropes, thread, grain, fish, and other distasteful goods'. The second thoroughfare was along the line of Tower Street, East Cheap, Candlewick Street, Budge Row and Watling Street, leading to St Paul's churchyard. According to Mancini, there 'you will find hardly anything for sale but cloths'; the textile trades were a major element in London's economy. His third street, 'which touches the centre of the town and runs on a level', did not actually originate at Tower Hill but ran from east to west along Fenchurch Street, Poultry and Cheapside, which effectively formed the city's high street and its widest thoroughfare, to Newgate Street. Mancini contrasted the various businesses in this third street with those in the other two long ones, with the observation that 'there is traffic in more precious wares, such as gold and silver cups, dyed stuffs, various silks, carpets, tapestry, and much other exotic merchandise'.[17] Cheapside was at the heart of a wealthy district that was the centre of the mercery trades and dealers in precious metals, and because of its proximity to both St Paul's and the seat of the city's government at Guildhall it was the setting for jousts, tournaments and processions, royal, religious and civic.

The shops of the goldsmiths and silversmiths naturally attracted attention and were taken to reflect the wealth of the country. Schaseck wrote that London contained 'a great number of goldsmiths, more than I have ever seen. The masters alone, without the journeymen, amount to four hundred, but they are never idle, for the size of the city and its wealth provide them with work in abundance.' Franciscius's impression was that 'working in wrought silver, tin or white lead is very expert here, and perhaps the finest I have ever seen'.[18] The entourage of Wilmolt von Schaumburg reacted in a similar way during a visit in 1489, for they thought that the goldsmiths' shops contained more precious plate than they had seen among all of the princes in Germany. An Italian analogy was provided by Trevisano, who reported that in Cheapside, which he misidentified as the Strand, there were fifty-two goldsmiths' shops, 'so rich and full of silver vessels, great and small, that in all the shops in Milan, Rome, Venice, and Florence put together, I do not think there would be found so many of the magnificence that are to be seen in London'.[19] Cheapside's primacy in the trade was demonstrated by the erection of Goldsmiths' Row in 1491 by Thomas Wood. The row contained ten houses and fourteen shops, and was four storeys high, 'uniformly built', with decoration on the street front that included the Goldsmiths' arms and lead figures of woodmen 'riding on monstrous beasts'. It was greatly admired, and at the end of the sixteenth century John Stow, topographer of London and a chronicler of its history, proudly described it as 'the most beautiful frame of fair houses and shops that be within the walls of London, or elsewhere in England'.[20]

London Bridge could also be described as a shopping street. It was built between 1176 and 1212, and a chapel dedicated to St Thomas à Becket, the City's patron saint, was built on it in the early thirteenth century and rebuilt in 1384–97. The bridge was just over 300 yards long, and Schasek described it as 'a long stone bridge, along whose whole length houses have been built'. In fact, many of them contained shops; by 1358 there were 138 shops, occupying prime sites as most travellers between London and

Southwark crossed the bridge rather than take a boat. Mancini wrote that on it were 'houses and several gates with portcullises: the dwelling-houses are built above workshops and belong to diverse sorts of craftsmen'. Franciscius was more fulsome with his praise. Having written that the Tower was 'a very strongly defended castle on the banks of the river', he went on, 'There are also other great buildings, and especially a beautiful and convenient bridge over the Thames, of many marble [sic] arches, which has on it many shops built of stone and even a church of considerable size. Nowhere have I seen a finer or more richly built bridge.'[21]

Franciscius also wrote that throughout the city 'are to be seen many workshops of craftsmen in all sorts of mechanical arts, to such an extent that there is hardly a street which is not graced by some shop or the like'. That gave the impression of an industrious population and a city that was 'exceedingly prosperous and well-stocked'. But the narrowness and condition of the streets tended to offset such favourable impressions, because they were all 'so badly paved that they get wet at the slightest quantity of water, and this happens very frequently owing to the large numbers of cattle carrying water, as well as on account of the rain'. The 'cattle' probably were the donkeys used by the water carriers. Because of the rain and spillage, and the fact that the streets did not drain well, a 'vast amount of evil-smelling mud is formed, which does not disappear quickly but lasts a long time, in fact nearly the whole year round. The citizens, therefore, in order to remove mud and filth from their boots, are accustomed to spread fresh rushes on the floors of all houses.'[22] The humanist scholar Desiderius Erasmus lived in London on several occasions during the early sixteenth century and he criticised that practice, because although the rushes were renewed occasionally it was done 'so as to leave a basic layer, sometimes for twenty years, under which fester spittle, vomit, dogs' urine and men's too, dregs of beer and cast-off bits of fish, and other unspeakable kinds of filth'.[23] London's environment was a smelly one, both without doors and within.

The atmosphere created by the narrow, crowded streets and tall houses, generally of three storeys in the centre of the city, was alluded to by Thomas More in a letter which he sent in 1504 to John Colet, who held the living of St Dunstan's in Stepney, and was soon to be made Dean of St Paul's. More contrasted rural life, which was then applicable to Stepney, with that in the city, where his own household was in Bucklesbury, close to St Stephen Walbrook church. One shortcoming of living in the city was that 'houses block out from us I know not how large a measure of the light, and do not permit us to see the heavens. And the round horizon does not limit the air but the lofty roofs.'[24] The sense of claustrophobia was increased by the upper storeys projecting above the street, a practice known as jettying; although civic ordinances regulated the height of such jetties, some householders were reported because theirs were too low and so presented a hazard to unwary passers-by, especially those on horseback.

In his account of the ideal commonwealth of *Utopia*, which he published in 1516, More wrote that in its chief city of Amaurote the 'very commodious and handsome' streets were twenty feet wide. But a street twenty feet wide was a narrow one; the widths specified for the rebuilding after the Great Fire of 1666 were that even the 'least' of the three categories of streets should be twenty-five or thirty feet wide, and that alleys were to be at least sixteen feet wide. Much had occurred in terms of town planning since the early sixteenth century, both in theory and practice, but in any context More showed limited ambition for his 'ideal' streets, surely reflecting his experience of early Tudor London.[25] Yet there were some similarities between the environments of More's native city and his imagined one, for London, according to Schasek, contained 'elegant gardens, planted with various trees and flowers, which are not found in other countries'. In Amaurote, behind the houses 'through the whole length of the street, lie large gardens enclosed round about with the back part of the streets', and its citizens 'set great store by their gardens. In them they have vineyards, all manner of fruit, herbs, and flowers, so pleasant, so well furnished, and so finely kept, that I never saw thing more fruitful nor better trimmed in any place.'[26] As well as the plots adjoining the citizens' houses in London, where they grew fruit and vegetables, there were gardens with flowers and herbs at the grand houses and in the monastic complexes within and around the city.

The area available for gardens had increased as the pressure on space was reduced by the fall in population in the aftermath of the Black Death. Even in and around Cheapside the number of houses declined and that trend was reversed only after the mid-sixteenth century.[27] If that were the case in this central and economically vibrant district, then other areas across the city were likely to have experienced a similar pattern.

Most of the houses were timber-framed, with lath and plaster infilling and perhaps an outer covering of plaster; brick was used and the chimneys were of stone. Trevisano described the houses as being 'of timber or brick, like the French', and not in the Italian style. Mario Savorgnano, a Venetian, was briefly in London in 1531 and his impression was that the houses 'are in very great number, but ugly, and half the materials of wood, nor are the streets wide'. Franciscius described how the upper floors were carried on six-inch oak beams 'inserted in the walls the same distance apart as their own breadth'.[28] The roofs were tiled, following regulations of the thirteenth century designed to reduce the incidence of fire. After a number of blazes the London Assize of 1212 stated that 'whosoever wishes to build, let him take care, as he loveth himself and his goods, that he roof not with reed, nor rush, straw nor stubble, but with tile only, or shingle or boards, or if it may be with lead or plastered straw'.[29] Despite the roofing regulations, which were enforced, fires occasionally erupted within the city. In 1502 there was 'a great fier at the ende of London Bridge next to St. Magnus', and the following year saw 'many grete fyeres in London in dyvers places, as at the brigge, Austyn freeres, sent Martyns grante, and Buttoll wharf' and in 1506 there was 'a great fier ... betwene the Custome Howsse and Billinsgate, that did great hurte'.[30] Tiles were imported from the Low Countries, as were bricks, although London was also supplied by domestic brick- and tile-makers. Paving stones were also imported for the ground floors of houses. In November 1480 the cargo of *The Mary*, of London, included 2,000 paving-tiles, and in September 1481 a ship from Middelburg unloaded twice that quantity at London.[31] Window glass, too, was brought in from Holland, Normandy and Venice. A building at Coldharbour, contracted for in 1485, was to be glazed with 'dusche glasse', 'Venys glasse', English and Normandy glass, indicating a degree of finesse in the choice of glass for the windows of the various rooms.[32] Wainscot was another relatively expensive item for buildings that was becoming more popular and, it was said, was imported, together with items of furniture: 'The Duchemen bryng over ... Weynskot ready wrought, as Nayles, Lockes, Baskettes, Cubbordes, Stooles, Tables, Chestes.'[33]

Because of the restricted space and the narrowness of the streets, it was convenient to prepare the timber frame for a building in an open space some distance away – even outside the city – before being taken to the site for assembly. A contract of 1510 to build a two-storey house in London, twenty-two feet wide and forty feet deep, with a jetty projecting from the upper storey, provided that the house 'shalbe in all thinges redy made and fraymed to the setting upp in Kinges Towne upon Thamys, and so from thens to be brought and sett up in London'. The owner was to pay the cost of the carriage, along the Thames from Kingston and then to the site.[34]

Not all property was in good repair and the buildings were replaced from time to time. A house in Thames Street was described in 1507 as being 'olde, febyll, ruinous, and at great decay', and when a new lease was granted in that year the lessees agreed to pull it down and replace it with 'a substaunciall newe tenement' of three storeys, built with 'gode and substaunciall newe tymbir'. The building was to contain a shop, a solar (an upper chamber), hall, parlour, kitchen, chambers and a privy, which the lessees undertook to see 'voydid and made clene from tyme to tyme and as oftyn as nede shall require'.[35] The description suggests that the property was characteristic of early Tudor London, with a shop on the street front and other rooms arranged over three storeys. Typically, there were workshops behind the rooms fronting the street and in some cases upstairs, to benefit from the light. The size of the buildings could be deceptive, according to Mancini, who found that 'the dwelling houses are built above workshops' and that the shops were 'not encumbered with merchandise only at the entrance; but in the inmost quarters there are spacious depositories, where the goods are heaped up, stowed and packed away as honey may be seen in cells'.[36]

That deceptiveness also concealed some of the larger and grander houses, those owned by the merchants and other wealthy citizens, which were inconspicuous, with perhaps only a modest gatehouse on the street front. Franciscius discovered this and commented that London contained 'very many mansions, which do not, however, seem very large from the outside, but inside they contain a great number of rooms and garrets and are quite considerable'.[37] Among the largest was Crosby Hall, built in 1466 on the east side of Bishopsgate by Sir John Crosby, a rich wool merchant, which Stow described as 'very large and beautiful, and the highest at that time in London'.[38] The house which Thomas More and his family occupied in Bucklesbury was also a 'great mansion', although until around 1495 it had been a public weigh-house and was then divided into tenements, until More managed to consolidate them into a single dwelling. Known as the Barge, it contained a great hall on the ground floor and on the first floor a gallery, a great chamber, which was the main reception room, and a parlour, chiefly for the family's use. Also on the upper floors were bedchambers, More's study, a counting house, where business documents were stored, and a chapel. On the ground floor were the service rooms, such as kitchen, pantry and larder; a summer parlour probably opened on to the relatively large garden.[39]

Opposite the Barge in Bucklesbury was Serne's Tower, which belonged to the Crown; in 1344 Edward III 'appointed his exchange of moneys therein to be kept', because it was a secure building located in the heart of the city. Private towers were not a feature of the skyline. The first citizen to build one was Sir John Champneys, Mayor in 1534–5, who added a brick tower to his house at the east end of Eastcheap, which John Stow mentioned as 'the first that I ever heard of in any private man's house, to overlook his neighbours in this city'.[40]

One of More's chief political rivals from the late 1520s was Thomas Cromwell, who lived from *c.*1522 in a house close to the city wall, within the precincts of the Augustine friary established in the thirteenth century, commonly known as the Austin Friars. The house was of three storeys and contained fourteen rooms. Success in the service of Cardinal Wolsey and then in that of the king brought Cromwell increasing wealth, part of which he invested in property by buying, in 1532, further houses close by fronting

Throgmorton Street. These he improved, and he also enlarged his garden by summarily moving the fence separating his property from those of his neighbours by twenty-two feet. He did not stop there and caused his men to reposition the house of Thomas Stow, in a process later described by his son John: 'This house they loosed from the ground, and bare upon rollers into my father's garden twenty-two feet, ere my father heard thereof.' When Thomas asked the surveyors directing the work what was going on, he was told 'that their master Sir Thomas commanded them so to do'. Both the house and the fences were moved arbitrarily and without warning, and because of Cromwell's status and position 'no man durst argue the matter, but each man lost his land'. Indeed, the incident might have passed without record but for the fact that when John compiled his *Survey of London* more than sixty years later the indignity which his father had suffered still rankled so much that he included this account in his description of the city. This was just a part of Cromwell's building programme, which culminated in an impressive new mansion built around three courtyards and containing fifty rooms; it cost at least £1,000.[41]

The size of Cromwell's new house was not at all typical and few other houses in the city were on such a scale, yet new construction within the walls and the extensive use of brick in the building were part of wider processes, reflecting the city's growth. It attracted an increasing number of the landed aristocracy and gentry, who had established seventy-five town houses there by 1520. Senior clergymen, too, maintained a house, known rather confusingly as an inn, in the city or its suburbs.

Scattered around the city among the houses, shops and warehouses stood more than a hundred churches, with their towers and spires, and there were also the buildings of thirty-nine religious foundations. Schaseck was moved to write that he had not seen 'more beautiful churches anywhere since we left home. Nor is a greater number of holy relics preserved and displayed in any city than here. In London there are twenty gilded tombs, decorated with precious stones.' Mancini's summary of the city's remarkable features included 'the adornment and opulence of the churches', and von Schaumburg and his party were shown churches 'the like of which they had never seen in any other kingdom or German land'.[42] Towering above them all was the great cathedral of St Paul's, begun towards the end of the twelfth century and, perhaps unsurprisingly given its scale, not finished until the mid-fourteenth century. The cathedral was indeed a large and impressive building, 596 feet long, with a nave of twelve bays which was 100 feet wide, and with a central tower topped by a tall slender spire that was 589 feet high. A detached bell tower stood at the north-east corner of the precinct, near Cheapside, and in the angle between the choir and the north transept was an open-air pulpit known as Paul's Cross, where, explained Sebastian Giustinian, the Venetian ambassador, 'the whole city is in the habit of assembling with the magistrates'.[43] South of the cathedral on the riverfront stood Baynard's Castle, rebuilt by Humphrey, Duke of Gloucester, after a fire in 1428. It consisted of four ranges enclosing a courtyard, with polygonal towers at the corners; Henry VII added five projecting towers to the riverfront *c.* 1501. Even so, it was a much less imposing building than St Paul's.

The Crown's only rival to the cathedral in London itself was the fortress of the Tower, a large and imposing complex covering eighteen acres, with concentric stone walls encircling the White Tower. Within the walls were a palace and military storehouses, as well as the workshops of the Royal Mint, depositories for bullion and government records, and the royal wardrobe, whose custody and maintenance of the royal household's possessions included care of the monarch's collection of exotic animals, including lions, leopards and bears. In 1515 the Venetian ambassador Piero Pasqualigo and his retinue were shown the menagerie and 'the king's bronze artillery, mounted on four hundred carriages, very fine and remarkable; also bows and arrows, and pikes for 40,000 infantry'.[44] As well as being a stronghold with artillery and a garrison, the Tower served as the state's prison and had a presence that could be used to intimidate the citizens. As could financial and legal pressure: three former Mayors were among the aldermen imprisoned by Henry VII's financial enforcers, Richard Empson and Edmund Dudley, in the closing years of his reign. Among those released on the king's death in 1509 was Sir William Capel, who had been Mayor in 1503 and was to be again in 1510. There were more strands to London's life and government than met the eyes of visitors.

The royal enclave was at Westminster, which was therefore the true capital of England. Edward the Confessor had re-founded the abbey of St Peter in the eleventh century and was buried in the newly built abbey church in January 1066. The church became a burial place for English monarchs, and from the coronation of Edward's successor, Harold II, all future rulers were crowned there. The exception was Edward V, who was deposed after a short reign in 1483, before his coronation. Henry III began the process of rebuilding the church, in a French style, and developed the cult of the Confessor, whose remains were placed in an imposing and richly decorated tomb. Schasek was so impressed by the church that he wrote that he had never seen 'more delicate and elegant carving' anywhere and described the Confessor's tomb as 'a golden tomb, large and adorned with gold and most precious stones'. The rebuilding of the church was not finished when Henry III died in 1272, and work thereafter was intermittent, with the west window and the clerestorey windows not installed until 1496; a new Lady chapel was erected between 1503 and 1510, replacing the early thirteenth-century one. It was begun by Henry VII and completed as his chantry chapel after his death in 1509, in a bold perpendicular style with a splendid fan vault, and containing the tomb and effigies of Henry VII and his queen, Elizabeth of York, made by the Italian sculptor Pietro Torrigiano.

Edward the Confessor also built a new palace at Westminster, which subsequent monarchs adopted as one of their principal residences; William II added Westminster Hall to the buildings in 1097–99 and it was remodelled in 1394–1401. Westminster also became the centre of the administration of justice with the establishment there of the central courts, as the body of common law evolved following the organisation of the English judicial system by Henry II. It was also the meeting place of Parliament, with the House of Lords assembling in the Queen's Chamber and the Commons in the abbey's chapter-house. To the north of the palace was York Place, the London inn of the archbishops of York. Around these clusters of ecclesiastical and royal buildings a community grew up which by 1520 was home to roughly 3,000 people and was served by a parish church dedicated to St Margaret. Westminster marked the limit of the metropolis upstream from London, but downstream creeping development continued beyond St Katherine's Hospital. Savorgnano's impression was that 'the population of London is immense, and comprises many artificers ... it is a very rich, populous, and mercantile city, but not beautiful'.[45]

2

An Organised Society

While the city's size and wealth impressed visitors, Londoners did not always give them a favourable impression. This also applied to the English generally because of their perceived pride and belligerence, but the citizens' industriousness was acknowledged and the diversity of the city's economy recognised. In judging the attitudes and disposition of the citizens, visitors were hampered by language difficulties and, for some of them, the shortness of their stay. They were unlikely to meet many people outside their own circle and gained an impression by questioning their hosts, as well as from observation, although they may not have fully understood and correctly interpreted what they saw.

Andreas Franciscius complained to his friend Jacobus Sansonus: 'Londoners have such fierce tempers and wicked dispositions that they not only despise the way in which Italians live, but actually pursue them with uncontrolled hatred.' He contrasted the way in which foreigners were received in Bruges, where they were 'treated with consideration by everybody', with the reactions of Londoners, who 'look askance at us by day, and at night they sometimes drive us off with kicks and blows of the truncheon'.[1] This was true more generally, according to Andrea Trevisano, who complained that 'the English are great lovers of themselves, and of everything belonging to them'. They acted as though there were no other men than themselves and no other country but England; a handsome foreigner was said to resemble an Englishman, with the comment that 'it is a great pity that he is not an Englishman', while if they shared any delicacy with a foreigner he would be asked 'whether such a thing is made in *their* country?'[2]

Individuals' experiences quite naturally coloured their reactions to London. In 1509 Andrew Badoer was appointed by the Doge to undertake a diplomatic mission to the city. To avoid attracting attention he travelled in the clothes he stood up in, two shirts worn one over the other and 'a certain doublet in the English fashion, all patched and moth eaten, without purse or pocket', and so was obliged to buy a complete outfit appropriate to the dignity of an ambassador when he arrived in London. He was mortified to find that no silks were made in England but were imported from Genoa, Florence and Lucca, so he had to 'take what I could get, and shut my eyes'. The clothes were costly, but even worse than the expense were the materials and the cut of the garments, which he would not be able to wear when he returned to Venice, 'my neighbours' gowns being of silk, and my own of frieze ... [and] it is all made more according to the English fashion than that of Italy'.[3] Franciscius also damned the style of dress with faint praise: 'They dress in the French fashion, except that their suits are more full, and, accordingly, more out of shape.'[4] Londoners would have taken that as a derogatory remark, for they despised French fashions. When Henry VIII replaced several senior members of his household in 1519, Edward Hall, a London lawyer, rejoiced and wrote that those displaced were unpopular because they were 'all French in eating, drinking and apparel, yea, and in the French vices and brags'.[5]

Visitors' reactions to English women were quite different. Schasek's summary of the country included the terse comment that it 'breeds women and maidens of outstanding beauty' and the Scotsman who composed the panegyric to London around 1500 mentioned its rich merchants' fair wives 'right lovesome, white and small'. In 1531, Mario Savorgnano was also much taken by the women's appearance: 'The women are all extremely handsome, nor did I ever see the like, save at Augsburg, and their head-gear is graceful.' Nikolaus von Popplau, in 1484, had gone further. Having noted that English women were very beautiful, as well as well-disposed towards Germans and willing to flirt with them, he added that they 'are like devils once their desires are roused, and when they take a fancy to someone whom they can trust they grow quite blind and wild with love, more than the women of any other nation'. His impression was that they were very forward, and when someone entered an inn the women came over to greet him and offer their lips to kiss. He wrote that kissing went on in the house, the street and even in the church. This may have been a misunderstanding derived from a cultural confusion. Other travellers noted the practice of using a kiss as a greeting, with guests expected to kiss the hostess and her whole household both when they arrived and when they left. Erasmus described the practice in 1499, adding that 'whenever a meeting takes place there is kissing in abundance; in fact whatever way you turn, you are never without it'. This was a fashion which, he thought, 'cannot be commended enough', while Schasek realised that it was the equivalent of shaking hands, which the English did not do. The practice continued, and Nicander Nucius, who was in London in 1545, wrote that women were kissed on the mouth not only by 'those who are of the same family and household ... but even those too who have never seen them. And to themselves this appears by no means indecent.'[6]

Savorgnano was also fascinated by the social contacts between men and women, and wrote that if a man spoke once or twice to a woman in the street, it was customary for him to take her to a tavern 'where all persons go without any reserve', or to 'some other place'. Her husband's reaction was not to take it amiss, 'but remaining obliged to you, and always thanking you, and if he sees you with her he departs'. Another aspect he noted was that if a man gave a woman flowers, she should wear them for three months, 'and should the man find her without them, he may exact what fine he pleases, so that you constantly see women with flowers of every sort'.[7] Yet from another perspective the men were said to be very protective of their wives. Andrea Trevisano wrote that 'the English keep a very jealous guard over their wives', but added rather enigmatically that 'everything may be compensated in the end, by the power of money'. He was critical of the emotional reserve and lack of outward affection that the English displayed, which was 'strongly manifested towards their children' because when they were seven or nine years old they 'put them out, both males and females, to hard service in the houses of other people, binding them generally for another 7 or 9 years'. He was here describing the apprenticeship system in place for the boys and domestic or other service for the girls, but he was mistaken about the ages of those who were apprenticed: the boys were in their mid-teens when they were bound to their master and served at least seven years, so that they were in their early twenties when they completed their term. Trevisano's references to the apprentices doing 'all the most menial offices' and the 'hard service' that they undertook were probably correct, but the purpose of the apprenticeship was to learn the trade or craft.[8] The stipulations of the Mercers' Company in 1510 were that a prospective apprentice should be at least sixteen years old, tall, lithe of limb and not physically handicapped, in other words someone who could carry out substantial work. Yet the ideal of big strapping youths was challenged by the reality that 'daily there be presented and also admitted divers apprentices which be very little in growing or stature'.[9]

After an apprentice had completed his term he could become a member of the appropriate livery company and a freeman of the City, which entitled him to set up in business on his own account, if that was feasible, and gave him the vote and qualification to hold municipal office. Roughly 90 per cent of those who held the freedom had achieved the status through completing an apprenticeship, although it could be claimed by a freeman's son or awarded to someone through a company, with payment of a fee.

The livery companies could attempt to restrict the numbers in their trades by imposing a high fee when an apprentice was enrolled, or setting other requirements. In 1478 the Goldsmiths' Company ordered its members not to take an apprentice 'wtout he canne writte and Rede', repeating the order before the end of the century, and the Ironmongers' Company set a similar literacy test with the stipulation that new apprentices had to register their names 'with theire owne hands, yf they can write'. The Mercers' Company regulations of 1489 required that apprentices 'must be able to read or write, or be taught these skills'. Once the apprenticeship was completed, the companies could limit the number who went into business independently by demanding that its members should hold a minimum value of goods before they set up in trade. In

1480 the Grocers' Company stipulated that the figure should be £40, and in 1503 the Mercers imposed a minimum of £100 in goods because many members 'for lack of a sufficient beginning have decayed and undone themselves'. Such restrictions could apply to aspiring journeymen at any age, but young men who had recently completed their apprenticeship would clearly have found them especially difficult to satisfy. One solution was a partnership, allowed by the Mercers in 1486 'for ii parsons taking oon shop to gether' with a half of the entry fee deferred, and another possibility was to set up in business with 'borrowed wares'.[10]

Some of those who were entitled to open a business never raised sufficient means to do so, and a typical City household would consist of the master, his wife and children, one or more journeymen and apprentices. It normally consisted of four or five people in total. The numbers of journeymen and apprentices depended on the master's status; his economic position was a constraint on the numbers that he could maintain, and so a limitation on the size of his business. Apprentices could benefit by a legacy from their master, allowing them to achieve financial independence. This also applied to widows, and although women were legally able to enrol as apprentices, in practice that was rare, so that many women who ran a business did so after they had been widowed. Yet Nicander Nucius was impressed by the extent of women's involvement in business, commenting that 'one may see in the markets and streets of the city married women and damsels employed in arts, and barterings and affairs of trade, undisguisedly'.[11]

Because of the need to complete an apprenticeship, young men were typically in their mid-twenties when they married for the first time; women were a few years younger. Many Londoners who were widowed then remarried, usually within a year; between a third and a half of brides were widows. With the restrictions of employment, such a those affecting servants, and perhaps a numerical imbalance between the sexes, partly as a result of a disparity in the numbers of internal immigrants, at any one time up to one-third of women were unmarried. Childbirth and the complications which ensued were common causes of death among young women, and the mortality rate among babies and young children was high, with perhaps as many as 50 per cent dying before they reached their fifteenth birthday. Infant mortality was higher in poorer families than in prosperous ones, and the number of children was lower in the poorer areas.

There were seventy-eight livery companies by 1500, ranged in order of precedence, with the major ones designated the 'Great Twelve'. By *c.*1475 at least twenty-seven of them had their own halls, many of them adapted from large houses donated or bequeathed to the company by a wealthy member rather than being purpose-built. Even a prominent company such as the Mercers', which had been recognised as a commonalty in 1304 and incorporated as a company in 1394, did not have a separate hall but met in the hospital established in the early thirteenth century on the site of the house of St Thomas à Becket's family in Cheapside. On the other hand, the Merchant Taylors' fraternity was established on a site at the rear of the south side of Threadneedle Street in 1347, where its hall was built by 1392 and the great kitchen was added during 1425–33. The Grocers' Company evolved from the guild of pepperers; it was incorporated in 1428 and built its hall soon afterwards on a site on the north side of Poultry. The Armourers existed as a guild by 1322 and built their hall on a site at the north end of Coleman Street acquired in 1428, although they were not incorporated as a company until 1453. In 1416 the Cutlers' Company obtained its first charter and occupied its hall in Cloak Lane for at least ten years before it was conveyed to the company in 1451; towards the end of the century the Blacksmiths were part-time tenants of the building. The hall was the focus for the social lives of a company's members, as well as the centre for its ceremonial and administrative functions. Building and acquisition of halls by the companies was a feature of London in the late fifteenth and early sixteenth centuries, and the number of companies which had their own hall had risen to forty-seven by 1540.[12]

A company's membership was divided into two classes, with the senior members described as being within the livery, or clothing, from whom the Master and Wardens were chosen, and the remainder, who worked for the better-off members, were known as the yeomanry, or bachelors. A further ranking was observed by, for example, the Cutlers' Company, with every freeman who had served as Master paying 20*d* for the annual membership fee and someone who had been Warden 12*d*, while 'those of the Clothing' paid 8*d* and 4*d* was due from those 'not of the Clothing'.[13]

A multitude of trades fell within the jurisdiction of the companies and, with the franchise and civic offices restricted to their members, they could keep such a tight control over economic matters that it was very difficult for someone outside them, described as a 'foreigner', to set up independently. They were discouraged in other ways; in 1463 the corporation even attempted to segregate them geographically by requiring 'all basket-makers, wine drawers, and other foreigners' to have shops in the district of Blanch Appleton, near Mark Lane, and nowhere else in the city or suburbs.[14] As new trades developed, through greater specialisation and innovation, either a company absorbed its practitioners or a new company was eventually created. The shearmen's organisation acquired a site in Mincing Lane in 1455, later known as Dunster Court, and it was incorporated in 1508. In 1528 the Shearmen's Company was merged with the Fullers' Company to form the Clothworkers' Company, which took its place as the twelfth of the Great Twelve companies and therefore assumed considerable standing in the City's affairs. Mergers could result from the decline of a trade, such as the pinners, who were in difficulties in the face of large-scale imports of pins; their company had just sixteen members when they proposed that it should be merged with the Wiremongers' Company. That was carried through in 1497, with the new company designated the Wiresellers' Company.

The companies themselves were regulated by the corporation and with the oversight of Parliament and the Crown. Because apprentices were drawn not only from London but from a wide area that covered virtually the whole of the country, the companies' practices and policies were of concern to the national government. In 1504 an Act of Parliament prohibited them from introducing ordinances that were 'against the common profit of the people'.[15] Their regulations had to be submitted to and approved by the Court of Aldermen, to whom they also made submissions requesting privileges, queried rulings on doubtful issues and made complaints. The ordinances of the company of 'graytawiers', the tanners of grey leather, were typical of those submitted in the early years of Henry VII's reign and related to the election of master and wardens and their right to oversee work, the number of apprentices to be allowed, the employment of journeymen, the setting up of a house or shop, and general obedience to the master and wardens.

Maintenance of standards was an important issue for all companies. They tried to uphold the quality of work through inspections and the sale of marked and approved items only. Completed articles had to be inspected before they could be sold; leather to be offered for sale in the city was first inspected at Leadenhall, for example. Such oversight extended to the details of the products, so that leather purses should be lined only with leather and not with paper of any kind. The Dyers' Company had received its charter in 1471, which gave it powers to search within twenty miles for dyed cloth, but in the following year its jurisdiction was reduced to the city and suburbs, which was confirmed in 1482. In practice, it was difficult for a company to enforce its standards much beyond the built-up area of the city, and perhaps even in Southwark. In 1487 the fullers drew attention to the 'low estate' of their company, which they attributed to 'the lax system of apprenticeship, the excessive influx of foreigners, and the want of proper supervision of work'. Their suggested remedies were that the number of apprentices should be restricted to four per master and that no former apprentice whose term had recently been completed, or indeed any other member of the company, should be able to set up in business without the recommendation of the company wardens and four other members. The woolmen and woolpackers sought to limit the number of apprentices per master to two, the curriers preferred a limit of between one and three apprentices, depending on the master's seniority within the company, and the fullers thought that no member of their company should employ more than six workers in the craft at any one time. The painters asked for approval of a rule that an apprentice at the end of his term should be examined by the company's wardens and four of its members to test his competence. If he did not meet the requirements, he should then be made to serve another full year, either with his former master or a new one.[16]

Some company ordinances related to the members' welfare. The hat-makers restricted their working week by an ordinance that no member of the company should display their wares for sale on any Sunday or feast day, and the bowyers requested that a fine be imposed on those working late on Saturdays and feast days. Similarly, the cutlers levied a fine of 1s 8d on those found 'working on a Saturday after 3 a clock at afternoon'. The wiresellers required that no member should open his shop on a Sunday, but with the proviso that 'if any estraunger will bye of his merchaundises on the Sonday he shall cause hym to come to his house and there shewe hym his ware for the ease of travallyng people'. They also ordered that no member of the craft should work after three o'clock in the afternoon on Saturdays and feast days, and showed consideration for the neighbours of those undertaking such noisy work as knocking and filing by stipulating that between 29 September and 25 March they should not engage in such activity between eight o'clock in the evening and five o'clock in the morning. But the prohibition of work during specified hours gave former apprentices and journeymen who were unable to set up in business the opportunity to join together, perhaps in a group of three or four, to work surreptitiously on their own account during those hours – this was done in defiance of the ordinances and avoided the process by which the quality of their work would have been checked. The saddlers pointed out that a journeyman might attempt to 'work in chambers or privy places to avoid examination of his work', and requested that the company should fine those discovered doing so to discourage them.

Levies were taken for charitable purposes, which in the founders' ordinances included 'kepyng of masses, buryng of poore brethern'. The loriners required the freemen of the craft to attend a requiem mass, in their 'most honest clothyng', at the deceased's church on the day after a death, and if the deceased, man or woman, had 'in their lyfe paied well and truly their quarterages and other charges' of the company then within eight days of their death they should have thirty masses sung for them by one of the four orders of friars, at the cost of the company. Attendance at a member's funeral was a requirement of other companies, but could be an unpopular obligation – if the pie-bakers' company was at all typical. It sought to introduce an order that should any member be asked to carry a corpse to the church, they should do so 'without any resistence grudge or geyneseyng of any persone or persones so commaunded'; the penalty of 3s 4d indicated how seriously the officers took the behaviour of the members on such occasions, which ought to be be appropriate to the company's dignity. That was also the intention of the pursers when they ordered that 'all suche Torches as be belongyng to the same Crafte be at buryall to brynge the body honestly to therthe [the earth]'.

Those producing and selling foodstuffs were subject to scrutiny and regulation in order to maintain supplies to the citizens at reasonable prices. It was accepted that fair prices would be achieved in an open market, where all produce was displayed to the customers and so the price agreed on the basis of its quantity and quality. London's weights and measures had long been taken as the standard across the whole of England, a standard that had been upheld by Magna Carta: 'Let there be one measure of wine throughout our kingdom and one measure of ale and one measure of corn, namely the London quarter, and one width of cloth ... Let it be the same with weights as with measures.'[17] But two activities in particular were regarded as threatening the process and steps were taken to suppress them. One was known as forestalling, when produce was bought from suppliers before it had reached the market, and the other as regrating, which was buying produce and selling it again at the same market at a higher price. The prices of staples were of particular concern, with a need to avoid profiteering and high prices that would cause hardship for the poor. The weight of a loaf was standardised, a weight fixed by the Mayor annually, when the quality of grain was known after the harvest. To guard against shortages, in 1455 the corporation built a granary at Leadenhall. It was a substantial stone building of four ranges with corner towers around an open courtyard, with an arcaded ground floor providing stalls for sellers of foodstuffs and the upper floors serving as granaries where the corporation stored its grain, which could be released if supplies were low.

By the 1490s the freemen bakers felt under pressure from non-freemen selling bread in the city, especially those from Stratford in Essex. They had been allotted fixed sites where they could stand their carts, from which they sold their bread. The Mayor and Aldermen issued an order in 1493 prohibiting the 'foreign' bakers from selling bread after noon and from keeping their carts in the city after that time. In the following year the freemen asked that a fine be imposed on those who persisted in keeping their carts on the streets after noon, as the confiscation of the offenders' bread had not proved to be an effective restriction. They also, and more seriously, complained that the 'foreign' bakers were not only selling inferior and underweight loaves made of 'evil and unwholesome paste', but were passing them off as the freemen's own produce. To make matters yet worse, they were also bringing horses into the city in addition to their cart horses, presumably so that they could sell, or 'hawk', their bread around the streets.

The Whitebakers' Company had the support of the Mayor and Aldermen in their campaign and were granted the restrictions on 'foreigners' which they asked for. In 1519 the corporation built additional garners within the Bridge House in Southwark and erected ten ovens there for making bread, 'of which six be very large, the other four being but half so big'. When the bakers complained vociferously that the grain from the garners at the Bridge House, which they were obliged to use, was 'not swete, but partly ynfecte and corrupt', the corporation responded with the assurance that the Mayor and his brethren had 'seen and tried the same whete and pronounced it good, swete, and holsom for manys [man's] body'. The complaining bakers were suspended from the Common Council, and the Mayor imposed an order that when any wheat was unsold at the Bridge House, the bakers were to use that for baking, at the price set by the Mayor.[18]

The plight of the 'Art or Mistery of Pastelers' was more difficult to deal with. They were pie-bakers and had seen their business decline as other fast-food outlets had taken to selling pies, such as those of the vintners, brewers, innholders and tipplers. Previously the pastilers had been able to maintain their guild, but as things stood towards the end of the fifteenth century there was a danger that they would no longer be able to do so, or to pay the charges due to the City.

The pastilers' problems reflected a change in social habits, not a newfound parsimony on the Londoners' part regarding their diet. Franciscius noted that they 'eat very frequently, at times more than is suitable' and that they were 'particularly fond of young swans, rabbits, deer, and seabirds. They often eat mutton and beef, which is generally considered to be better here than anywhere else in the world ... due to the excellence of their pasture.' He also commented that they enjoyed banquets and a variety of meat and food, 'and they excel everyone in preparing them with excessive abundance'.[19] Trevisano, too, remarked that they 'take great pleasure in having a quantity of excellent victuals, and also in remaining a long time at table'. Even when wine was served at such meals, the English preferred to drink ale and beer. He had enquired into the citizens' eating arrangements, which he criticised, with the comment that 'the English being great epicures, and very avaricious by nature, indulge in the most delicate fare themselves and give their household the coarsest bread, and beer, and cold meat baked on Sunday for the week, which, however, they allow them in great abundance'. Trevisano also noted that the countryside was productive enough to supply the population and that the English imported nothing for their subsistence, with the exception of wine.[20]

Price fluctuations and intermittent shortages did cause concern, but according to Thomas More Londoners were well provided by the 'confectioners, fishmongers, butchers, cooks, poulterers, fishermen, [and] fowlers, who supply the materials for gluttony'.[21] His own diet was described by his friend Erasmus: 'He preferred beef, salt fish, and bread of the second quality, well risen ... He has always had a great liking for milk foods and fruit: he enjoys eating eggs.' His favoured drink was water.[22] The physician John Caius commended a diet with a low meat intake, commenting that not 'all fishes, no more then al fleshes be so euil as they be taken for', and supporting his case by citing the vegetarian 'lusty chartusianes neuer in fleshes' and the 'helthful poore people more in fishe then fleshe'.[23] The diet at the priory of Holy Trinity, Aldgate, over the course of the year 1513–14 included fish on the three fish days of Wednesday, Friday and Saturday, and throughout Advent and Lent, perhaps with the addition of butter, eggs, or cheese. The fish included haddock, plaice, stockfish (cod, lightly salted and dried), flounders, shrimps, whitings, salmon, fresh cod, gudgeons, mackerel, soles, lampreys, red herrings, mullets, oysters, mussels, crabs, roaches, thornbacks, congers, sprats, gurnards, tenches, smelts, pike, bream and brills. The meat served was beef, mutton, lamb, pork, pigs and veal, as well as venison, rabbits, geese, chickens, pullets, teals, quails, cranes, capons, pigeons, larks and woodcocks. Parsley roots, parsnips, pies, and cloves, mace, currants, prunes, dates, ginger, cinnamon and saffron also formed part of the diet. Other payments during the year included those for 'sweet wine, red wine, claret, Rhenish, Malmsey, bastard, ale, and wheat, chiefly for the entertainment of strangers', and 'Holy cream and wine on Maundy Thursday'.[24]

The wardens of the Goldsmiths' Company gave a dinner each year on the occasion when their successors were about to take office. In 1497 this feast included roast capon, pike and baked venison, followed by cream of almonds, rabbit with chicken, turbot, pigeon and tarts, rounded off with strawberries and cream. At the celebration of the feast of St Dunstan, its patron saint, in the following year, the spiced cakes, buns and sweetmeats were washed down by thirty-two gallons of red wine, eight gallons of claret and two barrels of ale. That was a meal on a special occasion, but the regular eating habits of those attending court were found to be rather arduous, if a comment from Raimondo da Soncino is to be believed. Writing to his master the Duke of Milan in 1497 to provide the news of recent voyages of discovery in the Atlantic, he concluded his letter with the remark, 'Meanwhile, I stay on in this country, eating ten or twelve courses at each meal, and spending three hours at table twice every day, for the love of your Excellency.'[25]

The water supply from wells and the river was augmented by that from conduits; the great conduit in Cheapside was built in 1236–45 and rebuilt in 1286, and that at Cornhill was erected in 1282. A decorative conduit was built in 1491 by the executors of Sir Thomas Hill in Gracechurch Street. The corporation maintained the pipes and the conduits and defended its ownership of them, so that when, in 1478, a wax-chandler in Fleet Street was found to have 'perced a pipe of the conduit withynne the grounde, and so conveied the water into his selar', he was, rather imaginatively and cruelly, condemned to ride through the city 'with a condit upon his hedde', hopefully a model that was not too substantial.[26]

The Greyfriars at Newgate enjoyed piped water from the mid-thirteenth century, and there were conduits for St John's and

St Mary's in Clerkenwell before *c.*1430; St Bartholomew's also had a water supply by that date. In 1430 a conduit was erected at springs in Islington, and a pipeline, over a mile long, was laid to the Carthusian priory in Clerkenwell, paid for by a benefactor, William Symmes. Each monk's cell was given its own supply, and subsidiary pipes ran to the Hospital of St John of Jerusalem and St Mary's nunnery. Beyond the priory a pipe continued to the Windmill tavern, with surplus water running from there to the White Hart, and a separate branch supplied two other taverns, the Elms and Hart's Horn. In 1451 three brewers brought a case against Symmes's executors alleging that his intention had been that the waste water from the Charterhouse should serve the people in nearby parishes and that the prior was preventing this, but their claim was rejected.[27] The pipes continued in use after the dissolution of the priory in 1538 and until the 1760s. Another specific supply was laid on when Thomas Knolles made a bequest in 1467 to provide piped water to the prisons at Newgate and Ludgate. Newgate had recently been rebuilt after a fire there in the mid-1450s; the new building was completed by 1463 and a new administrative regime was put in place, all of which was done at the 'request, praier and desire of the weldisposed, blessed and devote woman Dame Agnes Foster'. Her husband Stephen was a wealthy merchant who had been Mayor in 1454–5, when the fire had occurred.[28]

The conduits were maintained, and when the alderman nominated as Mayor in 1542 for the coming year asked to be excused, £200 of the fine to release him from the duty was allocated 'to have the water brought more plentifully to the conduytes'.[29] River water from the Thames was taken around the streets by water-carriers in large tankards and sold to householders. The water-bearers formed themselves into a fraternity in 1496, but it did not become a livery company, perhaps because the work was entirely unskilled.

Thomas More's relatively plain fare might have been unusual for someone of his background; his father was a lawyer. But the Londoners' diet did not need to be dull, at least for those wealthy enough to buy imported wine and the more exotic provisions and flavourings. Wine imports into England rose steadily, from roughly 4,000 tuns per year around 1460 to roughly 12,000 tuns by the 1530s. London's share was generally more than 40 per cent of the total and in some years exceeded 50 per cent.[30] Foodstuffs landed at London in 1480–81 included grain from Seville, raisins from Corinth, sugar from Messina, garlic, dates (one vessel landed dates worth £194 10s), onions, green ginger, olive oil, pepper, prunes, nuts, apples, at least seventeen barrels of succade (fruit preserved in sugar), treacle, cloves, cinnamon, nutmeg and ginger.[31]

Fish were a staple and the Fishmongers' Company was a powerful and wealthy body. Regulation of the trade consisted partly in controlling fishing in the Thames, to help preserve stocks. An ordinance issued by the Common Council in 1486 laid down the size of various kinds of fish that could be caught and sold, and ordered that immature fish that had been taken should be put back into the river. The fish specified were barbel, flounder, roach, dace, pike and tench. At about the same date the Mayor and Aldermen ordered that 'false nets', that is those with a finer mesh than was specified, should be burnt as a warning to those fishing in the Thames with the unlawful nets designed to gather the smaller and younger fish. Herrings were an important part of the Londoners' diet and their price was taken to reflect the current level of prices in general. A chronicler noted in 1494 that white herrings were being sold at 3s 4d per barrel and that a dozen years later twelve herrings cost one penny. Franciscius wrote that, 'They have all kinds of fish in plenty and great quantities of oysters which come from the sea-shore.' Yet fish were also imported. In December 1481 a ship from Vlissingen landed herrings and salted fish, and another, freighted by the Hansa community at the Steelyard in London, brought in stockfish worth £100 and herrings worth £10.[32]

Supplies of fish from the Thames and its estuary, the North Sea and the English Channel could be relied upon so long as the weather was not too stormy during the fishing season, and the provision of agricultural produce, too, was dependable. London was well-sited within the agriculturally most productive part of the country, and was supplied by produce shipped coastwise from East Anglia and Kent and along the valleys of the Thames and its tributaries. The city's hinterland extended across south-east England and the

Midlands, with the area from which livestock were driven being wider than that for grain, malt, peas and dairy produce. But the quality of the harvest influenced the level of prices, and although fluctuations could be ameliorated by maintaining a stock of grain, arranging for imports when supplies were low and setting the prices of bread, ale, beer, wine, meat and poultry, they could not be entirely overcome.

Taking the price of wheat as a guide to the quality of the harvest, the early 1480s saw a run of poor harvests, with 1482 an exceptionally bad year. Thereafter, until the end of the century yields were good, with only one deficient harvest, in 1490, and abundant ones in 1494 and 1495. The new century opened with a run of four bad harvests in a row, from 1500 to 1503, but then good crops predominated through the remainder of that decade and into the following one, with deficient yields recorded in only two years, 1512 and 1519. The grain price was therefore steady and generally below the long-term average. This was an important factor in the Londoners' family economies, for the price of flour naturally followed that of wheat.

Similarly, overall price levels based on a composite of fundamental items, namely grain, malt, peas, mutton and herrings, charcoal, candles and oil, canvas, shirting material and woollen-cloth, show no perceptible rise before the late 1510s. From 1518 and through the 1520s prices did increase and did not fall back to previous levels, even in good harvest years, but they rose by only 22 per cent over the half century between the 1490s and the 1540s. Wage earners had benefited in the long aftermath of the plague epidemics in the 1340s and subsequent years because of the reduced supply of labour, which allowed them to obtain higher wages, and also the generally low level of prices as judged over the longer term. Only when prices rose and wage increases lagged behind did their living standards come under threat, an eventuality that seems not to have been the case to any great degree in London during the late fifteenth and early sixteenth centuries, when the annual rate of inflation was, on average, roughly one half of one per cent.[33]

Markets were held along the principal streets. From late Saxon times Cheapside was the principal market in the City, sometimes known as West Cheap to distinguish it from Eastcheap; the name Cheapside denotes 'the street alongside the market'. The adjacent streets also contained markets whose names indicated the specialities of their produce, such as Honey Lane, Bread Street, Milk Street and Wood Street; Friday Street was named for a fish market held there on Fridays. Cheapside continues eastwards as Poultry, where the poultry dealers were still trading until the early sixteenth century. At the other end of Cheapside, a corn market was held in the churchyard of St Mary-le-Querne, and beyond that Newgate Street was used by butchers for their slaughter-houses and stalls – a length of it was known as Newgate Street shambles.

To the east of Cheapside and just beyond Poultry was the Stocks market, which was held on ground adjoining the church of St Mary Woolchurch Haw. The church, which was rebuilt in 1462, took its name from a beam for weighing wool that stood in its churchyard. In 1282 a site on its north side was allocated by the Mayor, Henry le Waleys, as a market for meat and fish, and it was granted a charter by Edward I; the rents were to go towards the cost of maintaining London Bridge. The market was rebuilt in stone c.1406–11, with rooms in the upper storey; in 1543 it contained twenty-five fishmongers' stalls and eighteen for butchers, and had sixteen upper chambers. Eastwards from the Stocks market ran Cornhill, known as Cornhulle by c.1100, which indicates a grain market, and a general market was held in the street by the fifteenth century.

Along the line of streets connecting the bridge with Bishopsgate was Gracechurch Street, which contained a corn market where sellers from outside the city were allowed to trade. By the sixteenth century it had developed into a general market, used for pork (but not beef or lamb), dairy produce and fruit. Southwards, towards the bridge, a fish market was held in Fish Street Hill from the twelfth century; the street was also known as Bridge Street and was first referred to as New Fish Street in 1545. But the principal fish market was at Billingsgate, where an arcaded building with two upper storeys was built in the mid-fifteenth century to shelter goods on the quay, although the market itself was held on an open space. The marketing of fish was improved in 1502 when the River

Fleet was 'new cast', or scoured, so that the oyster and herring boats could be brought into the city as far as Holborn Bridge.[34] Crossing Gracechurch Street was Eastcheap, the site of one of the chief markets in the City. A patent of *c.*1324 provided for a market for flesh and fish, and both sides of the street came to be lined with butchers' shops; the butchers slaughtered the animals on or close to their premises. The westwards continuation of Eastcheap was Candlewick Street. Its name was a corruption of Candelewrithstret or Candelwrickstrete, where candles were made and sold for both domestic and ecclesiastical use. Across the river, a general market developed in the thirteenth century on the west side of what was to become Borough High Street.

The markets should have been adequately provisioned by pack-animals and carts. The carts had been the subject of civic orders from at least the thirteenth century, with a rule that their wheels should not be shod with iron nails. In 1485 the Common Council prohibited the use of long and square-headed nails and specified the use of flat ones. Vehicles used in the city were of two kinds: cars, which were twelve feet long and three feet wide and well-adapted to use in narrow streets and lanes, and long carts, which were fourteen feet long and four feet in breadth and, although able to carry larger loads and having greater stability, they were less manoeuvrable. The long carts were more serviceable for those responsible for administering the system of purveyance, by which the Crown acquired provisions for the royal court and commandeered transport for them and to move the goods of the royal household. The King's Wardrobe was based in St Andrew's Hill as well as in the Tower and serviced the principal royal palaces at Westminster and the Tower, and at Shene, where the royal residence was destroyed by fire in 1499 and rebuilt by 1501: 'Thys yere the kynge byldyd new hys maner of Shene, and changed the name and namyd it Richemonde, and he byldyd new his place called Baynyscastell in London [Barnard's Castle], and repayryd his place at Grenewyche with moche newe byldynge there and in diverse places.'[35] Those royal buildings were augmented by Bridewell Palace, built by Henry VIII close to the Thames within the City in 1515–23 following a fire in 1512 at Westminster Palace that had destroyed the accommodation there.

In 1512 the Court of Aldermen ordered that there should be forty carts within the city owned by freemen, and that each owner should have both a car and a cart. This was a difficult prescription to enforce, and the carters continued to prefer the smaller vehicles for transporting provisions and fuel, and for their other main role of removing the dirt and ordure from the streets. The upshot was that as the suburban and provincial carriers preferred the more capacious carts, the burden of requisitioning fell largely on them, so that they were reluctant to come into London in case their vehicles were appropriated. The problem was summarised by the aldermen with the comment that those who had previously brought victuals into the city 'as whete, malte, wode, cole and other thynges' had found that their horses and carts were being taken 'for the kyngs Caryage and purveaunce', as a result of which 'they often tyme absent and withdrawe theym selves from the seide Citie, which causyth the seid vitailles to be dere and of more excessive price then they have bene in tymes passed'. The solution was the establishment of the Fraternity of Saint Katherine in 1517. In return for providing carriage for the king when necessary, cleansing the streets and conveying provisions and fuel from the wharves and other places, they were given a monopoly of carriage within the city. Individual householders were permitted to keep a vehicle for their own use, and carriers from outside the City could join the fraternity. But it did not have regulatory powers, and there were complaints that still not enough vehicles were available for the king's use. And so in 1528 the fraternity was incorporated as a company, along with stringent regulations, which included the requirement that owners of wood-wharves, the street cleaners and those carrying building materials all had to join. The vehicles were marked by the symbol of a sword, and those owned by a woodmonger also carried 'the sygne of a ffaggott', while those belonging to the rakers, or street cleaners, displayed 'a sword and a donge forke'.[36] The carters carrying goods within the City and cleaning its streets had been brought into the livery company regulatory system, through a process driven partly by the need to curb price inflation caused by transport problems that threatened to restrict supply. Although there was a system of free-market pricing for provisions, there were also regulations governing the operation of the market-places, the prices of essentials and the carriage of goods.

Visitors were unaware of the organisation of London's economy and the role of the livery companies. They correctly adduced that it was a prosperous city, but could not be aware of the extent to which the workforce was regulated through supervision by the City and the companies. The structure imposed by those companies and their integral role in the City's government fashioned a coherent society in which Londoners' needs were recognised and addressed. The conduct of overseas trade was also organised in this way, and it made an important contribution to the city's prosperity.

3

Continental Connections

Overseas trade was a major element of London's economy, but its organisation was subject to various stresses, some of which had been evident in the Middle Ages, while others developed as the political and diplomatic contexts changed. Disputes between England and Flanders in the mid-thirteenth century had weakened the Flemish merchants' earlier dominance in English trade, especially the export of wool to the cloth-making towns in Flanders. The Italian merchants already had a toehold in the English economy as the collectors of Papal taxes and began to exploit the openings left by the Flemish, both in wool exports and the import of luxury items, such as spices and fine, expensive textiles. Trade with the Low Countries was of primary importance, and as cloth became England's principal export, much of it channelled through London, the Italian merchants were involved in the trade and supplied the cloth makers with essentials, including alum, dyes and soap.

By the fifteenth century a quarter of English trade was in the hands of a group of about seventy Italian merchants, most of them operating from London. They gave their name to Lombard Street, which had been known as Longbrod, and the word Lombard came to be applied to places where money transactions took place, for the merchants also acted as bankers. Italians were a visible presence in London's mercantile community at the end of the century, when Andreas Franciscius noticed merchants from Venice, Florence, Lucca 'and many from Genoa and Pisa', as well as those from Spain, Germany, the Rhineland and elsewhere.[1] That presence was enhanced by the properties which they held, which included Crosby Place, on lease from the prioress of St Helen, Bishopsgate to a Genoese merchant, before a new grant was made to Sir John Crosby in 1466 and the lease subsequently passed to Anthony Bonvix, alias Bonvise, a merchant from Lucca, who held it at the dissolution of the nunnery.[2]

The dislocation of trade with Flanders in the 1270s had also provided an opportunity for merchants from the Hanseatic ports. The Hanseatic League was formed in 1241 as a loose grouping of north European cities trading abroad, directed by a Diet that met in Lübeck. German merchants were operating in London by the 1150s and were granted concessions from the 1190s onwards, which included the freedom to trade throughout England and partial exemption from taxation. They were based at the Steelyard, or Stahlhof, a sample yard on the Thames alongside Dowgate. This constituted a *kontor*, effectively a defensible enclave within the city, with warehouses, dormitories, a tavern, houses and offices. By the late fifteenth century it covered three acres. At any one time there were eighteen to twenty Hanse merchants living there, leading quite separate lives from the Londoners and following their own rules. They handled between a quarter and a fifth of English broad-cloths sold abroad. The only other such privileged enclave for foreign traders in England was a much smaller Hanseatic depot at King's Lynn.

The trading privileges were disliked by the English merchants, especially the lower duties paid on cloth exports. From the mid-fourteenth century England's cloth-making industry had developed rapidly, while wool exports steadily declined. Cloth exports rose eightfold during the second half of the century, and then continued to rise during the fifteenth century. They had quadrupled by the 1490s, an overall rise from 5,000 to 160,000 cloths per year. As well as an increase in volume, during the fifteenth century there was an improvement in the quality of cloths exported through London. By the 1480s the general quality was much higher than it had been even forty years earlier, and the value was correspondingly greater. Cloth brought to London was sold at Blackwell Hall, close to the Guildhall, in a building acquired by the City in 1396. The market there was controlled by the Mayor, with sales permitted from Thursdays to Saturday mornings. The aims were to avoid dubious and dishonest bargains and to control the standards of the cloth. That was enforced by regulations, such as those issued in London in 1482 to curb 'falshode and deceite' in the making and finishing of cloth. All tenter frames for stretching cloth had to be placed at the Fullers' Company hall or at Leadenhall, where they were open to public view; in order that their operation could be overseen more easily, they were not permitted outside the walls.[3]

The Hanse merchants' rejoinder to the complaints was that London's connection with their network brought it benefits, especially the goods imported from the Baltic, where the Hanseatic traders had a near monopoly, including grain, flax, linen cloth and steel, and naval supplies, such as hemp, timber and tar. Such arguments may have had some validity, but were not enough in themselves to secure the merchants' position and, to preserve their concessions, the traders at the Steelyard had to maintain good relations with the monarch. The balance was upset in 1468, when Edward IV withdrew their privileges and a naval war followed. But the Hanse cities provided financial help for Edward's efforts to regain the throne in 1470, which were successful. The merchants were rewarded in the Treaty of Utrecht in 1474, with the right to pay only a half of the levy taken from English merchants on each broad-cloth exported, and freedom from the levy of a shilling in the pound payable on general commodities exported. Those and other concessions prompted Dominic Mancini's reaction that Edward IV 'was more favourable than other princes to foreigners who visited his realm for trade or any other reason'.[4] The treaty was confirmed by Richard III.

In contrast, Henry VII's policy was to reduce the privileges of the Hanse merchants, partly by making an agreement with Denmark which, by giving English merchants rights in the trade with Denmark and Iceland, encroached upon one of the Hanse's trading areas. A conference in Antwerp in 1491 changed little, but two years later the king attempted to prevent them trading between the Low Countries and England, and brought its merchants within the supervision of the London customs officers. His policy was matched by the Londoners' resentment of the privileged groups of traders from abroad, which produced attacks from time to time, with anti-Italian flare-ups in 1456 and 1457 and a protest against the Steelyard in 1462. A more serious incident occurred in 1493, which was described as 'a rysynge of yonge men agaynst the Stelyard'. Fearful that their employment was threatened, some cloth workers went there and 'beganne to rifle and spoyle such chambres and warehouses' as they could get into, and 'the Easterlynges had muche ado to withstand and repulse theym'. The assailants tried to break down the gates, but the defenders had shored them up so strongly that they failed. After two hours of this commotion word of what was happening reached the Mayor, and when he arrived with about forty armed men the attackers dispersed. The defenders had been assisted by 'Carpenters and Smythes, whiche came to their aide by water oute of the borough of Southwarke'; they could cross the Thames at such short notice because the watermen who plied the wherries carrying passengers on the Thames were also settled there.[5]

The English merchants involved in the cloth trade had gradually come to act together, and a 'Fellowship of Adventurers' had emerged among the members of the Mercers' Company by the 1460s. Similar groups developed in other livery companies engaged in the trade, and in provincial cities, such as York and Exeter. They operated in concert to arrange matters relating to the trade and elected a governor, who was most often a member of the London Mercers' Company, to oversee their affairs. The London merchants who petitioned Henry VII in 1485 with a request for privileges described themselves as 'the Merchant adventurers citizens of the city of London, into the parts of Holland, Zeeland, Brabant and Flanders'. They were awarded their concessions and by an act of Common Council in the spring of 1486 the Fellowship of Merchant Adventurers of London was recognised and its organisation was defined. The company did not operate on behalf of its individual members to sell their cloth, nor were their resources pooled. So far as their businesses were concerned, they acted on their own, selling through their factor in the mart town, which was the English town of Calais, or Bruges, and then Antwerp, as the diplomatic situation changed. But they shipped their cloth jointly in a fleet of vessels and the company arranged the freight charges and conditions with the ships' masters. The Londoners became dominant within the company, partly due to their policy of imposing a fee on any provincial merchants selling at the continental marts. By 1497, within a few years of its first imposition, the fee had risen from 3s 4d to £5, and it was alleged that the levy was taken 'by the felishippe of the Mercers and othre marchauntes and adventurers, dwellyng and being free within the Citie of London, by confederacie made amonge theym self of their uncharitable and inordinate covetise for their singular profite and lucre'.[6]

The Merchant Adventurers' company was not a livery company. The most important livery company among its members was that of the mercers, which provided a clerk and meeting room at their company's hall, although the Adventurers' headquarters were in Antwerp. The Mercers' Company's members held the largest share of the cloth trade – about 40 per cent of London's cloth exports until 1547 were by mercers. The other livery companies represented on the Adventurers' Court of Assistants were, according to a report of 1509, those of the grocers, drapers, haberdashers, merchant-tailors, skinners and fishmongers. The Merchant Adventurers' company was relatively small, with between 80 and 150 members at any one time, yet they could wield considerable influence because they were distributed among the various livery companies and so had their interests represented in each of them. In 1518 it was prepared to face down the Mayor, who protested that two aldermen had been chosen as the Adventurers' Assistants and so were serving abroad when they should have been carrying out their duties in London. The Mayor wrote to the Court of Assistants to make the quite reasonable point that the City's business was 'more ponderous and of gretter weight and difficulty then yours', only to be rebuffed with the reply that 'they wold noon otherwise do than they had doon'.[7]

The context of European trade changed around 1500, following the opening of the route to Asia around the Cape of Good Hope and the discovery of the Americas. Trade in Asiatic goods through the Mediterranean declined and new Atlantic routes were developed. Henry VII had not sponsored Christopher Columbus, but following his discoveries the king changed his policy and encouraged John Cabot and his backers in Bristol. Cabot's voyage to Newfoundland generated a burst of optimism, with the possibility that 'they could bring so many fish that this kingdom would have no further need of Iceland, from which place there comes a very great quantity of the fish called stockfish'. Even more profitably, Cabot reasoned, a sea route to the Spice Islands could be found, and so, as Raimondo da Soncino wrote to his master, the Duke of Milan, 'his Majesty will equip some ships, and in addition he will give them all the malefactors, and they will go to that country and form a colony. By means of this they hope to make London a more important mart for spices than Alexandria.' The hope and expectation of finding the North West Passage continued for centuries, but the North Atlantic fishing grounds did become an important resource.[8]

The more immediate concern was the outlet for English cloth in northern Europe. Antwerp was willing to admit English merchants selling cloth when the other Flemish cloth-making towns prohibited them, and so it, with its satellite Bergen-op-Zoom, developed a trade that they were able to sustain after those towns lifted their ban. Furthermore, its rival Bruges had been in decline for some time, with the silting of the Zwin, its outlet to the sea. Initially Damme acted as the city's outport, but it is also on the Zwin, and when the lower part of that waterway gradually became too shallow for sea-going vessels, Sluis took over that function. But with the shift of textile making from Flanders to Brabant and the continuing problem of silting, by the end of the fifteenth century Bruges had slipped into irreversible economic decline.

Once the English merchants had fixed their outlet at Antwerp its four great annual marts became the focus for their cloth exports, which came to account for nearly one-third of all imports to that city. In practice, the merchants took cloth to only three marts a year and attended the fourth to settle transactions and buy goods for shipment to London, including copper from Germany, linen from the Low Countries and Germany, thread from Oudenarde and Cologne, fustian from Tournai and silk from Bruges. Potters in Antwerp supplied decorative floor tiles, vases, jugs, bowls and dishes, its printers exported playing cards to London; the city was also the source for dyestuffs and fixing agents for use in the cloth-making process. Small domestic and personal items such as pans, thimbles, razors, shears, pins and spectacle cases came from northern Europe, as well as fine metal goods from the German cities

Augsburg, Nuremberg and Munich, with stoneware from Cologne arriving from around 1510. Mirrors came from Nuremberg and hats from St Omer; wine, iron, decorated ceramics and skins from Spain; malmsey wine from Crete; currants from Cephalonia and Zante; glass and fine textiles from Venice; woad and hemp from Toulouse; wine from Gascony; salt from Brittany; and grain from the Baltic. Trade between England and Spain increased in the 1470s and 1480s, and most of it passed through London.

Paper was not produced in England and had to be imported, and books were sent to London from Cologne, Utrecht, Frankfurt, Antwerp and elsewhere; the brothers Andrew and John Rue, from Frankfurt, owned a bookshop in St Paul's churchyard in the 1480s. In the early sixteenth century Franz Birckmann, from Cologne, sold books in both Antwerp and London and his sons, like the Rues, opened a shop in the cathedral's churchyard. Between 1492 and 1535 ninety-eight aliens paid customs dues on imported books.[9] William Caxton, a member of the Mercers' Company, set up his printing press at Bruges in 1472, printing books in English and shipping them to London, and in 1476 he moved to Westminster, where he established his printing business at the sign of the Red Pale. Caxton continued to bring books into England from France and Flanders. After his death in 1492 the business was taken over by Wynkyn de Worde, who had probably worked in Caxton's shop, as he took a lease of two tenements in Westminster in 1479. He moved the operation to the sign of the Sun in Fleet Street in 1500–01. Like Caxton, de Worde was an importer as well as a printer and exporter of books.[10]

Antwerp benefited greatly when Venetian dominance of the spice trade was undermined following the Portuguese opening of the route around the Cape of Good Hope into the Indian Ocean. Vasco da Gama's initial voyage returned to Lisbon in September 1499, and six months later a fleet of thirteen ships was sent out to begin trading in earnest. The Portuguese wrested control of the spice business from the Moslem traders and so cut off Venice's source of supply. King Manuel decided to use Antwerp as the distribution centre for the Portuguese trade in Oriental goods, and vessels laden with spices tied up on the Antwerp waterfront in 1501. Prices fell and so a wider market was opened for spices in London, initiating a reciprocal trade as the Portuguese vessels would return home with a supply of English cloth. But Venice was still the source for fine glass, and Italian merchants continued to bring to London silks, satin, velvet, carpets, soap, sacks of sponges and, importantly for the cloth trade, alum and woad. It had been the practice for Venetian galleys trading with Bruges to break their voyages at Southampton, but when that direct seaborne trade with the Italian cities was brought to an end in the early years of the sixteenth century the Venetians transferred their business to London.

London was dominant in England's overseas trade during the fifteenth century, and its share rose from 30 to 40 per cent before the mid-century to 60 per cent by the 1480s; by the early sixteenth century it had reached around 70 per cent. The third quarter of the century was a period of economic depression, though London recovered from the slump more rapidly than the rest of the country, partly because of its credit network, and so achieved a growing dominance in trade, with cloth the key element.[11] This in turn aroused complaints from provincial merchants that trade was being channelled through Londoners. Their grievances may have had some justification, especially after the various Merchant Adventurers companies were merged into one in 1505. But for such an important sector of the economy the government preferred to deal with a single organisation. It also intervened in the cloth trade, soon after Henry VII's accession, by imposing a rule that only cloths valued at less than £2 could be exported in an unfinished state. As the price of cloth rose, so the threshold was increased, and by 1542 it was £4 for white cloth and £3 for coloured. The objective was to keep the finer cloth in England to be finished before being exported, to provide employment for the fullers, shearmen, carders and dyers. Even so, the government maintained the privileges of the alien merchants and wished to encourage the supply of skilled craftsmen, such as joiners and glaziers, to work on building projects for the aristocracy and wealthier citizens. They were exempted from legislation of 1523 restricting anyone born abroad from taking apprentices, with peers or someone with property worth £100 per annum or more permitted to 'take and reteign Estraungers Joyners and Glasyers in their servyce from tyme to tyme to and for the excercysyng with them their craftes'.[12] The corporation employed 'Mathewe Peter, Spanyarde' to carve the arms of Sir John Thurston, a goldsmith, on stone shields placed on the new ovens at the Bridge House in Southwark, partly paid for by Sir John. It had earlier paid 'to a Frenchman dwellyng in the brugh of Suthwerk for a clocke and dyall, with all thynges ther unto belongyng, sett and occupied within the Briggehouse'.[13]

A tension existed between the maintenance of London's regulation of trades on the one hand and, on the other, the desire to introduce new techniques and so bring refinement to English products, and to provide a fitting, sophisticated, ambience within the houses of the wealthy. Underlying resentment at the preferential terms on which foreigners traded and allegations that they were taking work away from Londoners produced a simmering antipathy that boiled over in 1517; the Evil May Day riot in that year was the most serious outbreak of violence in London during the sixteenth century. Giustinian attributed the origins of the disturbance to an inflammatory sermon at Paul's Cross during which the preacher, one Dr Beal, 'commenced abusing the strangers in the town, and their mode of life and customs, alleging that they not only deprived them of their industry, and of the emoluments derivable thence, but disgraced their dwellings, taking their wives and daughters; adding much other exasperating language, persuading and exhorting them not to suffer or permit this sort of persons to inhabit their town'. But Giustinian's servant, Nicolo Sagudino, traced it to an incident in which a servant of the French ambassador had taken two doves from a stallholder without paying for them, claiming a right of purveyance. An Italian who had abducted a goldsmith's wife and purloined some of his silver was also blamed for fomenting the discontent.

Whatever the spark that ignited the smouldering resentment among the apprentices, the fact was that early in the morning of May Day they 'rose up and went to divers parts of the city inhabited by French and Flemish artificers and mechanics, sacked their houses and wounded many of them, though it was not understood that any were killed'. Giustinian added that they had ransacked the house of the king's French secretary and that they would have killed him if he had not 'escaped up the belfry of the adjoining church', an undignified but effective way of evading capture. The houses of Florentine, Lucchese and Genoese merchants were threatened but they were too well defended to be entered. According to Edward Hall's account, the response was that 'while this ruffling continued, Syr Richard Cholmeley knight, Lieutenant of the Towre, no great frende to the citie, in a frantyke fury losed certain peces of ordinaunce, & shot into the citie, whiche did little harme, howbeit his good wyl apered'. A letter despatched to Mantua a few days after the riot mentioned that 'Cannon were fired to intimidate the town'. Yet although the outbreak had been anticipated, it was not the City authorities who quelled the disturbance but the Duke of Norfolk, who led a force of armed men into the streets and dispersed the rioters. The government reacted sharply to the incident and 278 people were arrested; fifteen of them were executed. Giustinian summarised the riot as 'a great commotion, but the terror was greater than the harm done'.[14] He may not have been entirely correct, for a nervous Erasmus chose not to return to England in the aftermath of the disturbance and others may have been deterred for a similar reason. A city that relied upon regular contacts and an influx of people and business could not tolerate such a discouragement to the movement of individuals, and an awareness of that fact may partly explain the severity of the crackdown.

The court was receptive to influences and specialists from the Continent, and its connection with the commercial world could be a close one. Peter de Opiciis and his son Benedictus were recorded in Candlewick Street Ward in 1483, with Peter described as a 'broker', and in 1507, when he took a loan of £100 from Henry VII, he was then noted as a 'merchaunt' from the north-Italian marquisate of Monferrato. In 1508 he was acting as a broker for the Merchant Adventurers in Antwerp and had links with the English court, for in 1511 a letter from Henry VIII to Margaret of Austria, in Mechelen, recommended Peter and his children to her and was carried by his son Benedictus, an organist. Shortly afterwards Benedictus was given a position in Antwerp cathedral, and in 1516 he began serving Henry VIII as one of two new organists for the Privy Chamber.[15] The other was Dionysius Memo, who had been organist at the Basilica of St Mark's in Venice, the chapel of the Doge's palace, since 1507 and was lured to London by the king.

When Sebastian Giustinian wrote to the Doge in October 1516 he told him that he and the Imperial and Spanish ambassadors had been summoned by the king, who 'danced many dances' and then 'made the said ambassadors hear Master Friar Dionisius Memo play, as he did marvellously, being lauded by everybody: the King himself is so enamoured of him and pleased with his talent, that one could not wish for more'.[16] Memo was to prove useful to Giustinian as a source of information for the goings-on at court. Also in 1516, the king hired a new Flemish sackbut ensemble, which came to be described as 'the kinges olde sagbuttes' after Italian sackbut players were engaged in the early 1520s. In this he was continuing his father's practice of bringing musicians to England, to emulate the standard of display and entertainment experienced at the leading continental courts. In 1497–99, for example, payments were made to four French minstrels at court; the term 'minstrels' was used in a general sense.[17] Courtiers could not fail to be aware of Henry VIII's love of music and they made it a part of the ambience when they entertained him. George Cavendish, gentleman-usher to Thomas Wolsey, Chancellor from 1515 to 1529, recalled that when the king paid a visit 'as he did divers times in the year ... Then was there all kinds of music and harmony set forth.'[18]

Henry VIII's cosmopolitan music establishment was admired, for accomplished musicians from France, Flanders, Germany and Italy were persuaded to travel to England by the opportunities available at court and good rates of pay. In the 1530s the king enticed six brothers, Alvise, John, Anthony, Jasper, Baptista and Jacomo Bassano, to move to London from Venice. They were skilled wind musicians, members of a family that had lived in Bassano del Grappa on the River Brenta, roughly forty miles from Venice, before moving to the city. Alvise may have visited London in 1525, and he, Jasper, John and Anthony were in England in 1531, although the duration of their stay is unknown. If the king was impressed with their musicianship and the style of music which they performed, he either did not, or could not, persuade them to stay. But by 1538 Anthony had returned and held an appointment as 'maker of divers instruments' to the court.[19] Jacomo was with him, and in the following year their four brothers joined them. The English representative in Venice, Edmund Harvel, a merchant, arranged for their move to England and described the brothers as 'estimid above al others in this cite'. At the same time a consort of five violists also arrived at Henry's court, two of whom were fellow Venetians – the others were from Milan and Cremona. A sixth member was added to that consort in 1545 with the arrival of another violist, from Brescia, within Venice's mainland territories. They began to develop the violin as an instrument, distinct from the viol, and the two groups made an innovative contribution to English music.[20]

As well as the opportunities which Henry VIII's court offered, there were also the commercial possibilities of the market in England for musical instruments. These the Bassanos successfully exploited after they had settled in London, where they remained after Henry VIII's death. In 1547 they stated that they had invested approximately £300 in improving those buildings of the former Charterhouse where they had been lodged; clearly they were prospering, in both instrument-making and performing.[21] A tabor-pipe made of boxwood and bearing the Bassanos' mark has been recovered from the wreck of the *Mary Rose*, which sank in July 1545, and they evidently reached a wider market, for in 1571 the Bavarian court's collection of musical instruments included forty-five wind instruments 'made by the Bassani brothers' in London.[22] The Bassanos provided a successful example of what the government hoped to achieve by attracting skilled craftsmen and performers to London.

Henry VII's links with the Italian courts had attracted such specialists. The sculptor Guido Mazzoni, from Modena, was commissioned to model the effigies for the king's tomb in his chapel in Westminster Abbey. In fact, Mazzoni's design was not used, and the figures of Henry and his queen, Elizabeth of York, were by the Florentine Pietro Torregiano, who probably arrived in England in 1511. The tomb was surrounded by an iron grate by an English craftsman, Humphrey Walker, which was decorated with thirty-two bronze statues of saints by a Dutchman, known only as Thomas. Torregiano was also responsible for the effigy of Lady Margaret Beaufort, Henry VII's mother (who died two months after her son), which is also in his chapel. These are superb examples of Italian Renaissance sculpture. The tomb of Dr John Yonge, Master of the Rolls, in the Rolls Chapel in Chancery Lane, is in the same Florentine style and probably it, too, was by Torregiano. He was commissioned to design Henry VIII's monument, which was to be similar to, but of course larger than, his father's. But there seems to have been a falling out and Torregiano left England in 1522, leaving unfinished a high altar for the Henry VII chapel, which was completed by the Italian sculptor Benedetto da Rovezzano and installed in 1526.[23]

During a visit to Florence, Torregiano met the sculptor Benvenuto Cellini, who was impressed by his personality, although he 'kept talking every day about his gallant feats among those beasts of Englishmen'. Cellini admitted that he 'felt a wish to go with him to England', until his account of how he broke Michaelangelo's nose with a punch 'begat in me such a hatred of the man ... I now could never bear the sight of him'. So the English court gained artistically from Torregiano's time in London – but because of his bragging missed the chance of employing Cellini.[24]

The artist Hans Holbein arrived in London from Basel in 1526 by a different route, through an intellectual and artistic network. A member of a family of artists, he was born in Augsburg and was working in Basel by 1515. But commissions for both private works and church decorations fell away sharply after Reformation ideas reached the city and cut the demand for religious pictures; Erasmus wrote that 'the arts in Basel were freezing'. Holbein decided to try to ply his trade elsewhere. He had painted Erasmus's portrait a number of times, one of which Erasmus gave to Thomas More, and Holbein now carried a letter of recommendation from Erasmus to Quentin Metsys, a leading artist in Antwerp. Metsys's connections with the city's business community had produced the double-portrait known as 'The Banker and his Wife' of 1514. From Antwerp, Holbein travelled to London, where he made contact with More.

Erasmus had met More during his first visit to London in 1499. He also encountered the humanist scholar Pieter Gillis at Antwerp five years later, when Gillis was working for the printer Dirk Martens. Erasmus returned to London first in 1505 and again in 1509, when he wrote his brilliant satire *In Praise of Folly* while staying at More's house in Bucklesbury; its Greek title *Moriae*

Encomium is a pun on More's name. The work mocked and deflated the ecclesiastical establishment in particular, but also other groups with pretensions, self-satisfied claims to special knowledge or abilities, and a tendency to bask in mutual congratulation. He included schoolmasters, philosophers and writers (both those that we would describe as 'academic' and 'popular'), and he derided lawyers as 'the most self-satisfied class of people', with practices which 'make their profession seem the most difficult of all'. Erasmus's observations were universal and not targeted at his English hosts, but London provided an agreeable setting for the concentrated burst of writing that produced this corrosively satirical and influential work.[25] When More was in the Netherlands in 1515 on a diplomatic mission he spent some time with Gillis, who was by then secretary, or town clerk, of Antwerp. The episode stimulated More to complete *Utopia*, another enduring piece of Renaissance writing, which was published by Martens, under Gillis's supervision, in Leuven in 1516. Metsys painted Erasmus and Gillis in 1517 and they gave those portraits to More.[26] This network of prominent humanists facilitated Holbein's move to London.

More's reaction to Holbein's arrival was to write to Erasmus: 'Your painter friend, my dear Erasmus, is a wonderful artist. I fear he will not find English soil as rich and fertile as he hoped. But I shall do my best to make sure it is not completely barren.'[27] More was now a man with considerable influence at court; in 1521 he had been appointed to a post at the Exchequer and was knighted by the king. It was probably through his influence that Holbein had the opportunity to decorate large, but temporary, buildings at Greenwich that were being prepared as part of lavish entertainments for a delegation of French diplomats. This was a prestigious commission, for their visit was of major diplomatic significance. Holbein then went on to portray More and his family, with whom he stayed at the house in Chelsea that they had acquired a few years earlier. At Greenwich, Holbein was guided by Nicolaus Kratzer, a mathematician, astronomer and maker of scientific instruments from Munich, who had been recommended by Gillis to Erasmus and had travelled to London in 1517. He became a member of More's circle and tutor to his children; in 1520 he was described as 'deviser of the King's horologes' and he undertook a diplomatic mission to Antwerp. He and Holbein became great friends. Holbein's portrait of him, dated 1528, shows a range of mathematical and scientific instruments on the wall and upon a shelf behind the sitter, as well as on the table in front of him.[28]

Holbein went back to Basel in 1528, but the opportunities for artists had worsened as the fuse lit by Martin Luther in Wittenberg in 1517 fizzed across the continent. In 1529 the city guild ordered the destruction of all paintings in churches. Holbein had returned as a Protestant to London by the summer of 1532 and was appointed the king's painter in 1535, with an annual salary of £30. As well as executing portraits of the king, his parents, Jane Seymour and many members of the court, he was sent to European courts to 'take the likenesses' of potential wives for the king. Holbein was not the only foreign-born painter at Henry VIII's court; Lucas Horenbout, the son of an artist in the Low Countries, also had a role as court painter from at least 1525. Portrait miniatures by him included images of the king, and Katherine Parr's accounts include a payment to his widow 'for makynge of the Quenes pykture and the kyngs'.[29]

Like other office holders at court, Holbein lived in the city, not at Whitehall, where he was a resident of the parish of St Andrew Undershaft in 1541. Horenbout asked to be buried in St Martin's-in-the-Fields; the Bassanos settled in Norton Folgate and St Botolph's, Bishopsgate after leaving the Charterhouse buildings; and the emperor Charles V's ambassador in London during the 1530s, Eustace Chapuys, occupied lodgings adjoining the Austin Friars, at the opposite end of the metropolis from Whitehall Palace but close to Thomas Cromwell's new house.[30] Those from abroad who were attached to the court did not form a close-knit community within London, as the merchants did at the Steelyard, some of whom were depicted by Holbein, including a character known as Hans of Antwerp, who witnessed Holbein's will. Although an obvious target for those resentful of foreigners and their trading privileges, the Steelyard had escaped the attentions of the rioters in 1517.

During his stay in England in 1499 Erasmus had made friends with John Colet, an almost exact contemporary and a fellow humanist. Colet was a Londoner, son of Sir Henry Colet, a wealthy mercer who twice served as Mayor. His considerable influence on Erasmus's approach to scholarship included his insistence on the importance of the classical languages and literature, as a means of understanding the Scriptures. From that time Erasmus applied himself to acquiring a command of Greek. Colet had studied abroad in the 1490s, at Paris, Orléans, Rome and possibly Florence, and he was one of a small circle of fellow-scholars in England who had spent time in Italy and elsewhere, improving their knowledge of Latin and Greek. Colet and Erasmus maintained their friendship and shared an objective to improve the standard of education. After Colet's appointment as Dean of St Paul's in 1505 – the year in which his father died, leaving him a substantial sum – he could begin to ponder on a scheme to reinvigorate the cathedral's school. Its earlier good reputation had fallen away by the late fifteenth century, when the leading London grammar schools were those attached to St Anthony's Hospital in Threadneedle Street and the hospital of St Thomas of Acon, and at St Peter's, Cornhill and St Andrew's, Holborn. Teachers were licensed by the church, which thereby was able to maintain a strong control over secondary education.

In drawing up the statutes and curriculum for the new school, Colet was greatly assisted by Erasmus, as well as others who were advocates of the new learning and had studied in Italy, chiefly at Padua, Bologna and Florence. They included Richard Pace, a diplomat who became Latin secretary to Henry VIII, William Grocyn, William Lily, who had also studied on the Greek island of Rhodes, and Thomas Linacre, who took a degree in medicine at Padua in 1496. Lily was appointed as the school's first High Master. Colet acquired a site at the east side of the cathedral precincts, on which stood 'lowe howses of bokebynderes', and built a schoolhouse there in 1508; the school was opened in 1510, for 153 pupils, without fee. It was for boys 'of all nations and countries indifferently', although he favoured Londoners' sons. Perhaps surprisingly, he was able to wrest its control from the church and assign its management to the Mercers' Company, which had been his father's livery company. As might have been expected, Erasmus fully approved, commenting that its supervision had been entrusted 'not to the clergy; not to the bishop, not to the chapter; nor to any great minister at court; but amongst the married laymen; the Company of Mercers, men of probity and reputation'. According to Erasmus, Colet had done that because 'he found less corruption in such a body of citizens than in any other order or degree of mankind'. Erasmus was an active supporter of the school and compiled a textbook for its use, and other publications of his were adopted by Colet. The school was so successful that by 1525 the statutory number of pupils had been exceeded, and the Mercers' Company was informed that 'the school is surcharged with scholars and in especial them that come out of the country'. The response was that non-Londoners should be excluded to keep the number within the prescribed limit.[31]

Despite the popularity of St Paul's school, through the first half of the century St Anthony's school was 'commended above others'. Its scholars gave the best impression and won the prizes at the disputations held in the precincts of St Bartholomew's priory 'upon a bank boarded about under a tree'. The rivalry between the two sets of pupils led to exchanges of insults and even to clashes in the streets, when from 'questions in grammar, they usually fell from words to blows with their satchels full of books, many times in great heaps, that they troubled the streets and passengers'.[32]

Colet's friend Thomas Linacre was another member of the European-educated humanist circle in London to apply the experience that he had gained and establish a significant institution in his own field of medicine. Linacre was in Italy from 1487 until 1499, where he may have lived for some time in the house of the leading printer Aldus Manutius. After his return to London he was for a time a tutor to Prince Arthur, Henry VII's heir, who died in 1502. But Linacre did not secure a post at court under Henry VII and it was only after Henry VIII came to the throne in 1509 that he gained an appointment, as royal physician. His reputation rested chiefly on his translations of Galen's works from Greek into Latin; he was probably the first English scholar to gain a European recognition as a humanist. In 1518 Linacre, five other physicians and Thomas Cranmer petitioned Henry VIII for the establishment of a college for physicians in London and within an area up to seven miles around the city. Their petition was accepted and the Royal College of Physicians came into existence by royal charter in September 1518, with Linacre, who drafted its statutes, as its president. Its meetings were held in his house in Knightrider Street, where he allocated two rooms for its use, which served as a meeting room and a library. The barbers and surgeons already had their own organisations and the apothecaries operated within the Grocers' Company, but the physicians did not have a framework for oversight of their profession, and so this was a major step for medical regulation and education. It was also a development that would attract considerable, and long-lasting, opposition from the established groups, as well as from the two universities. By the time of Linacre's death in 1524 the college's original six members had increased to twelve, and by 1537 it had eighteen members. Its position in London was settled by an Act of Common Council of 1525, which gave it the authority to punish unlicensed practitioners within the city with up to twenty days in prison, and ruled that apothecaries should provide medicine only on a prescription issued by a licensed physician.[33]

It is likely that the establishment of the college owed much to the example of such institutions on the continent, and to a tacit acknowledgment in government circles that London, and by extension England, had lagged behind in medical organisation. New ideas and practices flowed from the Continent in this field, as in so many others, as part of a two-way process as London's overseas relations developed. Its integration into the Continent's economy and culture resembled a series of overlapping circles, centred on the commercial world of the City, the court's artistic interests and patronage, and the humanist intelligentsia's networks.

4

In Sickness and in Poverty

For most Londoners life consisted of the daily round of work and maintaining family life, with some time for social obligations and leisure. But problems could intrude into the regular pattern, such as ill health, injury and accidents, and wider disruptions could affect a neighbourhood, as in the case of a fire; there were even disasters that could engulf the whole city, as was the case during epidemics. Such events could be enough to tip someone's circumstances from equilibrium into crisis, without a family or a livery company to fall back on. The authorities in early Tudor London attempted to deal with the consequences of sickness and poverty and matters which they saw as related to those problems.

The needy poor included those who were sick, and London was much better provided for in that respect than any other English city. By the 1530s it contained 350–400 beds for the sick, spread across five hospitals. The Augustinian priory and hospital of St Bartholomew were founded by Rahere, a member of Henry I's court, and the site in Smithfield was dedicated in 1123. The hospital soon developed into an institution that cared for orphans as well as the sick poor. Disputes between the two branches of the foundation, especially over income, led to their eventual separation in 1420. St Thomas's Hospital in Southwark similarly originated as part of an Augustinian house, the priory of St Mary Overy; after a fire in 1212 the hospital was re-founded in 1215 on the east side of the high street, Long Southwark. As well as being a hospital for the sick it served as an almshouse for the elderly poor and provided hospitality for travellers. An important contribution was made in the early fifteenth century by Richard Whittington, three times Mayor, who paid for a ward with eight beds which was to be a refuge for unmarried mothers, described as 'young women that had amiss, in trust of a good amendment'.

The hospital of St Mary without Bishopsgate was founded in 1197 by Walter Brune, or Brown, and his wife Rose. It was run by the Augustinian canons to provide care for the sick poor and women in childbirth, and for the children of mothers who had died giving birth until they were seven years old. Initially there were twelve or thirteen patients, but in 1253 the hospital was re-founded on a much larger scale, with two infirmaries, one for men and one for women, each containing thirty beds. A church and accommodation for the lay sisters who nursed the inmates were built, as well as a cloister for the Augustinian canons. Both Henry VII and Henry VIII allowed the institution to acquire more lands and so increase its revenue. In 1534 there was a prior and eleven canons. The infirmary was again extended; when the hospital was surrendered to the Crown, in 1539, it contained 180 beds. On the south side of London Wall was the hospital of Elsing Spital, founded in 1329 by William Elsing, a mercer, for a hundred blind beggars. This was taken over by the Augustinian canons in 1340 and had its own chapel, dedicated to St Mary. Another institution with specialised care was the hospital of the priory of St Mary Bethlehem, commonly known as Bedlam. The priory was founded outside Bishopsgate in 1279, and by 1329 had incorporated a hospital, which from the 1370s took care of the insane.

These hospitals' contribution to poor relief was explained by the corporation in a petition submitted to the king in 1538, which pointed out that they were needed to help 'the miserable people lying in the streete, offending every clene person passing by the way with theyre fylthye and nasty savors'.[1] (Smelly air was equated with foul and dangerously polluted conditions that could spread disease.) But the beggars in the streets were only a small part of those Londoners who qualified as being poor – the numbers varied as prices and prosperity fluctuated. They included day-labourers who were short of work, perhaps temporarily, journeymen who had been laid off by their masters, or those with longer-term problems because of age or infirmity. Some were in need only for a short time, until employment picked up or their family or household circumstances improved; others were widows and widowers who were not provided for. They received help through their livery company, while those outside the companies could obtain assistance from the Mayor and Aldermen. In 1538 the Mayor, Sir Richard Gresham, instituted an annual collection on Sundays at Paul's Cross, with the proceeds distributed 'to them that had most neede thereof in the cittie of London, and a registre kept of the same'.[2] The parishes were conduits for bequests made specifically for the poor, to be distributed after the donor's death or annually, on specific days.

Personal injuries and accidents such as fires could be devastating for householders in the short term, and could lead to loss of life. During 'a great fire' in Bread Street in August 1485, the parson of St Mildred's church and another man failed to escape from the parsonage house and were killed. An even greater disaster struck the area occupied by basketmakers in St Margaret Pattens parish during 'a great fyre' in 1538, 'where were burnt and perished in three houres above a dossin howses and 9 persons of men, women, and children, cleane burnt to death, which was a pyteous sight'.[3] That was unusual, for even when a fire could not be doused, the flames should have spread slowly enough to allow time for the occupants to escape and perhaps to remove trade goods and other valuable items. But all such catastrophes were at the least disruptive and at worst ruinously expensive. Owner-occupiers faced the cost of rebuilding, as did some tenants by the terms of their lease, although the practice of the Bridge Wardens of remitting rent from the ruined buildings for a time may not have been unusual. Whatever the arrangements, many of the victims would have needed assistance.

A chronicler noted in 1504 'many grete fyers in London in dyvers places', including St Martin-le-Grand and at the north end of the bridge, where six houses were destroyed. Two years later there was 'a great fier in London betwene the Custome Howsse and Billinsgate, that did great hurte'. Adverse weather also contributed to the numbers requiring help. Around midday on 15 January 1506 'rose soche a tempest of wynd tyll it was twelve at mydnyth, that it blew downe tres and tyles of howsyes', as well as the weathercock on St Paul's Cathedral. That winter also saw such a severe and prolonged frost that 'men myght goo with carttes over the Temse and horse', and in 1517 'a great frost began the 12 day of Januarie & in suche wise that no bote might goe betwixt London and Westminster all the terme tyme. And from Westminster to Lambeth was a common way over the Themms upon the ise.' These conditions were disruptive economically and expensive for families in terms of the extra fuel consumed, and the frost in 1517 arrived during a drought that lasted from September 1516 until the following May.[4]

St Katherine's Hospital, to the east of the Tower of London, came to provide accommodation for those with long-term needs. Initially founded in the 1140s, it was re-founded by Eleanor of Provence, Henry III's queen, in 1273, accommodating a Master, chaplains, three brethren, three sisters, ten bedeswomen and six poor scholars. Henry VI's charter of 1445 gave it the status of a royal peculiar, and its rights were confirmed by Henry VIII in 1526. St Katherine's served as an almshouse for gentlewomen, retaining the patronage of the queen.[5] Henry VII's plans for his memorial chapel at Westminster Abbey included an almshouse to the south-west of the abbey, which was founded in 1500 and completed by 1504. It was for a priest, twelve almsmen and three almswomen, who were to be over fifty years old, literate and to have been loyal servants of the Crown. In return for their lodging, food, fuel and a pension, they were to pray for the souls of the king, his ancestors and relatives.[6]

The first almshouse in London founded as a separate establishment, rather than as part of a religious institution's provision for the elderly, was set up by the Merchant Taylors' Company from funds bequeathed by John Chircheman, who died in 1413. This became the new model, with a wealthy citizen providing the funds and an endowment and his livery company taking responsibility for the administration. An almshouse for thirteen poor men at St Michael Paternoster Royal was endowed by the bequest of Richard Whittington, in his will of 1421, and was administered by the Mercers' Company. In 1429 the Grocers' Company built seven almshouses near to its hall, for 'aged poor alms people', and the will of Thomas Beamond, a salter, in 1454 gave funds for six houses to be erected for 'six of the most indigent poor of his aforesaid art to dwell therein, if such poor should be found, and if not, then six other of the most indigent of other arts within the city of London'. The skinners, brewers, cutlers and vintners also had assumed responsibility for almhouses by the end of the fifteenth century, and the parish clerks, drapers, haberdashers and clothworkers had followed suit by 1540. Some residential accommodation provided by bequests was not extensive enough to be designated an almshouse. In the case of the haberdashers, the almsmen's accommodation was in rooms over the kitchens of the company's hall, which would have been warm at least, and the Girdlers' Company administered two rooms near to its hall, bequeathed by Andrew Hunt in 1431 for 'two decayed persons of the livery of the said Company', the elder of whom should also have 7d a week.[7] In 1544 a member of the Vintners' Company bequeathed a small sum to 'the almes pore peple adioynng to the Vynteneres Hall', who may have been in the almshouse, or just in rooms.[8]

A significant contribution to poor relief in the city was made by Henry VII in 1505 when he founded a hospital on the site of the Duke of Lancaster's former palace of the Savoy, in the Strand. It had been sacked by the rioters during the Peasants' Revolt in 1381 and not rebuilt. The new hospital was for 100 poor people, 'Sick or Lame, or Travellers; to be furnished with Lodging, Food, Firing and Attendance'. It was dedicated to St John the Baptist, and a statue of the saint was placed over the Strand gate. The buildings were completed between 1515 and 1517 and included a very long dormitory with transepts, a domestic range parallel to the river, the Master's lodgings and the Savoy Chapel. The hospital was staffed by a Master, four chaplains, a matron and twelve sisters. William Holgill was appointed the first Master, in 1517; when financial problems later became apparent, he was blamed for having spent both the initial sum for establishing the hospital and the whole of the reserve. Benevolent endowments were at the mercy of those who administered them, and donors relied on the probity and diligence of those who had oversight of the charity.

Problems of social disruption and poor relief were greatly increased by the intermittent epidemics of plague and the sweat.

Their incidence was erratic and could not be predicted. One of the worst outbreaks during the early Tudor period struck in 1500 with 'a great plague of pestilence wherof men died very sore in many places, especially in and about London, where died in that whole yeere (as it was thought) about the number of 30000 people'.[9] The number of deaths is implausibly high, given the total population, and a reasonable estimate is a death toll of 10,000 – still one-fifth of the population. At that time no record was kept of vital statistics, either in years without plague or in such abnormal conditions. In 1513 a 'great plague' afflicted London from the spring until the autumn, and another epidemic struck two years later; such outbreaks continued to occur throughout Henry VIII's reign. The sweat had appeared in 1506 and returned in 1508–9, the spring of 1516, during the second half of 1517 and again in 1528.

A letter to the secretary of the Marquis of Mantua in 1517 reported how the sweat lasted twenty-four hours 'more or less', with the victims who died passing away within twelve hours. Treatment was difficult because during the fit that seized the patient it was fatal to take any cold drink or to allow any air to penetrate the garments or bedclothes in which the patient had commenced perspiring. Great care had to be taken to keep air from reaching the armpits and the patient's arms should be crossed on his or her chest. More covering on the bed than usual was necessary, but with care not to suffocate the patient, and the bedchamber should have a moderate fire, not to heat the room but to keep it at 'a tepid temperature'. Neglect of those precautions 'insured immediate death'.[10] Sebastian Giustinian summarized the outbreak: 'This disease makes very quick progress, proving fatal in twenty-four hours at the furthest, and many are carried off in four or five hours. The patients experience nothing but a profuse sweat, which dissolves the frame, and when once the twenty-four hours are passed all danger is at an end.' Few foreigners had fallen victim, but 'an immense number of natives' had died. They included a friend of Erasmus, the poet and humanist Andreas Ammonio, who died during the epidemic in 1517, prompting Thomas More to write to Erasmus with the wry comment that there was less danger on the battlefield than in London. That August Wolsey explained to the king that he had not attended on him because he had been 'so vexed with the sweat he dare not yet come to his presence'.[11]

The sweat emerged quickly and disappeared within a short time, whereas a plague epidemic took a number of weeks to develop and could last for months. Those who had the opportunity and the means to do so, effectively the wealthier sections of society, avoided the plague by leaving London. This meant the plague came to be regarded as a disease of the poor, while the sweat, taking everyone unprepared, afflicted all social groups. Both plague and sweat caused great alarm at court, and the safest option during any epidemic was for the king to order its members to disperse and keep away from all infected places. But in 1514 the plague 'even had the effrontery to force its way into the royal palace itself, causing two or three deaths', and in 1517 the sweat claimed the lives of the courtiers Lords Clinton and Grey, as well as 'many other knights and gentlemen', two pages in the royal entourage and some members of Wolsey's household.[12]

Senior figures close to the court were afflicted during subsequent outbreaks of the sweat, so much so that the king came to take a close interest in the disease and offered advice on evading it. This was little more than 'to keep ... out of all air where any of that infection is', avoiding contact with those who may have the disease and regulating one's diet. Sir Brian Tuke, Clerk of Parliament, accepted that it was greatly to be feared and avoided – his wife had survived an attack – but he had no more idea than anyone else of its nature, concluding that it was 'rather a kind of a pestilence than otherwise, and that the moisture of years past hath so altered the nature both of our meats and bodies to moist humours, as disposeth us to sweat'. In his opinion many fell ill just through fear of the disease, so that when a man in good health came from London and talked of the sweat, 'the same night all the town is full of it, and thus it spreads as the fame runs'.[13] He was mocking the hypochondriacs and the pessimists' view that all news should be construed as bad news. Neither the king's solution nor Tuke's opinions could contribute usefully to the formulation of a policy to restrict the spread of epidemic diseases.

In the Italian cities well-considered countermeasures had been put in place virtually from the onset of the plague in the late 1340s.

Essentially, these consisted of isolating the sick and restricting movement, especially of merchants and their goods, particularly textiles, because plague was recognised as a disease of the trade routes. Pistoia introduced such restrictions in 1348 and Venice began the quarantining of shipping, passengers and cargoes in that year. From those beginnings more complex procedures were developed, although all were based on the same principles of restriction of movement and isolation, with the Italian communities most assiduous in observing them and the countries of northern Europe less so. No such steps were taken in England. Erasmus's parents had died of the plague and he was always understandably anxious about epidemic disease; in 1515 he wrote to Cardinal Wolsey's physician commenting that he was 'frequently astonished and grieved to think how it is that England has been now for so many years troubled by a continual pestilence, especially by a deadly sweat'. This he attributed to lack of ventilation and cleanliness in houses and the eating of too much salted meat, as well the need to have the streets 'cleaned from mud and urine, and the suburbs kept in better order'.[14] He was aware that the safest course was to avoid others and when he left London in October 1513 he did so without even visiting Colet, explaining by letter, 'I was in such haste to get away from there for fear of the plague that I decided not to enter even my lodgings. Again when I went back to remove my books, I got together all my books and my gear in complete solitude, and, having done this, by which time also I was quite late, I hurried away and never even slept in my room.'[15] A few months earlier a report sent to Venice included the terse observation that in London 'deaths from plague occur constantly'.[16]

In January 1518 Wolsey introduced the first measures in England aimed at reducing the incidence of plague. They were contained in a royal proclamation which stated that the 'resorting of persons not infected with the pestilence to other persons infected doth daily cause the increase of further infection, to the great mortality and death of many persons which, by reason of such resort one to another, have been ignorantly infected with the said pestilence'. To avoid unanticipated contacts with the sick, houses in London that contained persons infected with plague had to be marked for forty days with a bundle of straw on a pole at least ten feet long overhanging the street. When victims went out they were to carry a white rod four feet long, so that they could be avoided. The Court of Aldermen further ordered that no garments or bedding which may have come into contact with someone who had the disease could be removed from the house, or aired in any street or lane, and certainly not sold or given away. The bundle of straw, or 'wisp', to distinguish an infected house proved to be too elaborate and in 1521 was replaced by a headless cross, known as a St Anthony's Cross, fixed on the front of the building. The regulations were designed to clearly identify infected houses and individuals and so isolate the sick; a related order was issued for cleaning the streets 'for the avoiding of contagious infections'.[17] The street-cleaning functions specified when the Fraternity of Saint Katherine was established in 1517, taking over those duties from the wards, were described as 'to clense, purge and kepe clene all the Stretes and lanes of this Citie and Suburbes of the same of Donge and other filth'.[18]

Wolsey's orders followed soon after similar ones had been issued in Paris and they marked the beginning of the government's policy to prevent and restrict the spread of plague. To help the royal court identify the beginning of an epidemic, in 1519 Wolsey further ordered that a record of plague deaths should be made. This was done in future plague years; in 1543 the Privy Council admonished the Common Council for its 'slaknes used at this present' in not sending it the numbers of plague deaths, which were needed so that the king 'may surely knowe howe the sykenes dothe augment or decrease'. The Mayor's response was that he had indeed compiled weekly returns of the numbers, as his predecessors had done.[19] The returns were to develop into the Bills of Mortality, tabling the weekly number of deaths in the city by parish, distinguishing plague deaths and, as they developed, giving all causes of death. Although devised to safeguard the monarch, they were to prove of great value to the city's authorities. In 1538 Thomas Cromwell, acting as Vicar General, ordered that a record be kept of baptisms, marriages and burials in all parishes, which showed the varying number of deaths, and some clerks marked plague deaths.

The plague regulations may not have been easy to enforce; some Londoners were said to have 'murmured' and made seditious remarks about the proclamation of 1518. London continued to be stricken with epidemics from time to time, as were other cities, but the capital developed an especially bad reputation, so that in 1538 the French ambassador described it as 'of the towns in the world one of the most subject to plague'.[20] In 1548 the number of deaths was three times the average, and in 1554 the Venetian envoy Giacomo Soranzo wrote that there was 'some little plague in England well nigh every year, for which they are not accustomed to make sanitary provisions, as it does not usually make great progress; the cases for the most part occur amongst the lower classes, as if their dissolute mode of life impaired their constitutions'.[21] He had come to London in 1551, a year which saw an outbreak of the sweat when 'there dyde a grett multitude of pepull soddenly thorrow alle London'.[22] Parliament was prorogued in 1531 because of plague, and there were more epidemics in 1535 and 1537. When London was 'sore afflicted with the pestilence' in 1543 it was recognised that 'if great confluence of people should resort thither it might be occasion the rather to increase than diminish' the sickness. The humanist writer Thomas Paynell had explained a few years earlier that 'in a greatte multytude maye be some one infectyd the which may infecte manye'.[23] Church services were allowed to continue, but beggars were banned from churches during them.

Prohibiting assemblies of people was to become a mainstay of the government's plague policy. So, too, was household quarantine, with the sick confined to their houses rather than taken to isolation hospitals, known as pest-houses, as was the practice in many Continental cities. In 1543 a renewal of the orders stated once again that infected houses should be distinguished by a cross for forty days and that those who had been infected who needed to go out 'because of their poverty' had to carry a white rod, now just two feet long, also for forty days. Straw and rushes were not to be thrown into the street from the infected houses but should be burned on the premises or taken carefully at night into the fields to be burned, and there should be greater diligence in clearing rubbish from the streets and sweeping and washing them. The outbreak was blamed on sloth and negligence, which could lead to the 'corruption of the air', with the foul air emanating from filth and rubbish: the means by which disease was transmitted. Dogs were also suspected of being a cause of the outbreaks, and they were to be taken out of the city or killed, except for 'hounds, spaniels or mastiffs' that were needed for the security of the premises, in which cases they should not be allowed out.[24]

Those steps reflected current thinking on the prevention of disease. In More's *Utopia* the citizens did not allow 'anything that is filthy, loathsome, or uncleanly to be brought into the city, lest the air, by the stench thereof infected and corrupt, should cause pestilent disease'. There were four isolation hospitals outside the city walls of Amaurote, which were 'so big, so wide, so ample, and so large, that they may seem four little towns', designed so that the patients were not crowded together and so that those with diseases, 'such as be wont by infection to creep from one to another, might be laid apart from the company of the residue'.[25] The benefits of isolating those infected were understood, but the measure was difficult to achieve unless they were given practical support, which effectively meant a financial commitment and the organisation of helpers at a local level. This may have been recognised, but was not yet addressed.

Wolsey's orders had included the appointment of an official in London whose role was to search for beggars and vagrants, denizens whose malodorous qualities could be linked to the spread of disease. Other matters in London tackled by Wolsey during the 1510s included fixing the price of poultry, an investigation into the reasons for the scarcity of meat, setting the rates charged by the Thames watermen and tightening up the arrangements for the Watch. An order of Common Council aimed at protecting the fabric of the bridge was issued in 1517, prohibiting fishing with nets in the river within a specified distance of the bridge both upstream and downstream from it. Local administration, including the enforcement of environmental matters, was carried out by the overlapping jurisdictions of ward, parish, precinct and livery company. There were 111 parishes in the city and 242 precincts, and so administration was carried out in small units, with a high proportion of householders serving as one of the local officials at some stage. They were likely to be active and conscientious, both out of a sense of civic and local duty and because their own interests were fairly immediate in, for example, the notification of potential fire hazards or the accumulation of noxious filth.

Concern with diet and excessive indulgence was also evident in the years after Wolsey came to power, with the passing of new sumptuary laws. These attempted to limit extravagance in dining by setting the appropriate numbers of courses for meals for those with goods worth £500 or more, specified by social rank from cardinals downwards, including both senior churchmen and the laity. The civic elite were not exempt – the Mayor and Sheriffs of London were specifically mentioned – and, indeed, the scale of their hospitality attracted comments by contemporary visitors. This was not new: the first Act of Parliament addressing the problem of personal excess had been passed in 1334 and a number of later measures had attempted to deal with the issue, which included costly and overtly showy dress, as well as food and drink. Wolsey attempted to enforce the sumptuary legislation through the Star Chamber court, although the objective of controlling dress and diet by such means was surely unachievable. The underlying cause of the disquiet, expressed in an Act of 1515 relating to apparel, was that emulating the expensive clothing and trappings of others 'hath been the occasion of great impoverishing of divers of the king's subjects, and provoked many of them to rob and do extortion and other unlawful deeds to maintain thereby their costly array'.[26]

Crime was a problem, according to the Venetians. Trevisano, in 1500, thought that 'there is no country in all the world where there are so many thieves and robbers as in England; insomuch that few venture to go alone in the country, excepting in the middle of the day, and fewer still in the towns at night, and least of all in London'. He returned to the subject later in his account, commenting that people were arrested every day 'by dozens, like birds in a covey, and especially in London; yet, for all this, they never cease to rob and murder in the streets'. In 1509, Andrew Badoer's discontent with London was exacerbated by the servants he hired, 'who were common thieves'.[27] A Spanish visitor half a century later was also appalled at the scale of the problem: 'There are incredible numbers of robbers here; they go about in bands of twenty, and neither justice nor fear of God avail to hold them back.'[28] The murder in 1533 of two foreign merchants 'in a bote on the Temse' was the kind of incident that visitors would have found unsettling; a married couple were convicted and executed for the killings. Punishments were public and not uncommon; on one day in February 1537 ten women and four men were executed at Tyburn. Those convicted of poisoning met a more than commonly gruesome fate. The Bishop of Rochester's cook was executed in 1530 for attempting to poison the bishop and others: he was 'boylyd in a cauderne in Smythfeld ... lockyd in a chayne and pullyd up and downe with a gybbyt at dyvers tymes tyll he was dede'. A similar execution took place in 1542, when a woman was 'boyled in Smithfield' having been convicted of poisoning four people in three households with whom she had lodged.[29] Some executions took place in the street, close to the scene of the crime.

Thomas More attributed the causes of crime to 'bawds, queans, whores, harlots, strumpets, brothel-houses, stews ... wine-taverns, ale-houses, and tippling houses, with so many naughty, lewd, and unlawful games, as dice, cards, tables, tennis, bowls, quoits, do not all these send the haunters of them straight a-stealing, when their money is gone?'[30] His view chimed with that of the government so far as pastimes were concerned, and the offenders and causes of crime which he listed appeared in the censorious statutes and proclamations that were issued periodically.

Attempts were made to enforce the legislation. Patrick Russell of the parish of Holy Sepulchre was accused in 1498 of playing bowls in his house, and in the following year of keeping bowling alleys on the premises that were used by servants and apprentices. He was described as a gardener but may have been running a commercial bowling operation, not just a place for passing the time.[31]

Indoor gaming was the kind of transgression that came within Wolsey's line of fire for its detrimental social and economic effects, and in 1528 he authorised the destruction of gaming tables, as well as 'dice, cards, bowls, closhes [nine-pins], tennis balls and all other things pertaining to the said unlawful games'. Searches were carried out in London, with prosecutions brought against offenders; the citizens were said to have complained that the cardinal 'grudged at every man's pleasure saving his own'. Exception was made for the Christmas holidays, so long as the games were played in the master's house – in any event, control of games which could be played with no more than a deck of cards or a set of dice was well-nigh impossible. The government's fear was that games of chance were all too likely to lead to losses and then to indigence, especially for those who fell foul of professional cheats, and spending time playing rather than working was condemned.[32]

The courtiers should have anticipated the difficulties as well as anyone, for gambling was popular at court and was institutionalised, with the Knight Marshal of the Household acting as both the organiser and the bookmaker for the games of chance. Henry VIII was much given to gambling, especially when he was a young man, losing considerable sums at dice and even at shuffleboard, in which a coin, usually a groat, was slid along a table with the object of coming to a stop as close to the edge as possible.[33] Both he and his father also played tennis, as did members of the aristocracy, yet that too was on More's list of crime-related pastimes. The objection to tennis continued, and when William Griffiths, a 'King's servant', renovated a tennis-play in All Hallows the Less in 1542 and applied for a licence to permit its use, he stressed that it was for 'the use of strangers born out of the King's dominions' and he was not going to allow the king's own subjects to play there.[34] Primero came to be the favoured card game among courtiers and the elite; Shakespeare has Henry VIII playing with the Duke of Suffolk, although the game only became popular well into the sixteenth century.

The approved way for men to pass their free time profitably was archery, and the longbow remained the preferred weapon for the citizens – hence the order that if crossbows and handguns were being used for recreation they should be destroyed. Extra space beyond the walls for the archery butts was provided in 1489 when the gardens outside Moorgate were destroyed and the ground 'made a plain field'.[35] This had a serious, military aspect, for men between sixteen and sixty-five years of age were required to serve in the militia. Service was seen as a citizen's duty, and in 1522 the government initiated listings of men within the aforementioned age range and their weapons, making evasion difficult. Membership required giving a certain amount of time to training so that such a large number of men could assemble and manoeuver together, to avoid an embarrassing shambles at the annual Midsummer muster. An officer corps was provided by the members of the Society of the Artillery Garden in London, a military guild which received a royal charter in 1537, perhaps a formal recognition of an existing group. It was similar to urban military guilds or societies in north European cities; the earliest surviving group portrait of the members of a militia guild in the Low Countries was painted in 1529.[36]

At the muster in 1539, when fears of a papacy-inspired invasion were running high, the alderman of each ward supervised the process and 'turned such as were not meet to be archers to pikes and delivered their bows to such as were meet to be archers'. Each man had a white harness, a white cap with a feather, was 'cleanly shod' and had a sword and a dagger. The number of men mustered was estimated at 16,500, including a guard of twelve men for the City's standard, which was carried before the 'Lord Mayor', a term that was just coming into common use. They marched through the city from Stepney to Westminster to be reviewed by the king and were watched along the way by crowds in the streets and people at the windows. This was thought to be a great success: 'There was never a goodlyer sight in London, nor the citizens better besene, then this muster was, which was a great rejoycinge to the Kinges Majestie, and a great honour to the citye.' But the preparations and the parade itself were so expensive that the king cancelled the customary celebrations for the watch at Midsummer, which was disappointing, to say the least, because 'the mayor and sheriffes had prepared divers pageantes with lightes and other thinges for to have had the sayd watche, and had noe knowledge till two dayes afore Midsommer that yt should not be kept, which was a great losse to poore men'. Alternative entertainment was provided by a mock battle on the Thames at Westminster between two armed barges – one the king's and the other purported to be that of the Pope and his cardinals. After they had cruised up and down a few times they came to blows, and it cannot have been a surprise when 'the Pope and his cardinalles were overcome, and all his men cast over the borde into the Thames; howbeyt there was none drowned, for they were persons chosen which could swimme, and the Kinges barge lay by hoveringe to take them upp as they were cast over the borde, which was a goodly pastime'.[37]

The most exuberant annual festivities were held at Midsummer and Christmas and during the fairs. Considerable pride was taken in the Midsummer celebrations, such as those in 1529 when there was 'a goodly wache and two goodly pagenttes in Cheppe-syde'.[38] The largest of the fairs was St Bartholomew's, in Smithfield, established in 1123 by Rahere, with the tolls contributing to the priory's income. In 1445 the corporation and the priory came to an agreement making them joint lords of the fair. After the dissolution of the priory its rights passed to Sir Richard (later Lord) Rich. The fair was held on three days, centred on St Bartholomew's Day, 24 August. The event was very popular for both general entertainment and trading, especially in cloth, leather, pewter, livestock, and butter and cheese. The enjoyment came from the bustle and variety of people, the range of entertainments and attractions, such as puppeteers, conjurers, players, balladeers, wrestlers (a site in Clerkenwell was popular for wrestling bouts), tightrope-walkers and fire-eaters, and there were booths for eating and drinking. As well as legitimate trading and general jollity, the fair was long associated with cheating, petty crime and immorality. In 1537 three men were hanged 'for stelynge in Bartylmew fayer'; one of them was the hangman for the city, and the fact that he had gained the reputation of being 'a conninge butcher in quarteringe of men' gives an idea of the frequency of executions for treason, which involved the beheading and dismemberment of the corpse.[39]

St James's fair was established in 1290 and was held on the eve of St James's Day, 25 July, adjoining the leper hospital of St James the Less in Westminster. Southwark fair was held over three days around 8 September from at least the 1440s onwards and was granted a charter by Edward IV in 1462. During the fair stalls were set up on the bridge as well as in the streets; in 1499 a total of 7s 8d was collected from 'divers artificers stonding and selling their wares and chafres on the said bridge in the tyme of Oure Ladye Faire in Southwerke'. The strictures that were applied to Bartholomew fair were also applicable to that in Southwark, but a corrective to the impression of them as wholly boisterous events is given by the record of 3s 6d paid in 1528 to the choir of St Magnus the Martyr for 'singing evensong in the Chapel at our Lady's Fair before the Mayor and his brethren'.[40]

The fairs came to be seen as increasing the risk of a plague outbreak, due of the numbers of people crowding together. The government was inclined to order the Mayor to prohibit them when the risk was high, although the threat of plague had to be set against the economic disruption and popular resentment that the ban would cause. In 1535 the Mayor refused to cancel St Bartholomew's Fair because, he claimed, the extent of the disease was exaggerated 'by the sayenges of suche persons as resorte to the seid Citie'. More than that, there was a risk in the economic climate of the time that those who had brought their cloth to London would not be able to sell it, for 'the citizens of this Citie be nott stored with money, to dispatche the seid clothes, and other commodityes, yn the said Fear, as they have doen yn tyme past'. The Mayor asked Cromwell for a loan of £10,000 from the Crown, which the City would use to promote sales at the fair and so create work for those who otherwise would have to 'begge or stele'. His pleas emphasised the fair's commercial importance to London and to those from elsewhere 'that doo resorte to this seide Fear'.[41]

Londoners were likely to have been as protective of their fairs and festivities as were their rulers. The prolonged absence of the court from London in 1517 because of the sweat, and the failure to keep Christmas, when the citizens were permitted to come and watch the festivities, caused 'general discontent' in the capital. That was partly because the working regime for many of them was so strict that the holidays were a welcome relief from their routines. The patterns of work were reiterated from time to time, for example in an act of Common Council of 1538 that set out the daily round for those working in the building trades, gardeners and labourers. During the winter half of the year a worker in those trades was to begin at six o'clock in the morning and work until nine o'clock and then 'goo to hys brekefast & to tary therat but onely one quarter of an howre, & than immedyatly to resorte ageyn unto hys sayd worke'. He then continued until midday, when he had a break of an hour for his dinner, returning to work by one o'clock 'at the farthest'. At four o'clock he could 'goo to hys drynkeyng by the space of one quarter of an houre onely' and then return and work until six o'clock. He was to have 'none other houres or vacant tyme yn the hole day other than as ys aforesayd'. The maximum wage was set at 7*d* a day for building workers and 5*d* for gardeners and labourers, which rose to 8*d* a day for the building trades during the summer months, when work began at five o'clock and ended at seven o'clock in the evening, with the same breaks as in the winter.[42] With such a stringent regime and long hours, a man in those trades had scarcely any free time, although of course work could be fitful and not continuous, and wholly at the mercy of the weather. Even so, such regulation shows the inflexibility in the working pattern, which necessarily restricted other activities.

Thomas More was aware of this. He described how the task of the locally elected officials in Utopia was

> to see and take heed that no man sit idle, but that every one apply his own craft with earnest diligence. And yet for all that, not to be wearied from early in the morning to late in the evening with continual work, like laboring and toiling beasts. For this is worse than the miserable and wretched condition of bondmen. Which nevertheless is almost everywhere the life of workmen and artificers, saving in Utopia.

Did he have the London that he knew in mind? The Utopians worked a nine-hour day, had a two-hour break for dinner and slept for eight hours; the rest of the time could be given over to pastimes which were worthwhile and profitable, and not 'foolish and pernicious games' such as dice-play.[43]

The strict management of workmen was displayed in a mayoral decree directed at those 'obstinate and misruled and riotous Journeymen and Servants, and also apprentices' who would not work on a casual basis but insisted on being hired for a certain time, preferring to 'sit in Ale houses and haunt ill company, and also play at unlawful games, the which is great hurt and hindrance and an undoing to all young men and an ill example for many servants'. With such a fierce preamble, it was surely no surprise that the remedy was harsh. A journeymen who refused employment for that reason 'but had rather play and go up and down like a Vagabond' should be punished, with a day or two in gaol for a first offence, five days for a second, and for a third he was to be 'tied at a cart's Arse and beaten naked through the City like a vagabond And to be banished from the City for seven years and a day'.[44] Alehouses and gaming were among the chief targets of the city rulers in their drive to keep the citizens at work and so reduce the level of poverty.

Government and civic intervention, such as those measures initiated by Wolsey during the 1510s and 1520s, was designed to both regulate the citizens' behaviour and also to ameliorate their conditions. As well as being stern overseers of the Londoners' life and labour, the Mayor and Aldermen provided charitable help to those in need on an occasional rather than a systematic basis. Citizens were also integrated into the life of the church through their parishes and the monasteries, which were both almsgivers to the poor and beneficiaries of the citizens' charity.

5

Churches, Cloisters and Heretics

The Londoners' lives revolved not only around their families, trades and livery companies, but also their parishes and the weekly and seasonal cycles of services and processions. The year was punctuated by the celebration of civic elections and swearings-in, the church's festivals and saints' days. As well as the parish churches, the city contained monasteries, friaries and hospitals. The two worlds intermeshed, with some citizens worshipping in monasteries as well as in their churches, making donations to them and in some cases choosing a monastery rather than their parish church for their place of burial. And the clergy were conspicuous on London's streets, for as it was the centre of civil government, so was it the focus for ecclesiastical patronage and home of a class of clergymen who were also office-holders in the state.

London's parish churches varied in size according to the extent of the parishes, some of which were very small, especially those in the centre of the City. The largest of the monastic churches were bigger and grander than many of the parish churches. The largest church of the nine orders of friars in the city was that of the Franciscans, the Grey Friars, in Newgate Street, built in the early fourteenth century. At 300 feet long, 89 feet wide and 64 feet high to the line of the roof, it was the second largest church in early Tudor London; only St Paul's was bigger. Rather smaller, but still a large building, was the church of the Dominicans, or Black Friars, built in the late thirteenth century and measuring 220 feet by 45 feet; John Stow laconically described it as 'a large church'. Smaller again was the church within the monastery of the Augustinian friars, located on a site bounded by the modern London Wall on the north and Throgmorton Street on the south. Built in 1354, it had three aisles and nine bays and was 153 feet by 83 feet. Its chief glory was the central spire, rebuilt after a storm in 1362 and admired by Stow as 'a most fine spired steeple, small, high, and straight, I have not seen the like'. The Carmelites, known as the White Friars, were established between Fleet Street and the Thames, and their church, 260 feet long, had a tower that was also surmounted by a tall spire. Holy Trinity Priory's church was rebuilt in the late fourteenth century and was roughly 230 feet long, with side aisles and a long chancel. Across the river, in Southwark, the Augustinian priory of St Mary Overy was founded in the early twelfth century. Its buildings were replaced after a fire in 1212, with the priory church rebuilt. It was 'again newly built' in the late fourteenth and fifteenth centuries, but not entirely successfully, for in 1468 a part of the stone roof of the nave fell in and was repaired with timber.[1]

The Carthusians, whose priory was close to Smithfield, posed a contrast to the monastic orders which enlarged or rebuilt their churches with royal or aristocratic patronage. It had been established in 1371 on the site of a Black Death burial ground and had taken the modest cemetery chapel of 1349 as its church. This caused problems because the laity continued to attend services there, and even to wander around the cloister on festival days. For the Carthusians, with their exclusiveness and detachment from the world, the presence of the locals was undesirable, and a chapel for the laity was added at the west end of the monastic church in 1405 and a gate-chapel erected in the outer precinct in 1481. Before the chapel was added in 1405, the church was 97 feet by 38 feet; five side-chapels were built by 1520, but it was not substantially enlarged. Two of the side-chapels were built and endowed by Sir John Popham, an experienced soldier who was appointed Treasurer of the Household in 1437, and one of them, the chapel of SS Michael and John the Baptist, contained his tomb. In the early sixteenth century the side-chapel of St Katherine was endowed by Sir Robert Rede, an eminent lawyer, fellow of King's Hall, Cambridge, and from 1506 Chief Justice of the Common Pleas. He died in 1519, specifying in his will that he should be buried there.

Lay men and women were buried within the priory throughout its existence, as at the other monastic houses, some in the church and its chapels and others in the cloister. Many were benefactors whose wills included a request for burial there. And, despite their austerity, the Carthusians' church did display a certain richness by the early sixteenth century. At the high altar was a reredos of carved bone, possibly ivory, with the story of the Passion, flanked by images of SS John the Baptist and Peter. The front of the high altar was decorated with an alabaster carving with the Trinity and other images. The other altars were also embellished, with painted and gilt images, and those in the choir were separated by wainscot partitions.[2]

Other orders attempted to preserve the sanctity of their precincts and create the calm atmosphere conducive to holiness, worship and contemplation. But not all of them found that to be easy. For the abbey of St Peter's, Westminster, it was particularly difficult, for it adjoined the principal royal palace, where accommodation was in short supply, and so the abbey found itself lodging visitors, diplomats, senior churchmen and others, and providing space for meetings. The ample accommodation at the Black Friars included a guest house, the chapter house, and frater or great hall, 100 feet by 46 feet, a library, an infirmary and the prior's lodgings. The great hall was used by the Court of Chancery on at least four occasions during the fourteenth century, and in the fifteenth century by the Royal Council. Parliament met there in 1450 (hence its designation the 'Black Parliament'), 1523 and 1529. Emperor Charles V and his entourage occupied the guest house during his visit to London in 1522, when a wooden gallery was built across the River Fleet to connect it to the new royal palace of Bridewell, erected in 1515–23. When Henry VIII attempted to obtain a divorce from his first queen, Katherine of Aragon, on the grounds that the marriage was invalid because her marriage to his elder brother Arthur had been consummated, the case was heard at the Black Friars, in 1529, with the king and the queen both present. Cardinal Lorenzo Campeggio, absentee Bishop of Salisbury, presided, as protector of England at the papal curia, together with Cardinal Thomas Wolsey, Henry's Chancellor. On 31 July Campeggio announced that he was adjourning the hearing until 1 October because the court was part of the Roman consistory and so would keep the legal terms observed there. It never met again. There could have been no closer involvement with the most pressing matters of state than that.

For practical purposes, the monks or nuns necessarily had to engage with the citizens for supplies and specialist professional assistance, and they also shared their places of worship with them. At the friaries, involvement with the laity was needed to generate income, and whilst the friars were favoured in the early sixteenth century for their poverty and their preaching, the more reclusive orders found relations with the laity to be a problem. At St Helen's, Bishopsgate the nunnery church was built adjoining the north side of the existing parish church, forming a single building divided by an arcade. In the fifteenth century some nuns were admonished for waving over the screen that separated the two aisles to members of the congregation in the parish aisle, and the nuns were told to refrain from kissing secular persons and to wear plain, not showy, veils. The priory of St Saviour, Bermondsey erected a church nearby dedicated to St Mary Magdalene 'for the resort of the inhabitants ... there to have their Divine service'. It came to serve as a parish church. As with other houses, the priory provided accommodation for those who were of suitable rank. Elizabeth, widow of Edward IV, was sent there in 1486 by an order of the Council, where she died in the abbey in 1492. Other lay people came to live there. The Minoresses also accommodated aristocratic women, including Elizabeth, Dowager Duchess of Norfolk, who died in 1507, and Edmund de la Pole's widow, Margaret, after his execution in 1513. Houses were erected in the outer precinct of the Carthusian priory, at least one of which was leased to a layman, Sir John Neville, Lord Latimer. In 1532 he took a lease of the mansion, tenement, stables and gardens at the east end of the churchyard, formerly held by the Abbot of Pershore. John Leland, the topographer and King's Antiquary, was recorded at a tenement adjoining Lord Latimer's mansion between 1538 and 1546.[3]

The balance between the life of the cloister and accepting lay patronage was difficult to achieve. At Holy Trinity, Aldgate 'the prior kept a most bountiful house of meat and drink, both for rich and poor, as well within the house as at the gates, to all comers, according to their estates'.[4] One observer thought that there was greater and more varied provision for the guests than for the members of the priory. Fees were paid to twelve lawyers and wages to the servants, who were the steward, rent-gatherer, cook, master of the children, laundress, carpenter, butler, bell-ringer and gardener. Expenses for provisions at the prior's lodgings were varied but included cinnamon, ginger, cloves and mace, aniseed, spice bread, pepper, saffron, sugar, butter and eggs, with 3s 4d paid for 'strawberries for Trinity Sunday'. There were gifts to the queen and members of the king's household, the Mayor, the Sheriffs' yeoman and the Earl of Essex's minstrels. A significant contribution to the priory's revenues was provided by the dues payable to St Botolph's Church, just outside Aldgate, granted to it by a group of London burgesses in 1125. The priory keenly defended its rights to the church and it erected a new church building for the parishioners in the early sixteenth century. But its growing financial problems proved to be terminal, and it was the first monastic house in London to be surrendered to the king, in 1532.[5]

By contrast, the Charterhouse benefited from a period of careful economy. In the mid-fifteenth century it was pleading poverty and was certainly not a wealthy institution, even with the support of so prominent a patron as Cicely, Duchess of York and mother of Edward IV. Indeed, in 1482 the buildings were said to be in great need of repair.[6] The priory's receipts fluctuated considerably. In 1492–3 they were recorded as £589, including arrears of rent, but at the end of that accounting year the house was £101 in debt. Philip Underwood then became procurator, under whose careful management income rose sharply, so that by the end of 1495 the debts had been cleared. When Underwood completed his last account, in 1500, receipts had reached £1,150 per annum and the annual surplus was £150.[7]

Additions and alterations to the Charterhouse buildings indicate that the early sixteenth century was a relatively prosperous period. The priory attracted the patronage of Henry VII as one of eighteen religious houses he selected to perform anniversary services interceding for him and his family. This was agreed in 1504 and brought in a small annual fee, and the priory was allocated a bequest of £40 in his will.[8] Between 1490 and the early 1530s, a new cell for the prior was built, three extra monks' cells were added to the great cloister, the chapter house was rebuilt and a small court was created within ranges of service buildings. By 1534 the original complement of a prior and twenty-four monks had been increased by three, and the house maintained another thirty-seven 'religious'.[9]

Other houses enjoyed royal and aristocratic support, as well as that of the City. The 663 'persons of quality' buried in the church of the Grey Friars included four queens, four duchesses, four countesses, one duke, two earls, eight barons and thirty-five knights. St Katherine's Hospital received £40 at the funeral of Henry VII, and in 1517 St Bartholomew's priory was exempted from taxation to help finance the rebuilding of its church. Recovery from the double catastrophe which struck the Minoresses without Aldgate was greatly assisted by donations. The first calamity came during 'a plague of pestilence' in 1515, when 'there died in this house of nuns professed to the number of twenty-seven, besides other lay people, servants in their house'. As the complement of the house was an abbess and twenty-six sisters, this suggests that its population was wiped out. Soon afterwards fire swept through the buildings. Henry VIII gave £200 towards the rebuilding efforts; the Mayor, Aldermen and citizens added £133 6s 8d, and, later prompted by Cardinal Wolsey, the Court of Common Council gave a further £66 13s 4d, bringing the total up to £400. By 1539 the house contained an abbess and twenty-three sisters and so had made an almost full recovery from those disasters.[10]

The extent of the Franciscans' integration into the Londoners' world is shown by the presence of the graves of 107 London citizens there, and by the livery companies contributing to the cost of paving the nave of their church with marble. In 1514 it was agreed that the Mayor and Aldermen should process to the priory annually on St Francis's day.[11] The prior of Holy Trinity, Aldgate was the alderman for Portsoken Ward and, as John Stow was later to recall: 'These priors have sitten and ridden amongst the aldermen of London, in livery like unto them, saving that his habit was in shape of a spiritual person, as I myself have seen in my childhood.'[12] At the Black Friars, 211 testators requested to be buried in the church, eighty-four of whom were London citizens, who preferred to be interred in a monastic church rather than in that of their own parish. This applied to the other houses, too. Sir John Skevington, an alderman, who made his will in 1524, donated £50 towards the rebuilding of the church of the Crossed Friars and asked to be buried 'within the high choir', although he was a parishioner at St Mary Woolnoth.[13] The City had promoted the rebuilding of the friars' church in the early 1520s, and Sir John Milborne, Mayor in 1521-2, was buried there. In his will, proved in 1515, Sir Thomas Thwaites, a mercer, asked to be interred in the chapel of St Jerome in the Carthusians' church, and he bequeathed to the priory all the 'jewels and stuff' from his own chapel.[14]

In the 1520s over a third of the wealthier London citizens made a bequest of some kind to a monastic house. Through such legacies the possessioner houses built up considerable property portfolios. The Benedictine nuns of St Helen, Bishopsgate came to own almost the whole parish and had property in sixteen other parishes; in 1535 about a half of the income of the collegiate church of St Martin-le-Grand came from its London rents, and by the same date Holy Trinity, Aldgate had property in eighty-seven London parishes. In 1535 St Mary Overy's annual income was £624 6s 6d, of which 45 per cent came from rents of property in Southwark. Between 50 per cent and 85 per cent of the income of a cross-section of London's monastic houses were from London property. Chiefly through bequests, monasteries outside London had also come to own property in the city, and by around 1530 roughly one-third of properties within the walls were owned by the Church.

The citizens' relationship with the Church was not only as worshippers and benefactors, but as tenants. This could create difficulties. The Crossed Friars were alleged to have received 'great sums' from Peter and Margaret Johnson, and to have entered into an agreement in 1511 to pay their daughter an annuity of £3 6s 8d, but in 1535 Margaret, by then a widow, claimed that the payments had not been made for the last ten years. She also alleged that the priory had failed to honour an agreement of 1518, whereby in exchange for other donations a house was to be built for her and her husband within the precincts. The priory offered to settle the case by giving Margaret permission to live in the precincts with an annual pension of £3 and an annuity of £1 to her daughter after her death. The house had also borrowed more than £25 from John

Watson, a mercer, who allowed it to keep the money for more than ten years before petitioning 'to recover my dues'. A further debt was to George Tadlow, a haberdasher, from whom it had borrowed £27 10s 0d in 1527.[15]

Whatever the rights and wrongs of such cases, they were no different in nature from disputes between the citizens and other landlords. The clergy behaved like the laity in other respects, going with prostitutes and even brawling among themselves, such as when two priests had a bloody fight in the church of All Hallows, Bread Street. After an unexplained death at the Austin Friars in 1525, 'dyvers of the Austyne freeres [were] put in the tower of London for a freer [friar] that dyde in prisone amonge them'.[16] In these and other ways respect for the church and the relationship between the clergy and the citizens could be tarnished; the Dean of St Paul's, John Colet, told his fellow clergy that heresies were 'not so pestilent and pernicious unto us as the evil and wicked life of priests'.[17]

Despite such tensions the citizens contributed to major projects, such as the building of the new parish church of St Andrew Undershaft in the 1520s, which was supported by Sir Stephen Jennings, Mayor in 1508–9, William Fitzwilliams, John Kerbie and John Garland, all of whom were merchant-tailors, and Garland's executor Nicholas Levison, a mercer. The donors' contribution was commemorated in heraldic glass in the heads of the aisle windows.[18] Sir John Shaa, a goldsmith who was Mayor in 1501–2, made a bequest for the church of St Peter the Apostle to be rebuilt. He died in 1508 and another goldsmith, Thomas Wood, also contributed to the cost, marking his donation, it was assumed, by the 'images of woodmen' that supported the roof of the middle aisle. All Hallows, Gracechurch was rebuilt by John and Robert Warner, father and son, with assistance from the pewterers. The building was finished in 1516, with a bell tower added in 1544. The stone porch was a piece of architectural salvage, brought from St John's priory in Clerkenwell after its dissolution, as was the frame for the bells – the bells themselves, although purchased, never arrived because the contractor for moving them died and his son refused to carry out the work. And so at the end of the century 'that fair steeple hath but one bell, as friars were wont to use'.[19]

St Mary Aldermary Church was rebuilt in 1510–18 at the initiative of Henry Keble, a grocer who was Mayor in 1510–11. He donated £1,000 towards the cost, with Thomas Hinde, a mercer, giving lead for the roof of the principal aisle. John Stow described the building as 'a very fair new church'; Keble had been buried there after his death in 1518, 'with a fair monument raised over him'. But by the time that Stow wrote his account, in 1598, Keble's monument had been destroyed and 'his bones are unkindly cast out', to make room for the bodies of two later Mayors, Sir William Laxton, who died in 1556, and Sir Thomas Lodge, who died in 1585. They were buried in Keble's vault 'with monuments over them for the time, till an other give money for their place, and then away with them'. Stow's displeasure with the process, which was not unusual, is evident from his account.[20]

Much charitable giving in the late Middle Ages was geared towards reducing the time that the soul of the benefactor and his or her family would spend in Purgatory. Provision was made for thousands of 'private Masses', with prayers offered for the soul of an individual, celebrated by a single priest and a server, not necessarily to any congregation at all and not a part of the regular pattern of services. The number of such Masses, or the period of time for which they should be said, was specified in some cases, while others were to be performed in perpetuity. The chantries established for such Masses were within the parish churches but were served by a sub-group of clergy, designated chantry priests. In his will of 1503 John Long, a tailor, bequeathed property in Birchen Lane to the parish of St Edmund the King, the rents from which were to support two such chantry priests. Their stipends could be much less than those of the parish clergy, but their duties allowed them time to spend on other duties, perhaps teaching, which supplemented their incomes. In 1546 there were 317 chantry priests in London.

London's livings were highly prized and relatively rewarding. Less than a third of London parishes were worth below £15 per annum, at a time when the national proportion was almost three-quarters. The holders of the London benefices were much better educated than their counterparts across England, but they did not necessarily serve their parish and in many cases were pluralists, holding the living of more than one parish. Of the 326 men who held London benefices between 1521 and 1546, at least 112 were pluralists. The actual pastoral duties were carried out by assistant clergy, who were less well remunerated and not so well educated, although that did not prevent them from executing their responsibilities efficiently and properly and in a humanitarian manner. But the system did not always work well. In the mid-1540s at the parish of St John Zachary, with 240 communicants, the rector was 'not resident upon the same but a French priest not able to serve the cure', and at St Matthew Friday Street the chantry priest was a seventy-year-old who was described as 'meanly learned'.[21]

Beneficed clergymen and others held posts outside the church, in the royal service, for example, as administrators, or as diplomats, a practice which had continued through the Middle Ages. Others served as chaplains in the households of wealthy families, which had become so common that in 1529 Sir Thomas More sneered with the phrase, 'Every mean man must have a priest in his house to wait upon his wife, which no man almost lacketh now.' There were numerous other posts open to clergymen both within the church and outside it, and many of them were situated in or close to London, or could be obtained by soliciting the great men who dispensed such positions, whose lives revolved around the city and the court. And so supplicants for those positions gravitated to London, which served as a kind of clearing house for those seeking an ecclesiastical post.[22]

The citizens' piety also found expression through lay fraternities, or guilds, which existed in parallel with the parishes and friaries; their rules were confirmed by the Bishop of London. They were associations providing mutual support for their members, through prayers and charity, and were open to anyone of good character, both men and women. Altars were dedicated to a saint, or saints, and lights were maintained there, Mass was celebrated on the saints' days and other special days and on the death of a member of the fraternity. The members attended the funerals of fellow members and prayers were said for the souls of the deceased. Fifteenth-century London saw the establishment of perhaps as many as 176 such fraternities; more than eighty were in existence in the 1530s, when roughly one-quarter of Londoners included a fraternity in their will.[23]

The citizens maintained their churches and their clergy through regular payments, the principal of which were tithes, a tenth of all produce, but in London commuted to cash payments based on house rents. They had been fixed by an agreement of 1453 yet continued to generate disagreements. Disputes that were serious enough, or were pursued tenaciously enough, to require hearings in the church courts occurred in over one-third of City parishes between 1520 and 1546. Some tithes and other payments to the church went unpaid, perhaps because of resentment of such levies or a habitual evasion of any taxes whenever possible. Even citizens who were wealthy enough to pay them without any hardship neglected to do so, and 70 per cent of those who made a will admitted to the fact.[24] In 1508 Richard Martin bequeathed to his parish of St Martin-in-the-Vintry just 4d 'for my tythys and offryns neclegent forgottyn'; in 1523 a haberdasher of the same parish, Robert Collins, allocated 6s 8d 'for tithes and offerings forgotten by him'; and in the following year Sir John Skevington assigned £1 'for tithes forgotten' while he lived in the parish of St Michael, Cornhill.[25] They were not large sums for such wealthy parishioners, who were prepared to make other donations, for church or monastic buildings and for services. Perhaps they and others preferred to make high-profile personal contributions, which would attract the respect of their peers, rather than routine and obligatory ones.

A range of other dues was payable to the clergy, including oblations and fees for weddings, churchings of women after child-birth, and burials. One Londoner was so exasperated by the church's financial demands that 'he termed the Church of Paul's a house of thieves, affirming that the priests there were not liberal givers unto the poor but rather takers-away from them of what they could get'.[26] This may have been an unduly harsh judgement. The parishes distributed alms, in kind and in money, allocated by bequests, and the monastic communities made donations to the poor. A survey of the monasteries in 1535 showed that their average contribution to charity nationally was 3 per cent of their income, and a sample of nine London houses indicates their average to have been below 2 per cent. But the figures may undervalue their contribution, with much of the giving being of an informal kind, such as that noted at the Charterhouse, where the poor were permitted to enter the precincts to collect alms from the buttery. In the 1530s bread, ale and fish were given to strangers at the buttery as well as bread and ale to beggars at the gate. At St John's priory in Clerkenwell, too, the poor received alms 'at the door and in the hall of the priory', and it claimed to give the equivalent of £1 a week in alms.[27]

The church's insistence on collecting its dues in full could be irritating, which was especially true while Richard Fitzjames was Bishop of London, between 1506 and 1522, for he was strongly protective of the church's rights. Fitzjames was theologically a conservative and was vigorous in pursuit of heretics; in 1513 he even threatened John Colet with charges of heresy, on the grounds that he had rendered the Lord's Prayer into English. It was an offence to translate any passage of Scripture into English without the express consent of a bishop, or to possess a copy of the Bible in English, but Fitzjames was surely taking these injunctions a bit too literally when he employed them against his own dean. They were aimed chiefly at heretics known as Lollards, who followed the teachings of John Wycliffe, an Oxford theologian who had died in 1384. Wycliffe and his followers had produced a translation of the Bible in the 1380s, and one of the Lollards' key demands was the availability of the Bible in English. As in other European states, religious conformity was regarded as essential and those who sought to deviate from the prevailing orthodoxy attracted the full venom of the Church and State. Lollardy had adherents living in London and their persecution seems to have increased after around 1500. The executions for heresy in the diocese of London were mostly carried out in Smithfield, as they had been from the late fourteenth century. Charles Wriothesley's chronicle contains the laconic entry for 1510: 'Two heretiques burned in Smithfield on St. Luke's day.'[28]

Attention was drawn to the defiance of the clergy in London by the case of Richard Hunne, a wealthy tailor. In March 1511 his infant son died and the rector of his parish, St Mary Matfellon, Whitechapel demanded, as was his due, the most valuable of the deceased's goods. As an infant the only item that could be claimed was the boy's bearing-sheet, which Hunne refused to hand over on the grounds that it belonged to him, not to his son. Although the item was surely of pitifully low value, the priest, faced with Hunne's obdurate refusal to surrender it, passed the case on to the Archbishop of Canterbury's court, so that the rights of the church should be maintained. The court duly found against Hunne. The matter then rumbled on, with Hunne taking the case to the court of King's Bench, on the basis that the church was encroaching on the Crown's jurisdiction. Eventually, in October 1514 diocesan officers raided Hunne's house, where they found heretical writings, including a copy of the Wycliffe Bible. He was examined by Fitzjames on suspicion of heresy, by denying tithes and having heretical material in his possession, and imprisoned in the bishop's prison at St Paul's, known as the Lollards' Tower. There, on the morning of 4 December 1514, he was found hanged in his cell by his silk girdle. The bishop and his Chancellor claimed that he had committed suicide and carried out a posthumous trial, presided over by three bishops and a suffragan bishop, at which Hunne was condemned as a heretic. A few weeks later his body was exhumed and burned at Smithfield, and all his goods were forfeit. Meanwhile, a coroner's jury had concluded that there had been a struggle, Hunne had been tortured and throttled, and that the hanging had been carried out after his death. This, then, was a case of murder, and the Chancellor and the bishop's Summoner were arrested, but not put on trial.

Nothing was proved and, although the Londoners suspected that Hunne had been murdered while in the church's custody, his widow failed in her claim for restitution of his property and goods. The case had attracted such attention that the king ordered an enquiry by his Council, while the matter of jurisdictions was discussed by the House of Commons. Bishop Fitzjames expressed his sense of the prevailing antagonism towards the clergy in London when he wrote to Wolsey that any jury would 'cast and condemn my clerk though he was as innocent as Abel'.[29] Indeed, a delegation from the City went to the bishop to complain about 'certain perilous and heinous words as been surmised by him to be spoken of the whole body of the city touching heresy'.[30] The popular reaction was summarised by Polydore Vergil, who wrote to a friend that Hunne's death had 'created great outcry', as well as Richard Arnold, who noted that Hunne 'was appeached of heresy, and put into the Lollar's Tower, at Powles, and therin was founde hangyd in prison, whereupon grete exclamacyon was amonge people, how, by whom, or by what means, he was hangyd'.[31]

The church's attempts to suppress heresy in London became more difficult with the spread of the ideas and writings of Martin Luther and other reformers during the 1520s. There was a developing trade in imported Protestant books, especially after William Tyndale's English translation of the New Testament became available; it was printed initially at Cologne, then at Worms, in 1526, and was reprinted in Antwerp by Hans van Ruremund. Cuthbert Tunstall, the Bishop of London, and Sir Thomas More were opposed to the availability of the Bible in English, and copies of Tyndale's New Testament were seized and burned, so that importing them became a clandestine operation, albeit within the regular trade across the North Sea. More harassed booksellers in London, destroying their stocks and condemning them to stand in the pillory. He organised a raid on the Steelyard in 1526 in a search for illicit Lutheran publications, on the assumption that its residents were bringing them into England. Some were found there and four merchants were arrested. John Foxe related an anecdote concerning Tunstall and Augustine Packington, a mercer. While Packington was in Antwerp he was told by the bishop that he was willing to buy copies of the New Testament, to which Packington responded, 'I know the Dutchmen and strangers that have bought them of Tindall and have them here to sell.' The bishop bought those copies from Packington in order to destroy them, and indeed everyone was happy, because 'the bishop had the books, Packington had the thanks, and Tindall had the money'. Tyndale used the income from the sale to finance a new printing of the corrected text 'so that they came thick and threefold into England'.[32]

In 1528 'John Raymund, a Dutchman', who probably was Hans van Ruremund, was imprisoned in London for 'causing fyftene hundredth of Tyndales New Testament to be printed at Antwarpe and for bryngyng fyve hundredth into England'. He certainly supplied 725 copies of the New Testament to Franz Birckman, a bookseller-cum-publisher with outlets in Antwerp, London and Cologne, and he sold 300 copies for the equivalent of just *9d* each. Hans was later released, but Christofell van Ruremund, from Eindhoven, died in prison in Westminster in 1531, having been arrested for supplying the book to dealers in England. In London the books were distributed by the convinced Lutheran William Lock, mercer and merchant adventurer, who traded with Antwerp and in 1527 received a licence to import silks, jewels, and mercery wares for court revels, and Robert (or Thomas) Forman, who resigned the post of President of Queen's College, Cambridge to become rector of the small church of All Hallows, Honey Lane, near Cheapside.[33] It seems to have been an improbable career move, but his motive becomes clearer when it is realised that, while he held the living, All Hallows effectively became a centre for the distribution of Tyndale's New Testament. The books had no set price and were sold cheaply; it is likely that the buyer was charged according to his or her means, or perhaps the copies were given away, for there was an unquenchable demand in London for Tyndale's Bible and other Protestant texts despite the risks.[34] Forman's status did not save him in 1528 from arrest and a grilling by Tunstall, when he admitted that he had illicit Lutheran books in his possession, but he disingenuously claimed that was so that he could familiarise himself with their contents before condemning them. He was suspended from his living and died later that year.[35]

Tunstall did manage to gain an admission from one John Tyball that in September 1526 he and a companion had visited the religious controversialist Robert Barnes at the Austin Friars with the intention of buying a copy of the New Testament. Barnes was under a form of house arrest there after having to do penance for his errors, but nevertheless he was not afraid to sell them a copy, for *3s 2d*, although he 'desired them to keep it close'.[36] The risks of such distribution continued into the following decade. Rose Hickman later recalled that, when she was a girl of about nine or ten, her mother 'came to some light of the gospell by meanes of some English books sent privately to her … from beyond the sea: whereuppon she used to call me with my 2 sisters into her chamber to read to us out of the same good books very privately for feare of troble bicause those good books were then accompted hereticall'.[37]

Importing of Bibles may have been the reason for one of the earliest recorded murders using a handgun. On the misty morning of 13 November 1536 Robert Packington, the Upper Warden of the Mercers' Company and an MP, was shot dead as he was crossing Cheapside on his way to the company's hall. Packington had links with evangelical groups on the Continent and was involved in importing copies of the Bible in English. He was later remembered as 'a merchant who used to bring English bybles from beyond sea', and they could have been embedded in his customary trade goods from Antwerp. Dr Vincent, Dean of St Paul's, was said to have made a deathbed confession that he had hired an Italian assassin to do the deed, but a felon condemned to be hanged at Banbury a few years later also confessed to committing the murder. The confessions are incompatible and responsibility for the crime remains unclear.[38]

The inflow to London of Tyndale's works and other Lutheran literature showed how difficult it was for the government to control such imports, to say nothing of the difficulties of censoring the interchange of ideas and opinions. Indeed, the city's role as a North European trading city facilitated the movement of a range of goods, licit and illicit, and the arrival of specialists who enlivened society and intellectual debate. Aware of the prestige which Erasmus gave to his court, in 1527 the king reminded him that 'you used to say that England should be your refuge in your old age', and he told Erasmus that his own objective at that stage was to support the Church: 'I have myself felt for some years the same desire of restoring the faith and religion of Christ to its pristine dignity, and repelling the impious attacks of the heretics, that the word of God may run on purely and freely.'[39] Much was to change in the coming decade.

6

Dissolutions and
New Foundations

The balance began to veer away from the religious conservatives with the king's pursuit of Anne Boleyn and his attempt to end his marriage to Katherine of Aragon. Cardinal Wolsey fell from favour and lost the position of Lord Chancellor, as did his successor, Sir Thomas More, who was executed in 1535. One of Wolsey's former servants, Thomas Cromwell, came to prominence and engineered the annulment of the king's marriage, the break with Rome and the dissolution of the monasteries, all within just a few years.

There was little opposition from the clergy or members of the monastic orders to the changes that made the monarch the head of the English church. The strongest resistance came from the Carthusians of the London Charterhouse. The priory's achievements and reputation at that time were attributable in large part to the influence and leadership of William Tynbygh, prior from 1500 until 1529. His successor, the elderly John Batmanson, died in November 1531 and was succeeded by John Houghton, who had left the house six months earlier to become prior at Beauvale, in Nottinghamshire. It was Houghton and his monks, a half of whom were under thirty-five years old when he became prior, who had to face the Henrician changes to the English church.[1]

In 1534 the Carthusian monks subscribed to the first Act of Succession, thereby acknowledging the annulment of Henry's marriage to Katherine and the legitimacy of Anne's children. Nevertheless, their misgivings were such that Houghton and the procurator, Hugh Middlemore, were briefly incarcerated in the

Tower before they were persuaded to swear, and it required three visits to the Charterhouse by the king's commissioners to obtain the oath from all of the monks. But many members of the community who had taken that step felt unable to acknowledge the king as head of the English church, expressed in the Act of Supremacy of 1535, and satisfy the commissioners appointed for that purpose.

Houghton was the first to be imprisoned and tried. Convicted of treason, he was executed at Tyburn in May 1535, together with the Carthusian priors of Beauvale and Axholme. His body was dismembered and one of his arms fixed above the gateway to the Charterhouse. During that summer three other senior members of the house were imprisoned and then executed. In 1536 fourteen monks and lay brothers were removed to other Carthusian houses and the Bridgettine abbey at Syon – two of whom were subsequently executed – and in the following year ten more were imprisoned in Newgate, where nine of them died in the dreadful conditions; the tenth was executed in 1540. In all, ten monks and six lay brothers of the London Charterhouse lost their lives; no other monastic community in England suffered such losses.

The Break with Rome was followed by the Dissolution of the Monasteries, which in London mostly took place in 1538–40. Despite the Carthusians' high standing in London, neither the citizens nor their masters intervened to object to their fate or the subsequent moves to dissolve the priory. In June 1537 the Court of Aldermen reversed an earlier resolution to press for the continuance of the house and decided 'that no labour shalbe made by thys Cytye yn that bihalf'. Nor had it raised an objection to the dissolution of Holy Trinity, Aldgate in 1532, despite the fact that the prior was one of its number, perhaps because Parliament had pre-empted any such complaint with the comment that the grant to the king was made 'because the Prior and Convent had departed from the monastery leaving it profaned and desolate for two years and more'.[2] The first lay alderman of Portsoken Ward was chosen in 1538, replacing the prior. Another reason may have been because the aldermen were among the beneficiaries of the redistribution of property that followed the dissolution of the religious houses. Alderman Martin Bowes, a goldsmith, bought the White Horse tavern and adjacent properties in Lombard Street, which had belonged to the Minoresses, and property in Shoreditch that had been owned by the Charterhouse. Moreover, in some cases the inmates acquiesced in the dissolution of their house. When St Mary's priory was closed in 1539, Cromwell's agent told him that 'we put the Duke of Norfolk's servant in custody of Clerkenwell and have fully dissolved it to the contentation of the prioress and her sisters'.[3]

At the Charterhouse a new prior was appointed and monks were transferred there from elsewhere, so that when the house was closed in 1538 it contained the prior and sixteen monks, all of whom were granted pensions. St Peter's, Westminster had twenty-four monks in 1536, compared with twenty-eight in 1381; there were three more nuns at St Helen, Bishopsgate in 1539 than there had been in 1379, and two more monks at St Mary de Graces over the same period. Other houses had maintained their numbers, but the mendicant orders were much reduced in strength by the time that their houses were closed. The Franciscans were down to twenty-one friars, the Dominicans to seventeen, the Carmelite and Augustinian houses both had thirteen and the Crutched Friars just six. In the autumn of 1538 'all the orders of fryers in London chaunged the[ir] habits to secular preistes habits', removing their distinctive presence from the city's streets.[4]

The pensions allocated to the heads of the houses displaced at the dissolution may have been adequate to allow them to subsist quite comfortably. John Gybbes, the prior of the Carmelite friary, was paid an annual allowance of £10, and the Franciscans' prior, Thomas Chapman, one of £13 6s 8d. The abbess of the Minoresses was awarded a much more substantial pension of £40 per annum for life, but the other members of the house received considerably less; for the twenty-three nuns the pensions were between £2 and £3 3s 8d, and a novice was granted only £1 6s 8d per annum. This was the approach at the other houses: the prior of the Charterhouse received a pension of £20 per annum and the monks £5 per annum each. Some of those displaced did receive other help, including bequests from citizens, such as the twenty-three former London Carthusians who were each allocated 5s 0d in the will of Richard Billingsley of St Sepulchre's parish that adjoined the Charterhouse, which he drew up in 1541. Some may have found openings as clergy; twenty-seven of the 317 London chantry priests in 1546 held pensions as former members of the monastic orders, and eighty-two such 'religious' were granted dispensations to hold benefices between 1536 and 1546. Of course, those openings were not a possibility for the displaced nuns, for whom there were few alternative livelihoods.[5]

As well as seeing the closure of the monasteries and in some cases the monastic churches, the citizens witnessed both liturgical and physical changes within their parish churches during the later years of Henry VIII's reign. From being proscribed, the Bible in English received official sanction. Tyndale was burned at the stake in Brabant in 1536 before he had finished his translation of the Old Testament, but Miles Coverdale produced a complete English Bible in 1535, followed by another in 1537, edited by John Rogers and known, somewhat confusingly, as Matthew's Bible. Matthew was the pseudonym Rogers adopted to protect his identity in those still uncertain times, when both reformers and conservatives were burned as heretics. Rogers's version gained the royal approval and carried on its title page the clear statement: 'Set forth with the king's most gracious licence.' By an order of 1538 an English Bible was to be placed in all churches, and a new Great Bible was issued in 1539. Six copies of the Great Bible were placed in St Paul's, 'fixed with chains for all to read that would', and 'any that had an audible voice' would read aloud from them. John Porter could read well and large groups assembled to hear him, which attracted the attention of the recently consecrated Bishop of London, Edmund Bonner. He questioned Porter and, claiming that 'he had made expositions upon the text, and gathered great multitudes unto him to make tumults', consigned him to Newgate, where he was found dead a few days later.[6]

Jewels and lights were gradually removed from churches. In 1538 an order was issued that 'the lightes of waxe in every church to be taken downe, saffe onely the roode-loft light, the light afore the sacrament, and the light afore the sepulchre'.[7] As the word replaced the image as the focus of worship, pictures and statues of the saints and the Virgin Mary, which had been among the Lollards' long-standing criticisms of the church, were now painted over or destroyed. The rood loft became a target for the reformers.

This was across the chancel arch, separating the chancel from the nave, and had the rood or crucifix in the centre with the figures of the Virgin Mary and the Apostles to the sides. As recently as 1525 one had been carved for the church of St Martin-in-the-Fields, and a payment of £3 6s 8d was recorded by the churchwardens 'for the Carvyng and garnysshyng of the Rode looft, & for the makyng of the Image of J'hus & of our lady, & the xijth p'phetts'.[8] Some were taken down with official sanction, while others were destroyed in a rougher manner, such as that in St Margaret Pattens Church, which one night in May 1538 'after midnight … was broken all in peeces with the house he stoode in by certeine lewde persons, Fleminges and Englishe men, and some persons of the sayd parishe'. Three months later 'the roode of the north in Paules was taken downe by the Dean of the same church, which was the Bishop of Chichester, by the Kinges commandement, because the people should doe noe more idolatry to the sayd image, and the image of Saint Uncomber also in the same church'.[9]

Destruction within churches included tomb wrecking, which was a feature of mid-sixteenth-century London. Stow mentioned the process in several City churches, such as his laconic entries for St Botolph, Billingsgate, which was 'a proper church, and hath had many fair monuments therein, now defaced and gone', and St Peter's in Cornhill: 'Monuments of the dead in this church defaced.'[10] In the small church of St Mary Bothaw he deduced from the coats-of-arms in the windows that 'divers noblemen and persons of worship' had been buried there, yet it contained only 'defaced tombs and prints of plates torn up and carried away'. In All Hallows Stane Church the tomb of Sir Richard Tate, buried there in 1554, was the only one remaining, 'the rest being all pulled down, and swept out of the church'. When its tombs were destroyed the churchwardens had to pay 12s 0d for brooms to sweep up the rubble and dust, 'besides the carriage away of stone and brass at their own charge'. The name of John Cosyn, who had died in 1244, was 'painted in the church roof; if it had been set in brass, it would have been fetched down'. The monuments in the Franciscans' church were also destroyed. Some were of alabaster and marble, and the grandest ones were surrounded by an iron grate, 'all pulled down, besides sevenscore grave-stones of marble, all sold for fifty pounds, or thereabouts, by Sir Martin Bowes, goldsmith and alderman of London'.[11] He was the alderman who had bought the Minoresses' and Carthusians' properties: a leading figure in the Goldsmith's Company and with a senior role in the administration of the Mint, he became extremely wealthy and served as Mayor in 1545–6 and as MP for London in 1547. The removal of monuments and brasses was primarily done to sell the materials for profit rather than to destroy figures or images of saints or angels; the removal of roods and other features presented the opportunity to similarly deface or destroy the tombs. Whatever the reasons, the process disfigured the interiors of some churches, although not all of them suffered in that way. Stow found that in the small church of St George's in Botolph Lane 'the monuments for two hundred years past are well preserved from spoil', and three 'monuments of antiquity' survived in St Leonard's, Foster Lane even after the rebuilding caused by a fire in 1548 that had destroyed the church 'so far as it was combustible'.[12]

Changes to church services included an increase in preaching, which was derided by the conservative clergy, such as a curate who preached at Bethlehem in 1535 and made the comment that 'these new preachers now-a-days that doth preach their iii. sermons in a day have made and brought in such divisions and seditions among us as never was seen in this realm, for the devil reigneth over us now'. In any case, these sermons gave conflicting messages, summarised in a letter written in the same year: 'It is preached here that priests must have wives, and that the sacrament of the altar must be received in both kinds. Some preach that purgatory is tribulations of this world, others punishment in another world, and some say there is none.' The irreverent reply was to thank the writer for his news regarding priests being married, 'which I would a been gladder of 20 year agone, that I might a made some priest cuckold'.[13] Despite that jocular response, the times remained hazardous and the religious melting pot continued to simmer.

The liturgical position depended on the monarch, as the head of the church, and the form of his devotions was taken notice of, as a guide to his current thinking and therefore the practices that all should follow. A letter from the city written in May 1539 included the information that someone had been executed for eating flesh on a Friday, against the king's command, and that the king 'receives holy bread and holy water every Sunday, and daily uses all other laudable ceremonies. In all London no man dare speak against them on pain of death.' In 1543 the Council instructed the Mayor and Aldermen to search the city for those who were eating flesh in Lent and they supplied a summary of the examinations and depositions of all the butchers, with the quantity of meat sold in Lent and to whom it was sold. Shortly afterwards twenty-five booksellers were ordered to provide lists of books in English that they had bought in the previous three years, and 'what Englisshe bokes of ill matter they have knowen to have been browght in to the Realme, and by whome'.[14] In September 1546 there was a fire at Paul's Cross of 'a gret multytude of Ynglych bokes, as testamenttes and other bokes, the wych ware forbodyn by proclamacyon by the kynges commandment before'.[15] Henry VIII's vacillations over how far reforms should go created uncertainty for the clergy and, indeed, for all worshippers. On the other hand, the effects of the dissolution of the monasteries and the destruction of features within the churches were obvious and could not be reversed.

The buildings of the dissolved monasteries were a visible reminder of the changes, as they were taken over by the Crown, together with their properties in the city. A new body, the Court of Augmentations, was established to administer their revenues and lands. The treatment of the Charterhouse buildings may have been typical of those of the other monasteries. The plate and ornaments were appropriated by the king's commissioners, glass was taken down to prevent it being stolen (filling twenty-two cases), and six cisterns and twenty-two new lead pipes were removed for safekeeping. The contents of the monks' cells, including the wainscoting, were also removed, so that already by November 1537 some cells were 'deffasyd' and 'spolyd'. Much of the wainscoting was taken away by the monks themselves, who were authorised to remove 'suche thynges as was meyte for them'. Nor were the gardens and orchard spared: the king's gardener took cuttings from at least ninety-one trees and removed three loads of bay trees for the royal garden at Chelsea. Other items were sold to help defray the commissioners' costs, including seven seats from the church and the great clock. Despite these depredations, in March 1539 the bells and some of the lead remained, and the buildings themselves seem to have survived intact in the years immediately after the priory was dissolved.[16]

In 1545 the Charterhouse was granted to Sir Edward North, Chancellor of the Court of Augmentations. Soon after acquiring the property North demolished large sections of the monastic buildings, including the priory church, and erected a mansion there. Other grantees used the sites of monastic buildings to erect new houses. Sir Thomas Pope acquired Bermondsey Abbey and demolished most of its buildings, although some of the monastic fabric was incorporated into his new building, which John Stow described as 'a goodly house built of stone and timber'.[17] Pope was Treasurer of the Court of Augmentations and so was well-placed to pick out that particular plum. Sir Thomas Audley obtained Holy Trinity, Aldgate and demolished the church, steeple and other buildings to erect his mansion. Other sites were developed differently. The Austin Friars was granted to William Paulet, later Marquess of Winchester, except for the nave of the church, which in 1550 was granted by the Crown to the Dutch community in London. The remainder of the church was used as storehouses until it was demolished in 1600. The marquess had sold the tombs for £100, and the splendid spire became unsafe because of neglect and was dismantled in 1613. The winding street set out there after the dissolution of the friary perpetuated the name of Austin Friars, the house on the site of the Carthusian priory is now an almshouse and retains the name of the Charterhouse, and Blackfriars and Whitefriars are districts where the friaries once stood.

The Franciscans' church was granted to the corporation in 1547 and made a parish church, but the existing parish churches of St Nicholas Shambles in Newgate Street and St Ewin, Newgate Market were then demolished. In 1540 the priory church in Southwark was dedicated as the parish church of St Mary Overy and two adjoining small parishes were added to it. The church was bought by the inhabitants 'with the bells of the same, to their great charges, which now is the largest and fairest church about London'.[18] At St Bartholomew's the nave of the church was demolished, but the choir, crossing and Lady chapel were retained and became the parish church. Blackfriars' priory was granted to Sir Thomas Carwarden, the son of a London shearman and fuller who made a career at court, probably under Thomas Cromwell's patronage, becoming Keeper of the King's Tents and Master of the Revels. He turned the parish church, which was within the precincts, into a store for the royal tents and pavilions, and then pulled down both that church and the friars' church. During Mary's reign (1553–58) he came under pressure to provide a church for the parish and so 'allowed them a lodging chamber above a stair, which ... in the year 1597, fell down'. At St Martin-le-Grand, within Aldersgate, the secular college, consisting of a dean and up to thirty priests, was dissolved in 1542, and the church was demolished in 1548. According to Stow, a 'large wine tavern' was built on part of the site, and on much of the remainder 'many other houses were built and highly prized, letten to strangers born and other such'.[19] At All Hallows the Great, in Thames Street, Stow noted a large cloister on the south side of the church 'but foully defaced and ruinated', and at St Augustine's, London Wall, 'the church ... was pulled down, and in place therof one Grey an apothecary built a stable, hay-loft etc. It is now a dwelling house.'[20] Some monastic sites were redeveloped only slowly, so that in 1554 the Venetian ambassador, Giacomo Soranzo, could write that 'the city is much disfigured by the ruins of a multitude of churches and monasteries belonging heretofore to friars and nuns'.[21] In January 1549 a meeting of Common Council agreed that the surveyors of the bridge 'shall to-morowe begyn to cause the chappell upon the same brydge to be defaced, and to be translated into a dwellyng-house'. But in 1553 it was demolished – an act that made a particular impact, for Becket, born in Cheapside, was the Londoners' own especial saint.[22]

Demolition was carried out in order to replace the monastic complexes with new buildings and in some cases so that the empty structures would not have to be maintained. But owners who anticipated making a profit from selling the materials could be disappointed, as Stow explained in the case of Sir Thomas Audley at Holy Trinity. Audley offered the church, with its peal of nine bells, to the parishioners of St Katherine Cree in exchange for their church, which he intended to pull down to provide a street frontage for a new house. When they refused, the priory church was made available to anyone who would demolish it, but there were no takers and so Audley had to carry out the task himself. He was then

> fain to be at more charges than could be made of the stones, timber, lead, iron, etc. For the workmen, with great labour, beginning at the top, loosed stone from stone, and threw them down, whereby the most part of them were broken, and few remained whole; and those were sold very cheap, for all the buildings then made about the city were of brick and timber.

With the stone from the monastic sites not being wanted for building it was put to another use: 'At that time any man in the city might have a cart-load of hard stone for paving brought to his door for six pence or seven pence, with the carriage.'[23] Sir Edward North's builders at the Charterhouse reused stone from the priory buildings for his new house on the site, including some from the tomb of the priory's founder, Sir Walter de Mauny, buried in its church in 1372, and a statue of St Katherine from the side-chapel dedicated to her in the early sixteenth century.

Coincidentally, during the 1530s the London residences of bishops and abbots along the Strand were transferred into lay hands. Henry VIII acquired York Place in 1529, following the fall from power of Cardinal Wolsey, Archbishop of York. The king extended and transformed it into a royal palace, which then became the centre of the court and the government – the Strand was conveniently close by for its courtiers and administrators. The senior churchmen were displaced from their large houses, usually by a process of exchange, which were granted to senior figures at court who then rebuilt or enlarged them. They were occupied by members of the aristocracy and their entourages, and used to lodge royal visitors from abroad or their ambassadors.

Among them was the residence of the Bishop of Coventry and Lichfield in the Strand, known as Chester Inn (the diocese included the future diocese of Chester until 1541). This was taken by the Crown in the mid-1530s and by February 1537 had been assigned to Edward Seymour, Earl of Hertford, who treated it as his London residence. His family's rise to prominence followed the marriage of his sister Jane to Henry VIII in May 1536. Their son, Edward, was born in October 1537, but Jane died twelve days after the birth. With the death of Henry VIII in 1547 and the accession of Seymour's nephew as Edward VI he became Lord Protector, and before the coronation he was created Duke of Somerset. In the mid-1540s he enlarged the site with the acquisition of the inn of the bishopric of Worcester, Strand Inn (an Inn of Chancery), St Mary-le-Strand church and its churchyard and other properties. Many of those buildings were demolished, including the church, and a new mansion was built on the site, known as Somerset Place. It was incomplete at Somerset's execution in 1552 and passed to the new Lord Protector, John Dudley, Duke of Northumberland, but he exchanged it for Durham House, former residence of the bishops of Durham, which had been assigned to Princess Elizabeth. She was then allocated Somerset Place, which thus became a royal palace. A parish church to replace that demolished was not built until 1714–17. Somerset's building plans extended to St Paul's, where, in April 1549, the cloister on the north side of the cathedral, known as Pardon Churchyard, was 'pullyd downe ... wyth the chappelle that stode in the myddes, to bylde the Protectores place withalle'.[24] As well as deliberate demolition, the number of ruined churches was increased by a fire that swept through St Giles, Cripplegate on 12 September 1545, 'with the steple and bells ... the stone walles onelie saved, which could not burne'. In November 1548 St Anne's near Aldersgate suffered the same fate. Both were rebuilt; Stow described St Giles's as 'a very fair and large church' and noted that because of the fire it contained few monuments, but at St Anne's 'there remain a few monuments of antiquity'.[25]

The dissolution led to the closure of the hospital of St Mary within Cripplegate, or Elsingspital, which was served by the prior and ten canons, and the sisters who nursed the blind and sick poor. The nurses were allotted a house in the close, and the hospital and the prior's and canons' residences were adapted as a house, while 'the lodgings for the poor are translated into stabling for horses'. The principal aisle of the church was pulled down and replaced by four houses, and the remainder was adopted as the parish church of St Alphage, the existing church being demolished and replaced by a carpenter's yard.[26] The Mercers' Company took over the chapel of the hospital of St Thomas of Acon, and its school, for twenty-five poor boys, became the company's school.

The almsmen of St Anthony's hospital were expelled by the Master and given a pension, and their houses rented out; he appropriated so much of the endowment that the school declined 'both in numbers and estimation'. But its chapel, on the north side of Threadneedle Street, was let to the French church, established by royal Letters Patent in 1550, the year that the Dutch church was assigned the nave of the Austin Friars' chapel.[27] Refugees from the Low Countries and France had arrived in London in increasing numbers following the Peace of Crépy in 1544 between France and the Empire. Edward VI's grant explained that the Strangers' Church was being established from 'compassion for the state of exiles and foreigners ... banished and cast out from their own country for the sake of the gospel of Christ'. But there were other motives, for Cranmer and the reformers wished to slow the pace of change in the English church, as well as to counterbalance the influence of Anabaptists within the immigrant community. They also hoped to create a 'living model' for the reformed English church, and the Polish reformer John à Lasko was appointed as superintendent of the Strangers' Church to oversee the Dutch and French congregations, with two pastors for each congregation. They were permitted to use their own rites and ceremonies, despite the Act of Uniformity of 1549 and the opposition of the Bishop of London, Nicholas Ridley. The churches were outside the bishop's jurisdiction, but Mary's accession in 1553 caused à Lasko and his associates to emigrate to Denmark. After Elizabeth came to the throne five years later the churches were re-established and provided a focus for the immigrant communities thereafter.[28] The French church became the largest such church in England and had considerable influence in terms of both theology and organisation. Its order of worship, prepared by Nicholas Des Gallors, pastor in the 1560s, was held by some Puritans to be the form that should be adopted by the English church.

Anticipating the possible closure of London's other hospitals when the monasteries were dissolved, the Mayor, in 1538, and the Court of Aldermen, in 1539, petitioned the Crown, asking that they and their endowments should be granted to the City.

This did take place, but only after a long delay. St Bartholomew's priory was dissolved in 1539 and the hospital continued to operate, although in a reduced condition, so that by 1546 it had just forty bedsteads, but not enough bedding for all of them. In 1544 and 1545 Henry VIII nominated new Masters for St Bartholomew's, effectively re-founding the hospital, although probably with the intention that it should be a shelter for the poor rather than a place for the treatment of the sick. In 1546 it was indeed presented to the City and was 'hereafter to be called the House of the Poore in West Smithfield in the suburbs of the City of London, of King Henry VIII's foundation'; the title was retained until 1948, although it continued to be commonly known as St Bartholomew's. The new establishment was governed by the four aldermen and eight common councillors who had negotiated the transfer to the City, including most of its existing property. The hospital was served by three surgeons, a matron and twelve sisters, who were to tend the sick poor, keeping them 'sweet & clean as in giving them their meats & drinks'. The post of physician was created later.[29]

Bethlehem Hospital was also transferred to the City in 1546 and was continued as a mental asylum. The chapel, which stood in a small churchyard, was taken down later in the sixteenth century. The institution rarely had more than fifteen to twenty inmates at a time. It came to attract visitors who went there out of voyeuristic curiosity rather than pity, to stare at the inmates. Sir Thomas More had written, 'Those shalt in Bedlam see one laugh at the knocking of his own head against a post, and yet there is little pleasure therein.' The only one of the five principal hospitals in London to be closed was St Mary-without-Bishopsgate. John Stow regretted its dissolution, as it had been 'well furnished, for receipt of the poor; for it was an hospital of great relief'.[30]

In contrast to Bethlehem, where its existing function was continued, at Bridewell there was a complete and really rather dramatic change of use. Although the palace was described by Stow as 'a stately and beautiful house', it had not been popular with Henry VIII or his son Edward VI because of its location. The ground on which it had been built was marshy and, according to John Howes, 'there was no coming to yt but throughe stinking lanes and over a fylthye ditche which did so continually annoye the house that the kinge had no pleasure in it'. An apparently audacious plan was put forward to convert the royal palace into a shelter for the poor, but the proposal made little progress until a letter from the Bishop of London, Nicholas Ridley, to the king's Secretary, William Cecil:

> I must be a suitor unto you in our good Master Christ's cause ... He hath lain too long abroad (as you do know) without lodging in the streets of London, both hungry, naked and cold. Now, thanks be to Almighty God! the citizens are willing to refresh him, and to give him both meat, drink, clothing and firing: but alass! Sir, they lack lodging for him. For in some one house I dare say they are fain to lodge three families under one roof. Sir, there is a wide, large, empty house of the King's Majesty's, called Bridewell, that would wonderfully well serve to lodge Christ in, if he might find such good friends in the court to procure in his cause.[31]

His sentiments reflected a concern among senior churchmen about the lack of provision for the poor and their overcrowded living conditions. In a sermon which he delivered in 1548 Hugh Latimer, the former Bishop of Worcester, included criticism of the rich citizens for their lack of charity: 'In London their brother shall die in the streets for cold, he shall lie sick at the door ... and perish there for hunger. Was there ever more unmercifulness?'[32]

Edward VI did grant the palace to the City, just before his death, in 1553, as a workhouse for the poor and vagrants; the City took possession in 1556. This was unique in contemporary Europe. The Trinity Hospital in Paris, established in 1545, provided religious instruction, education and work, chiefly for children, and that may have been an inspiration, but nowhere was there an institution that exactly carried out Bridewell's functions.[33] From 1557 Bethlehem Hospital and Bridewell were administered jointly; Howes later described them as 'nere kinsemen in condicions'. He alleged that Bridewell in particular had come under attack from the bishops during Mary's reign and 'they did all they might doe to discountenance & to discreadit that house'. He claimed that their hostility was because they were afraid that the conduct of priests would be revealed during the interrogation of prostitutes who had been sent there, and 'theire owne consciences accused them of some fowle matters which they feared shoulde come to lighte by examinacon'.[34] The harassment should have ended with the changes to the episcopate following Elizabeth's accession in 1558, but nevertheless Bridewell did develop an unsavoury reputation for the treatment of the inmates, which it retained. Yet there was an aspiration in the mid-century to improve conditions. In 1555 a new counter, or prison, was built by the corporation in Wood Street, and prisoners from the existing counter in Bread Street were moved there.

The re-founding of St Thomas's Hospital in Southwark also took a long time to achieve. In 1538 it was investigated by Richard Layton, the king's commissioner, who discovered that the Master had sold some of the silver plate and other items, and had taken excessive fees. Layton also accused him of living immorally, and described the hospital as 'the bawdy hospital of St Thomas's in Southwark'. The hospital was shut down in 1540 and the staff and the forty patients were dispersed. A proposal in 1546 to reopen St Thomas's for twenty 'impotent and lame soldiers and suchlike poor persons' did not succeed. But when Sir Richard Dobbs, the Mayor, and Ridley presented an appeal to Edward VI in 1551 they had a positive response. The site and any of the remaining estate of the medieval foundation that had not been disposed of were sold by the Crown to the corporation, which then re-founded the hospital. As St Thomas à Becket had fallen out of favour at the Reformation, St Thomas the Apostle was adopted as its patron. Its modest endowment was increased by the transfer of the estate of the hospital of St John at the Savoy after it was suppressed in 1553, as well as all its beds and bedding. The closure of the Savoy was not unduly controversial, as it had become, in Raphael Holinshed's phrase, 'a lodging of loiterers, vagabonds and strumpets'.[35] At first St Thomas's was governed jointly with Christ's Hospital and Bridewell, but from 1557 was administered separately, by fifteen governors. It had ten wards and some 250 patients initially were admitted, but that proved to be an unrealistically high number and it was soon reduced to around a hundred.

Some of the medieval functions at St Thomas's were discontinued. In 1562 the governors ordered that no woman with child was to be admitted, because 'it is a house erected for the relief of honest persons and not of harlots to be maintained there'. Before the end of the century it had ceased to accommodate elderly pensioners and early in the seventeenth century lodging for travellers was also withdrawn, so that St Thomas's had become a hospital for treating the sick. Guard had to be set to keep out casual callers hoping to cadge a lodging for the night or longer, and those who were begging for a donation also had to be discouraged. One supplicant had a letter from the queen to support his claim for an almsman's place, and a former sailor, with supporting letters from the Privy Council, was trying to raise money while he learned to play the trumpet.

The mid-century concern with social welfare extended to the city's orphans. Henry VIII granted the Greyfriars buildings to the corporation, an act confirmed by Edward VI when he established an orphanage there for 'poor fatherless children'. The buildings were quickly adapted and the first children were admitted in November 1552. The initial intake of 340 was soon increased to 380 and then to 400, and within a few months the institution became a school as well as an orphanage. At first the children wore a russet-coloured costume, but within a few months this was replaced by a blue one with yellow breeches and stockings, and the institution, Christ's Hospital, duly became known as the Blue Coat School. Governors and individual citizens added to the endowment through gifts and bequests, further income was received from the poor rates, the profits from the corporation's management of the cloth market at Blackwell Hall, and from 1582 onwards the fines and rents arising from its 'rule charge oversight and government of all the Carts, Carres and Carmen' in London.

St Katherine's Hospital lost much of its property, yet continued to serve as an almshouse for gentlewomen and it retained its royal patronage. Its chapel became the parish church of St Katherine-by-the-Tower, but the choir was demolished; Stow described it as having been 'not much inferior to that of Paules'.[36] From 1549 its Masters were laymen, not clergymen. Dr Thomas Wilson, who was appointed in 1561, sold the rights of the annual fair on Tower Hill to the corporation for £466 13s 4d. He served as an administrator, diplomat and privy councillor under Elizabeth until his death in

1581, and the dedicatory letter of his *A Discourse upon Usury* was written at St Katherine's and dated 1569.

The establishment and re-founding of these institutions in London during Edward VI's reign was a major effort in terms of public welfare and provided a model followed by many provincial towns, in adapting their former monastic buildings for charitable purposes. Winchester, Coventry, Gloucester, Ipswich, Canterbury and Oxford all undertook similar schemes.[37] As well as establishing the welfare organisations, the corporation further extended its responsibilities by acquiring Southwark from the Crown, and thereby 'they shall have all the whole towne of Southwarke ... as free as they haue the City of London'. It became the City's twenty-sixth ward, designated Bridge Ward Without. An aldermen and deputies were appointed in a short time, 'for the better order to be kept there, and for the more quietnes of the Mayors hereafter to come, and the good order of the Kinges subjectes there, according to the lawes of the city'.[38]

By the end of the mid-century period of change, the monasteries had been closed and a few parish churches demolished. St Katherine's Hospital was continued, as were the Mercers' Company's school and St Paul's School, but the hospital of St Mary, Bishopsgate, Elsing Hospital and St Anthony's Hospital were lost; the other hospitals were re-founded and the city's asylum was maintained, while a house of correction and an orphanage and school were established. There had been a major shift in the administration of welfare responsibilities away from the church to lay institutions, and the challenge for the citizens was to provide charitable donations to at least match, and preferably to exceed, the previous level of financial support for social provision in the city.

7

Troubled Times

The religious pendulum continued to swing during the ensuing reigns. The accession of Edward VI gave the reformers confidence, for he was a young king and the Protector during his minority was the Duke of Somerset, who was known to support further reform. But Edward's reign lasted only six years, and that of his sister Mary who succeeded him was an even shorter one of just five years. Under Mary there was a return to the Catholic rites, but when her sister Elizabeth came to the throne they were abandoned and the English church followed a Protestant path once more. Londoners weaved their way through these changes to worship to continue worshipping at their churches, as well as adjusting to the alternating pattern of curtailment and revival of public religious festivals and processions.

Masses and prayers interceding for the souls of the dead were abhorrent to the reformers, and the chantries were surveyed during Henry VIII's final years with a view to their abolition. This was implemented by an Act of Parliament of 1547, after Edward's accession, justified partly because chantries maintained 'vain opinions of purgatory and masses satisfactory'. Yet bequests had continued to be made to them during the years leading up to their closure. When George Hide of the Steelyard made his will in 1544 he bequeathed to the church of All Saints 'to the high alter 12*d.* and to the Fraternity of St. Mary in that church 3*s.* 4*d.*'. In the previous year Nicholas Grove, a barber, left three great gilt goblets to the

Company of Barber Surgeons, requesting that 'thay for ten yeres ensuyng yerely to kepe a obett yn the parishe churche off Saynt Peters in Cornehyll for my fathers and my mothers sowles and myne and all Chrystyn sowles'.[1] The livery companies sponsored priests and obits in over sixty parish churches in London. Among the Mercers' Company's commitments was oversight of lands and tenements given by William Brown for his soul in perpetuity, which generated £50 19s 4d annually, and the Fishmongers' Company was responsible for Henry Jurden's legacy of lands producing £40 10s 6d per annum for obits in St Botolph Aldgate and St Nicholas Cole Abbey. But most endowments brought in much smaller sums. Following abolition, at first the companies were required to undertake the payments on those properties with which they had been entrusted to support the chantries, effectively as tenants of the Crown. But then

> the kinge ... having occasion to levie a great masse of money, did require the companies to purchase those rentes, which they were lothe to doe, but beinge urged by their dutie of love and service to the kinge, the companies accordingly purchased those rents, for which they paied to the kinge allmost xix thousand pounds. For the raisinge of this somme of £18,700 they were enforced to sell divers of the said landes and tenements to paye for the reste.

In the case of the Merchant Taylors, the lands sold were worth £2,006 2s 6d and those bought produced an annual rental of £102 0s 10d.[2]. This step effectively enforced each company into switching its investments from one set of properties to another, without having choice of the new ones. While some wealthier members may have done well economically by buying ex-monastic properties, the companies themselves probably did not benefit from the dissolution.

The pace of change within the parish churches accelerated as roods, stained-glass, images of the saints, relics and statues were removed, walls were white-washed, the Ten Commandments were displayed and service books in English were acquired. Rather than a reluctance to comply with the changes, some Londoners gave the impression of being ready and willing to undertake them. At St Martin, Ironmonger Lane, within days of Henry VIII's death the rood was taken down and images of saints were removed, texts from Scripture were placed on whitewashed walls and the royal arms was installed 'in stede of the image of the crucifixe'. That was a little precipitous and the churchwardens had to justify their actions to the Privy Council, explaining that the roof had been in such a dangerous state that it had to be taken down 'for feare leest it would fall on the peoples heddes', continuing that the crucifix and other images 'being olde were so rotten by the tyme that the Churche rowfe was repayred that they fell to powder and were nat apte to be sett uppe againe'. They got away without punishment and were merely told to set up 'an image of the crucifixe'.[3] In May 1547 the choir in St Paul's 'with diuers other parishes in London song all the service in English, both mattens, masse, and even-songe; and kept no masse, without some receaued the communion with the priest'. In the cathedral the great rood was taken down in November 1547 and its statues removed, and in that month 'all images in euerie parish church in London were pulled downe and broken'. By the time that the order to replace stone altars with wooden tables was issued in May 1550, one-third of London parishes had already made that change, and by the end of the year all parishes in the city had only one altar, which was 'a table made in the quire for the receiving of the communion'.[4] A prayer book was issued in 1549 and a revised version in 1552, both the work of Thomas Cranmer, Archbishop of Canterbury from 1533, and Henry VIII's favoured theologian. The parish of St Matthew, Friday Street adopted the 1549 prayer book as soon as it was introduced into the House of Commons, and 'Poules quire, with divers parishes in London and other places in England, begane the use after the said booke in the beginning of Lent, and putt downe the priuate masses as by the acte is ordayned', although the Act of Uniformity that specified its use required it to be introduced at Pentecost, three months later.[5]

At the central parish of St Mary at Hill the churchwardens paid 5*s* 0*d* for 'taking downe of the Rode lofte', 13*s* 4*d* for 'taking down of the tabernacle ouer the vestry doore, being all stone, and other stone workes in the churche, and for making vppe therof, and for lyme and sande', and spent a further 1s 4d for the removal of all the iron work. Other expenses included £4 for 'paynting of the Rode lofte with scriptures', new psalters in English for the choir and four 'songe bokes of te deum in Englisshe', a prayer book, two 'bookes of ye new service' and a copy of Erasmus's *Paraphrases*. The organ was replaced with a new one. But money was raised to offset this outlay by the sale of the gilt from three images, silver from 'claspes of bokes and the busshops myter', a silver bell, a gilt chalice and a pax, and the altar table, which together raised £13 8s 3d; the sale of books brought in a further £2 6s 8d.[6]

Festivals and processions were also curtailed, and traditional objects were destroyed. The titular shaft in the name of the church and parish of St Andrew Undershaft was a maypole, set up in Leadenhall Street outside the church every May Day until the Evil May Day riot of 1517. It was then hung beneath the eaves of a row of houses until 1549, when the curate of St Katherine Cree condemned it during a sermon at Paul's Cross, on the grounds that, as its name was incorporated in that of the church, it had become an object of worship. That Sunday afternoon, those who lived in the houses where it was stored 'sawed it in pieces' and then burned it. The companies also removed items now deemed to be offensive: a silver-gilt statue of St Dunstan, patron saint of goldsmiths, was removed from the screen in the company's hall, and the Angels of the Annunciation was taken out of the the Cutlers' Company's hall.[7]

Edmund Bonner was deprived of the bishopric in October 1549 and replaced by Nicholas Ridley. It was he who ordered the replacement of altars to 'turn the simple from the old superstitious opinions of the popish mass' and to implant the perception of the Lord's Supper as a godly meal. Ridley examined 'euery parson and curate himselfe in his owne house privately of theyr learninge, and gave them 4 dayes to make theyr aunswere'. He promoted reformers, although he was anxious that reform should not proceed too far and was among the theologians who attempted to persuade Joan Bocher, an Anabaptist known as 'Joan of Kent', to recant her beliefs; she refused and was burned for heresy in Smithfield.[8] In 1552 marriage of the clergy, hitherto tolerated, was formally permitted and copes and vestments were forbidden; only surplices were to be worn by the clergy. Linen from the chantries was handed over to the Commissioners of the Court of Augmentations; the Merchant Taylors' Company surrendered three vestments, two curtains and two altar-cloths. The Duke of Northumberland was approached and asked if such linen from London's churches could be given to help the poor, and he passed the request to the Secretaries of State.[9]

Lack of respect for the clergy became common enough to attract attention. On the streets, and in Westminster Hall especially, 'servinge men and other yonge and light persons and apprentesses of London' taunted priests and 'those that goe in scollers gownes like priests'. This had become so frequent by November 1547 that it was brought to the notice of the Privy Council, probably because, although a minor issue in itself, it typified a declining respect for those in authority. Those who resembled clergymen presumably were lawyers, especially as the harassment occurred in Westminster Hall, where sat the principal courts. The Council wished to check such disrespectful behaviour and so ordered that it should cease, even though the incidents seem to have amounted to little more than banter, snatching off their caps and capes and 'tossinge of them'.[10]

Although the reformers' changes were implemented in London, they were not universally welcomed, or they produced uncertainty. That was apparent on the festival days in 1549 and 1550, when some shops were closed, as before, and others remained open as on a normal day, which was the new practice. On the Feast of the Assumption in 1550 there was 'soche devision thorrow alle London that some kepte holy day and some none ... this was the second yere, and also the same devision was at the fest of the Nativitie of our Lady'.[11] In 1552 a maypole was set up in Fenchurch Street, painted green and white, with Morris dancers, men and women, who danced around it wearing baldrics of the same colours, but on the day that it was raised the Lord Mayor issued instructions that it should be taken down and destroyed.[12] Morris dancing was curbed by the Lord Mayor in 1553–4. The new order was much more strongly resented elsewhere, with rebellions in the West Country and Norfolk in 1549 that required the deployment of armies to suppress them. As a precaution, during these rebellions artillery was placed at the city's gates and the houses and gardens that had been built close to the walls were cleared away. A watch was kept, including two artillerymen at each gate, and all householders were warned to ensure that their families and men-servants kept the curfew and that all were 'of honest rule and behavior during this time of unquietness'. One consequence of the rebellion in East Anglia was that trade with Essex was interrupted during the summer and so the only cheese for sale at Bartholomew Fair was 'soch as came owte of dyvers mens howsys within London that was not good'.[13]

Edward's reign came to an early end with his death from tuberculosis in July 1553. Earlier in that year John Dudley, Duke of Northumberland, who had ousted Somerset as Protector, had moved to strengthen his hold on power by marrying his son Lord Guildford Dudley to Lady Jane Grey, the daughter of Henry VIII's younger sister Mary and a possible claimant to the throne. The wedding was celebrated on 21 May at Durham House in the Strand. Edward did name Jane as his successor, with the intention that she would reign as a Protestant monarch rather than his half-sister Mary, daughter of Katherine of Aragon and a Roman Catholic. After his death on 6 July Jane was proclaimed queen, but Northumberland had not secured Mary, who quickly raised an army in East Anglia and was widely regarded as the legitimate claimant. Northumberland set out with a small force to disperse Mary's supporters, but as he and his men marched through Shoreditch the crowds gathered ominously at the roadside did not shout any encouragement or words of support, as he admitted.[14] He had not only failed to detain Mary but also had not convinced Londoners that Jane was Edward's legitimate successor. His support drifted away and it was he, not Mary, who returned to London as a prisoner. Jane and Guildford had been moved from Durham House to the Tower of London in preparation for the coronation, following the traditional practice, and it now became their prison. Jane was deposed on 19 July, when Mary was proclaimed queen. Mary had come to the throne with the support, or at least acquiescence, of the citizens as well as the country's political leadership, a popularity that influenced the degree of confidence with which she implemented her policies in the early stages of her reign.

The Protestant reforms were reversed in the parishes as services in Latin, clerical vestments and the Mass and other sacraments were reintroduced, but the repossession of monastic lands was a sticking point; it would not be until Cardinal Pole arrived in England in November 1554 with an absolution from the Pope that the issue was resolved. It surely would have been a political impossibility to dispossess the owners of the former church property. By the time Pole reached England the queen had married Prince Philip of Spain, heir of Charles V, King of Spain and Holy Roman Emperor, in Winchester Cathedral on 25 July. The initiative for the alliance had come from her, although the proposal had been taken up by the emperor with enthusiasm – he foresaw England and his possessions in the Low Countries united as a block to French ambitions. Mary and Philip processed through London on 18 August. As was customary for such an event, pageants, or structures with celebratory embellishments, had been erected at a number of points. That was not without controversy, for on one of them the queen was shown holding a book with the text '*Verbum Dei & Misericordia*'. Some claimed that originally the book had been shown in Henry VIII's hand, and so it was he who had presented the Word of God, in English, and when the bishop saw this he compelled the painter to change it and show the book in Mary's hand, because she, not her father, had restored the Word of God in the Church. The marriage was not popular, nor was the influx of the members of Philip's large entourage. For their part, they alleged that the exchange rate for currency had been set very much to the London merchants' advantage, prompting the protest that there were 'great thieves among them, and they steal openly. They have this advantage over Spaniards, that we do it by cunning and they by force.' When Philip's followers were billeted in London there were disputes: they complained that they were refused lodgings, and when they did obtain some they were then over-charged for rent, and that they and their priests were openly mocked. On the other hand, the Londoners felt threatened by the numbers of outsiders who had suddenly appeared in their city. Simon Renard wrote to his master Charles V telling him that 'disagreeable incidents are of daily occurrence'. Philip had foreseen the problem, and the subsequent steps he took to check the ill-feeling did succeed in reducing the tensions.[15]

As part of the reversal of the changes made under Edward, the Savoy Hospital was revived, although the earlier problem of inadequate funding was not solved. Ridley was deprived of the bishopric almost immediately and Bonner was reinstated, having spent the previous three years in the Marshalsea prison. On 23 August the Mass, sung in Latin, was celebrated at the parish church of St Nicholas Cole Abbey, and over the following two days it was celebrated at another four or five City churches – not by order, it was said, but 'of the people's devotion'.[16] The Mass was not officially restored until December. At St Mary at Hill surplices and albs were made, a chrismatory and an incense burner were bought (though both were of pewter), the altar-stone, which had been placed in the kitchen, was restored to its place, and a Mass book costing 13s 4d and books of the homilies and sacraments were purchased. The accounts also mention the 'borrowynge' of a cross, two candlesticks and a censer, all of which were of silver, for Lady Day. The churchwardens also spent 1s 8d on 'puttyng owt of the scrypture in the roode lofte', the large sum of £11 4s 8d was laid out for a new rood, with the figures of Mary and John, and 6s 0d for 'mendyng of the Canapye over the hygh alter wherin the sacrament hanges and for the sylke'. Singers were hired to supplement the choir and a priest to take the services on the Sunday after the curate died 'and lefte vs desolate'.[17]

In that parish, as in the others, the old forms were restored and 'all copes of cloth of gold that was taken owt of all chyrches' and kept at Whitehall were returned 'to them that cowld know them'.[18] Nevertheless, the reintroduction of the Catholic service and priestly vestments met with some opposition in London. One Sunday in August 1553 someone threw a dagger at the preacher during the sermon at Paul's Cross, when he spoke in favour of Bonner and was very critical of Ridley; nobody claimed responsibility, nor did anyone come forward with information

on the identity of the thrower and so claim the offered reward
of £5. A few weeks later members of the Privy Council were
at the sermon there with the Lord Mayor, aldermen and senior
members of the livery companies, as were the captain of the
royal guard and 200 of his men, who 'stoode about the pulpit,
with their halberdes'. Twice within a month the parson of
St Ethelberga, Bishopsgate Street was placed in the pillory and
had his ears nailed to it, for speaking seditious words regarding
the queen.[19] In St Giles-in-the-Fields a man shaved his dog's head
in mocking imitation of a monk's tonsure, and on a Sunday in
April 1554 a dead cat 'havinge a clothe lyke a vestment of the
priest at masse' was found 'hanged on the post of the gallowes
in Cheape[side] ... and a bottle hanged by it'. Nobody was ever
caught for that 'villanouse fact'. A few weeks later a handgun
was fired from close to St Vedast church in Foster Lane, near to
St Paul's churchyard, during the Sunday sermon at Paul's Cross.
The shot hit a wall close to where the Lord Mayor was sitting.
He was Sir Thomas White, who was described by the Imperial
ambassador as a Catholic, and he implemented the queen's
policies in the City. A suspect was interrogated but denied the
fact and, as no evidence could be brought against him, he was
discharged. But when an ex-monk stabbed the officiating priest
in St Margaret's, Westminster on Easter Day 1555 with a wooden
knife he was apprehended. The priest was struck on the head and
wounded so badly that 'the bloud ran downe and fell both on the
challes and on the consecrated bread'; his attacker had his hand
cut off before being burned at the stake.[20]

Dissatisfaction with Mary's policies and her marriage, which
raised fears of a Catholic dynasty and England's subservience to
Spain, together with concern that the power of local magnates
and gentry would be eroded, generated enough resentment for
subversive plots to be hatched. The dissent was encouraged by
Antoine de Noailles, the French ambassador, and other French
diplomats in London, for the diplomatic conjunction of England
with Spain and the other Habsburg possessions threatened French
interests. Uprisings were planned, but the government was aware
of them and made a number of precautionary arrests in London
in early 1554; the intended rebellion in Devon did not even get

started, and only in Kent did one take place, led by Sir Thomas Wyatt. When a force of Londoners sent to suppress the uprising defected to him, he was encouraged to think that he might be able to capture London, and the rebels entered Southwark on 3 February. But Mary and her government stood firm; she had gone to the Guildhall and rallied the citizens with a speech, in which she shrewdly claimed that Wyatt's objectives included seizure of the Tower, where the richer citizens stored their wealth for safekeeping. Sir Thomas White and the Londoners supported the queen and prevented Wyatt's men from crossing London Bridge by closing the gates and raising the drawbridge. The rebels were fired on by the artillery at the Tower, described as 'great peces of ordenance', which were directed 'full against the foote of the bridge and agaynst Southwarke, and the ij. Steples of saincte Tooles [Olaf's] and sainct Marie Overies'. The inhabitants of Southwark pleaded with Wyatt to withdraw his men, to prevent 'the utter desolation of this boroughe, with the shott of [the Tower] layed and chardged towardes us'. Vulnerable to that artillery fire and thwarted by the Londoners' refusal to allow his force across the bridge, Wyatt was compelled to march to Kingston and cross the bridge over the Thames there. His men then advanced into London from the west without opposition, through Temple Bar and along Fleet Street, but they found Ludgate closed to them – there was no uprising within the City as Wyatt had hoped. Realising that the game was up, he retreated along Fleet Street with the remainder of his force, only to be defeated at Temple Bar. In the aftermath Wyatt was executed, as were Lady Jane Grey and Lord Guildford Dudley.

Nevertheless, the Spanish ambassador was well aware of rumbling dissatisfaction in London, which in his opinion was stirred up partly by the French ambassador and Protestants, playing on the citizens' resentment of a proposal for Parliament to meet in Oxford, which would deprive them of much business. He even feared an insurrection and an attack on the Tower and, as he put it, 'if the Tower is lost London is lost'; the aim should be to conciliate rather than alienate the city. His fears were chiefly for the safety of Prince Philip, who was due in England for his marriage to Mary. Evidently the Londoners' discontent was dangerous enough to be taken seriously.[21] Londoners of both religious affiliations had stood by the queen and she had promised them her favour, but, as one of them wrote, 'none of us got anything, although she was very liberal to many others that were enemies to God's word'. An uneasy state of mutual mistrust existed between the queen and the citizens.[22]

Bonner was not to be daunted by opposition within London or the rebellion and set about enquiring into the morals, beliefs and practices of his diocese and attacking heresy, condemning to death those convicted. This he did with such thoroughness that he earned the title 'Bloody Bonner' and perhaps greater resentment than any of the Marian bishops. During the reigns of the first three Tudor monarchs, between 1485 and 1553, 102 heretics were burnt, only two of them during Edward VI's reign. But it was the burnings during Mary's reign that made the deepest impression, and the Protestant martyrs long remained in the popular memory, partly because of the unprecedented number of victims. The first such execution took place in February 1555 with the death of John Rogers, who had been rector of Holy Trinity the Less and St Margaret Moses, and by the time that they were halted, in June 1558, 283 people had been burned, seventy-eight of them in London, of whom fifty-six were executed in Smithfield. Although only roughly a fifth of the victims were executed there, 'the fires of Smithfield' came to symbolize all of those burned to death during Mary's reign. Among those executed by burning were Cranmer, Ridley and Latimer, at Oxford. Rogers and Ridley were among forty-four of those executed who can be identified as Londoners. In almost all cases their offence was denial of the Mass. They included former priests, schoolmasters, a lawyer and the grandson of a Lord Mayor, whereas others were more junior, including William Hunter, who was a nineteen-year-old apprentice. Roger Holland was from a gentry family in Lancashire, who was apprenticed to a merchant-tailor in Watling Street and was in his late twenties. He was said to have refused the invitation to recant that was offered to all of the convicted Protestants and he maintained that 'as for the Mass, transubstantiation, and the worshipping of the sacrament, they are mere impiety and horrible idolatry'. Some did recant faced with the prospect of such a ghastly death and some died in prison, but the persecution on the whole had been fruitless and the officers given the task of identifying offenders had carried out those duties in an increasingly lukewarm manner.[23]

Despite the threat of execution or a long period of imprisonment – and at least 200 were jailed for their faith – some Protestants met in secret to worship. One of them recalled that 'some were preserved still in London, that in all the time of the persecution never bowed their knees unto Baal, for there was no such place to shift in this realm as London, notwithstanding there great spyall and search'. A number of places were later remembered to have provided refuge for groups to gather clandestinely, including ships on the river and rooms in the house that Sir Thomas Carwarden, Master of the Revels, had built on the site of the Blackfriars monastery. Rose Hickman's parents provided a haven for 'well disposed Christians' at their house, where they met together in a chamber 'keeping the doors close shut for fear of the promoters, as we read in the Gospel the disciples of Christ did for the Jews'. But they, like others, eventually went into exile, choosing Antwerp as their place of refuge; others went to Germany and Switzerland. The Edwardian services were celebrated in the prisons and prisoners spent time singing psalms or in prayer. As they were already undergoing punishment they had little to lose, and of course by bringing and keeping them together the government risked such behaviour. By receiving visitors, the prisoners also helped to maintain the web of contacts among defiant Protestants in the city, and some City officers, including a former sheriff, assisted those suffering persecution.[24]

Protestant writers made much of their and the citizens' righteous indignation at the persecution and burnings. The corporation had inadvertently contributed to the recording and dissemination of news of the martyrs' fate when, in 1549, it leased Aldersgate to the printer John Day. He used it as both his printworks and home, expanding the accommodation; Stow wrote that he 'built much upon the wall of the city towards the parish church of St. Anne'. The most notable works printed by Day were the *Folio Bible* of 1549, the martyrologist John Foxes's massive and very influential *Acts and Monuments*, popularly known as the *Book of Martyrs* (1567 and later, and ever-longer, editions), and his edition of the works of the reformers William Tyndale, John Frith and Robert Barnes (1572–3), Roger Ascham's seminal text entitled *The Scholemaster* (1570), and a translation of Euclid's *Elements of Geometry* (1570). Foxe used Day's printing house as his base and address for correspondence; on one occasion he referred to it as 'our printing treadmill'. Day died in 1584 and Foxe in 1587, when he was buried in St Giles, Cripplegate. Bonner had again been deprived of the bishopric after Elizabeth's succession and was imprisoned once more. According to Foxe, who was not a friendly witness, 'after he had long feasted and banqueted in durance at the Marshalsea, [he] died in his bed unrepentant'.[25]

Mary underwent a phantom pregnancy following her marriage, and her failure to give birth to a child indicated that she would not do so. From 1556 it was thus certain that her half-sister Elizabeth would succeed her, unless she pre-deceased Mary. Following Mary's death on 17 November 1558, Elizabeth was swiftly proclaimed queen. In the afternoon of the day that her accession was announced, 'all the chyrches in London dyd ryng, and at nyght dyd make bonefyres and set tabulls in the strett, and ded ett and drynke and mad mere for the newe quen Elsabeth'.[26] When her sister died Elizabeth was at Hatfield House. She travelled to London a few days later and, arriving from the north, went directly to the Charterhouse, entering through the back gate to avoid the muddy streets. Her informality and lack of decorum in doing so appealed to the Londoners. She stayed there for five days before making her ceremonial entry to the City and going to the Tower.

Elizabeth's succession was followed by another swing of the religious pendulum, and Bonner's successor, Edmund Grindal, was to bear the responsibility for implementing the Elizabethan church settlement in London. It was assumed that Elizabeth was a Protestant who had conformed to her sister's faith against her will and would restore the Church to the condition in which Edward had left it. Some indication of her inclinations came from a proclamation that authorised the use of the English litany, as was done in the Chapel Royal. The City took this up and the Lord Mayor and Aldermen issued an order, on 1 January 1559, that the clergy in every London parish should read the epistle and gospel of the day in English. The queen also signified her approval for the reformers' practices when

Above: London in the late fifteenth century looking west; a painting by John Fulleylove based upon a contemporary illustration. (Author's collection)

Below left: The Court of King's Bench in session in Westminster Hall around 1460. (Courtesy Jonathan Reeve JR1579b4fp564 14501500)

Below right: Arms of the Barber-Surgeons' Company, granted by Henry VII and illustrated in 1492. (Author's collection)

Above left: The entrance to Staple Inn, Holborn, erected in 1586, painted by E. W. Haslehust around 1924. The inn was the largest of the Inns of Chancery. (Author's collection)

Above right: Portrait of Desiderius Erasmus, among the leading intellectuals of the European Renaissance and a frequent visitor to London, by Hans Holbein. (Author's collection)

Below: Henry VII's chapel in Westminster Abbey, completed after the king's death in 1509; painted by John Fulleylove. (Author's collection)

A chalk drawing by Hans Holbein of Thomas More, a Londoner who was a lawyer, a prominent intellectual and Chancellor of England 1529–32. (Author's collection)

Sir Brian Tuke was appointed Treasurer of the Chamber in 1528. He had a house in St Margaret's, Lothbury, was a member of the Common Council and in 1536 organised the postal service between the capital and the north. He was buried in St Margaret's in 1545. The portrait is by Hans Holbein. National Gallery of Art, Andrew W. Mellon Collection acc. 1937

Portrait of George Gisse, merchant of the Steelyard, the Hanseatic League's site alongside the Thames in London. The portrait, by Hans Holbein, is dated 1532. (Author's collection)

Above left: Portrait of William Tyndale, translator into English of the New Testament and the first books of the Old Testament, who was executed in Flanders in 1536; artist unknown. (Author's collection)

Above right: Portrait of Nikolaus Kratzer, 1528, by Hans Holbein. Kratzer was a mathematician, maker of mathematical instruments and astronomer; he came to England in 1517 and was employed by the crown for a variety of assignments. (Author's collection)

Below: In his play *Henry VIII* Shakespeare set a scene in Blackfriars priory when the case for the king's divorce from Queen Katherine was being heard; she accuses Cardinal Wolsey of being the prime mover of the divorce. This performance by the Kemble family around 1817 was painted by George Henry Harlow (1787–1819). © RSC Theatre Collection

Above left: An early Tudor town house, imagined by Margery Whittington. (Author's collection)

Above right: Portrait of Henry VIII in 1542, by Hans Holbein. (Author's collection)

Below: Henry VIII granting the arms of the Barber-Surgeons' Company in 1540, after Hans Holbein. (Author's collection)

Above: Cardinal Wolsey was the most powerful man in England after the king and is shown here on his way to Westminster Hall; the painting by Sir John Gilbert was exhibited in 1887. (Author's collection)

Left: Much of London's trade in the early and middle sixteenth century was through Antwerp and its merchants, such as the couple depicted by Quentin Matsys. The artist was a member of a network of humanists who helped to arrange Hans Holbein's journey to England. (Author's collection)

The French ambassador, Jean de Dinteville, with Georges de Selve, Bishop of Lavaur, probably painted at Bridewell Palace in 1533, by Hans Holbein. (Author's collection)

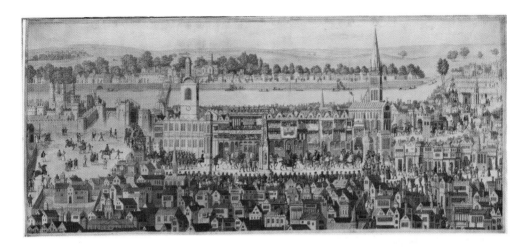

Above: The coronation procession of Edward VI in 1547, passing through Cheapside, London's principal street. (Courtesy Society of Antiquaries of London)

Right: Bermondsey Abbey was replaced by a grand house, which still displayed monastic features in the late eighteenth century. (Author's collection)

A portrait of Edward VI at the age of six, by Hans Holbein. (Author's collection)

A London street in the sixteenth century, imagined by Margery Whittington. (Author's collection)

St James's Palace was built by Henry VIII in the 1530s; the Tudor gatehouse survives and was painted by E. W. Haslehust in the early 1920s. (Author's collection)

Merry making on Tower Hill on the day of Edward VI's coronation in 1547. (Courtesy Society of Antiquaries of London)

Above: While a wife berates her husband in the kitchen, their son warms himself at the fireside and servants look anxiously through the doorway. The scene was depicted by Joris Hoefnagel in London in 1569. (Author's collection)

Below: Plan-view of London around 1585. The Tower is prominent, as is St Paul's cathedral, without its spire, destroyed in 1561. On Bankside, in the left foreground, the two animal-baiting arenas are shown. (Author's collection)

Above left: Portrait of Lord Burghley, Elizabeth's chief minister, who took a close interest in London and its government. The artist is unknown. (Author's collection)

Above right: The Savoy Hospital was established by Henry VII in 1505 and was closed by Edward VI in 1553; by the late eighteenth century parts of the buildings were in ruins and the site was cleared in 1816–20. (Author's collection)

Below: A feast at Bermondsey around 1570, depicted by Joris Hoefnagel. Food is being prepared in the open-fronted buildings and musicians beneath the tree are serenading the guests. (Courtesy Society of Antiquaries of London)

Above: An imagined view of Southwark in Tudor Times, showing tall buildings with jettied and decorated fronts. (Author's collection)

Below: Gray's Inn hall, built in 1556–8. (Author's collection)

Above: The Great Hall at the Charterhouse, built in 1546 and modified by the fourth Duke of Norfolk in 1571. Painted by Thomas Hosmer Shepherd *c.* 1830. (Author's collection)

Below: The central section of London Bridge in the late sixteenth century, looking downstream. It was supported on piers, or starlings, with only narrow gaps between them, while the structure carried substantial buildings. (Courtesy Jonathan Reeve, JR1062b1prelims 16001650)

Above left: Westminster around 1585; north of the abbey is Whitehall Palace. On the opposite side of the river is Lambeth Palace, the Archbishop of Canterbury's residence, but few other buildings. (Author's collection)

Above right: Portrait of Queen Elizabeth in 1592, artist unknown. (Author's collection)

Below: Revels at Elizabeth's court; the queen dancing with the Earl of Leicester, artist unknown. (Author's collection)

The gateway of Lincoln's Inn was built in 1518; the adjoining range was erected shortly afterwards. This painting is by E.W. Haslehust. (Author's collection)

Portrait of Sir Francis Drake, sailor and privateer, who owned a house in Dowgate from 1588 until 1593. (Author's collection)

Statue of Queen Elizabeth, originally on Ludgate and now on the exterior of the church of St Dunstan-in-the-West. (Author's collection)

Portrait of George Clifford, Earl of Cumberland, courtier, privateer and the Queen's Champion, as he was depicted by Nicholas Hilliard, perhaps in 1590. (Author's collection)

Portrait of Elizabeth I and Robert Devereux, Earl of Essex. Miniatures by Nicholas Hilliard. (Author's collection)

The building on the left, looking towards the church of St Helen's, Bishopsgate, was traditionally said to have been lived in by members of the Boleyn family. The scene was painted by Philip Norman just before the building was demolished in 1894. (Author's collection)

Above: The densely built-up riverside close to London Bridge in the early seventeenth century; redrawn in the late twentieth century by C. S. Tallant. (Courtesy Library of Congress)

Below: Memorial bust of John Stow (1525–1605), historian of London and chronicler of English history, in the church of St Andrew Undershaft. (Author's collection)

she instructed the celebrant of the service in the Chapel Royal at Christmas 1558, the Bishop of Carlisle, that he should not elevate the Blessed Sacrament; he refused and so she left the service after the reading from the gospel. And on her way to her first Parliament in January 1559 she made clear her opinion on candles as part of the Church's paraphernalia with a brusque remark, dismissing the traditional escort of the monks of Westminster by saying, 'Away with these torches, we see very well.'[27]

The religious settlement did indeed restore practices as they had been in 1553, before Mary's accession, but it took time and some management of Parliament before that was put in place. The Mass was discontinued, the rood and images were removed, clerical vestments were changed, communion tables replaced and torch-bearing processions came to an end once again. From Whitsuntide 1559 the English prayer book used under Edward VI was restored until a new prayer book was introduced at Midsummer, and 'the administration of the sacraments in our vulgar tongue was restored to be done as in the time of King Edward the Sixth', with the service of holy communion reinstated.[28]

The churchwardens of St Mary at Hill responded to the injunctions by taking down the rood with its figures of Mary and John and removing the altars. Images and other items were collected together to be burned. A communion table was made, the pulpit and reading desk were repaired, books of plainsong were bought for the choir, service books in English were acquired and a shilling was paid for 'the changing agayne of the sayd bookes'.[29] At St Martin-in-the-Fields similar changes were made, with the rood taken down, the altars removed and the floor where they had stood paved, a communion table was made, a service book and new psalters were bought, 3s 0d was paid for 'the whytenge of the Churche' and 5s 0d more 'for the payntenge of the ten Com'aundymentes'.[30] Similar changes were made across London. In the course of the year 'was alle the rod-loftes taken done in London, and wrytynges wrytyne in the sam plase'. Also removed were 'copes, crosses, sensors, alter-clothes, rod clothes, bokes, baners, bokes, and baner-stays, waynskott, with myche odur gayre', and the churchyard crosses were taken away.[31] In September 1559 'were burned in Paules Church-yarde, Cheape, and divers other places of London, all the roodes and images that stoode in the parishe churches. In some places the coapes, vestments, aulter clothes, bookes, banners, sepulchers, and other ornaments of the churches were burned.' The chronicler Charles Wriothesley noted that they were items which had been acquired during the previous reign, at a cost that he estimated at more than £2,000. The removal of images extended to the statue of Thomas à Becket on the street front of the Mercers' Company's hall in Cheapside, which, one morning in January 1559, was 'fownd broken and cast downe'.[32] Not all of the changes involved destruction, for a proclamation issued in September 1560 prohibited the 'breakinge or defacing Monumentes of antiquitie, being set up in Churches'. It emphasised that monuments were erected for remembering the dead and providing a memory for posterity of those buried there; they were not to be equated with 'monuments of Idolatry, and false fayned Images in Churches and Abbeyes'.[33]

The arrangements put in place in 1559 were not reversed, as Elizabeth enjoyed a long reign, unlike her siblings. But, as in the 1540s and 1550s, the settlement hung on the sovereign's life, for Elizabeth did not marry and the heir to the English throne was Mary, Queen of Scots, a Catholic and the widow of Francis II of France. After Mary's return to Scotland a complex political situation developed that, along with her own questionable judgements, saw her first imprisoned and then fleeing to England in the spring of 1568. Her arrival raised a number of problems for the government; she was not allowed to go to London, but was held in virtual house arrest in country mansions. A major plot to unseat Elizabeth promoted by Roberto Ridolfi, a Florentine banker, was thwarted, and Thomas Howard, fourth Duke of Norfolk, who had agreed to marry Mary and head a planned rising and invasion by Spanish troops, was executed in June 1572.[34] The political situation had been further complicated by a rising in the north of England in the autumn of 1569, which was subsequently quelled, and a Papal Bull issued by Pius V in the following year that proclaimed Elizabeth's excommunication and called for her deposition.

The Bartholomew's Day massacre in Paris and other French cities in August 1572, along with the brutalities during the Habsburg attempts to suppress Protestant rebels in the Netherlands, hardened Londoners' opinions against Catholicism. Other plots against Elizabeth by Catholic sympathizers followed, but they were nipped in the bud, and none depended upon or sought to foment unrest among the Londoners. The citizens and their rulers had embraced the Elizabethan church settlement and accepted the forms of the Church of England – and they had equally pressing matters to deal with, including prices and trade.

8

Prices and Trade

In many ways the mid-century period was a disconcerting one for the citizens, as they experienced the effects of religious changes at a time of economic insecurity, with war, unprecedentedly high taxation and price rises all impacting on their lives. Yet it also saw a growth in the cloth trade, and the turbulent years were followed by a more stable period, with an expansion and widening of overseas commerce that had a positive effect on the city's economy.

Henry VIII went to war with France and Scotland in 1542, defeating the Scots and fighting a successful campaign in France during which Boulogne was captured (the territory was retained until 1554). Mary also began a war with France, in 1557, at Philip's behest, and early in the following year Calais, England's foothold on the continent for over 200 years, was lost. The diarist Henry Machyn's reaction was that this was 'the hevest tydyngs to London and to England that ever was hard of'.[1] The military campaigns, the cost of maintaining garrisons and the navy, and the renovation and building of coastal fortifications added hugely to the Crown's expenditure. Between 1540 and 1552 wars cost almost £3.5 million, with the capture and maintenance of Boulogne accounting for £1,342,000 and the campaigns and garrisons in Scotland absorbing £954,000. This was far beyond the Crown's ordinary revenues and several expedients were employed to bridge the enormous gap. Roughly two-thirds of the monastic lands were sold, raising approximately £800,000 between 1539 and 1547, and direct taxation was granted by Parliament and supplemented by the aptly named forced loans and benevolences. Short-term loans were raised on the Antwerp money market, chiefly from the Fuggers of Augsburg, bringing in £272,000 in 1544–6, but at rates of interest that were never below 10 per cent and at a consequent cost of £40,000 a year.

The charge of servicing the debt was exacerbated by a fall in the value of the pound on the international money market.[2] One expedient that the government adopted was the debasement of the coinage by reducing the amount of precious metal in the coins; the advantage of debasement to the Crown was that its bullion went further and so it made a profit from the process. This shortfall amounted to £1.2 million pounds between 1542 and 1551, which contributed a significant part of the Crown's income during the years when its need for money was pressing. There were no further debasements after 1551, although the currency's true value was not restored until 1561.

Among the loans raised by the Crown was £21,263 6s 8d from the livery companies. But the City's contributions were not made without complaints. Taxation invariably raised howls of protest, and two aldermen refused to pay the benevolence in 1545. The king's commissioners for the levy in London sat at Baynard's Castle 'calling all the citizens of the same before them, beginninge first with the mayor and aldermen'. One of the aldermen, Richard Reid, balked at the levy and 'would not agree to pay as they set him' and so he was sent to fight with the army in Scotland, where he was captured. He was released only after his wife successfully petitioned the Privy Council that he should be exchanged for a Scottish prisoner in the Tower; she offered to pay the ransom that the king would lose by the prisoner's release. Another alderman, Sir William Roach, protested that the benevolence was illegal on the grounds that such levies had been condemned by an Act of Parliament in Richard III's reign, and he was accused of using 'uncivil and seditious words' to the commissioners. He was consigned to the Fleet prison until he bought his way out. The absence of those aldermen from their wards for a time risked impairing local administration, including the collection of taxes. Nevertheless, the king summoned the Lord Mayor, William Laxton, to Whitehall, knighted him and 'gave him and the aldermen great thankes for the benevolence to him by them given'.[3]

The wars affected Londoners in other ways. Men were levied to serve in the armies, but the practice of substitution was permitted, with a citizen who was due to go paying another man to take his place so that he could continue his business without interruption. In 1543 the capital sent 100 men, thirty of them archers and the others 'billmen', with the costs shared among thirty of the livery companies. The requirement was much higher in the following year, when London had to enlist 500 men, the cost of which was again 'borne amonge the craftes of the sayd citye at theyr owne costes and charges'; that year 'the Kinge would have no watch kept at Midsommer because the city had bene divers ways charged with men toward his warres'.[4] After that, the Midsummer Watch, which had been a regular feature of the city's life, became so intermittent as to virtually come to an end, and although attempts to resuscitate it were tried occasionally until 1585, it never resumed as a regular annual event. In 1545 London sent 100 men to serve with the fleet, and when a French force landed on the Isle of Wight 1,500 men were raised in the city and sent to Portsmouth. When they reached Farnham news arrived that the invaders had withdrawn and so they were ordered to return; each man was given 3s 0d when he set out and 2s 0d for his return from Farnham. These and the other costs were levied on the wards and paid by the aldermen, who then collected them from the householders.[5] As well as troops raised within London, the city was a staging point for others on their way to take shipping for the Continent, and foreign soldiers were among those billeted, such as a detachment of Spanish troops, consisting of a captain and 177 men, lodged with 'diverse hostes in London' in the spring of 1549.[6]

Oversight of the markets and prices became difficult and contentious tasks during the mid-century period of high inflation. In 1541 the clerk of the Drapers' Company grumbled that 'for every groat in the past we now pay five'; he could not know that ahead lay an unprecedented surge in prices.[7] Among the causes of the inflation, critics of London did not fail to point the finger at its wealth and high levels of consumption, described by Sir Thomas Smith in 1549 as 'excesse in apparel and fare'. He alleged that it was in London, 'the head of this empire, wheare suche excesses, by reason the wealthe that is of all this Realme is heaped up, as the corne of the field into a barne, be most used'.[8] There was indeed increasing demand as the population grew, and so pressure on supplies. But the major inflationary factors were not the Londoners' level of consumption and their alleged self-indulgence but the successive debasements of the coinage, the greater quantity of specie in circulation in Europe as the Spanish exploited their silver mines in the Americas, and England's balance of payments surplus, all of which increased the amount of money in circulation. This rose from perhaps £850,000 in 1542 to £2,170,000 in 1551, before falling back after a reduction of the 'base' silver content in the coinage and then rising again, to £1,390,000 in 1562 – an overall increase of 64 per cent over the twenty years.[9] As the precious metal content of the coins was reduced, so suppliers asked for more of them to maintain their income. The bulk of the small coins with which everyday transactions were conducted was of 'base' silver; the groat was originally worth 4*d* but was reduced to 2*d* in 1551; and so with the smaller coins. These smaller pieces were the ones which, as Edward VI noted in his journal, were 'to serve for the poor People, because the Merchants make no Exchange of it', as they dealt in higher denomination coins.[10]

Tinkering with the coinage also decreased confidence in it and so contributed to the instability in prices. The overall level of prices for consumers was roughly 9 per cent higher in the early 1540s than it had been in the 1530s, whereas in the later 1540s it was 39 per cent higher, and prices continued to rise so that in the 1550s they were 86 per cent higher than they had been in the 1530s. Prices did not subsequently fall back to their earlier levels. In London the highest rises were for flour, meat, poultry and dairy produce, with lower increases for fish, fuel and drink, and of course there were considerable short-term fluctuations for all goods.[11]

The system by which the Lord Mayor and his officers set the market rates for produce was partly designed to reduce such variations but it was vulnerable to criticism at a time of rising prices. The author of a tract issued in 1549 entitled *Policies to Reduce this Realme of England unto a prosperus Wealthe and Estate* was especially hostile to the practice, alleging that it could reduce the amount of grain brought into the port and that the system was open to abuse. He argued that if the Lord Mayor set a low price on grain brought in, aware that the storehouses were full, it would discourage merchants and shipowners from bringing in more, and so 'whan by souche means he hathe dryven awaye all the Corne vitallers, thene he will sell his owne at what price hime selfe listeth'. Similarly, at market the Lord Mayor might cause a pig to be taken from 'a poore womans hande', then that pig could well be sold to his officer's wife at half the price it would have fetched in the market, and the same with other produce. His argument was presented in crude terms but he concluded that it would help to reduce prices if the Lord Mayor, or any other officer, did not have the authority to intervene in setting them.[12]

What may have been even more irritating for consumers was that grain supplies should not rightfully have been a long-term problem, as there were few poor harvests during the inflationary years. The harvest in 1535 was a bad one, but a run of good or average harvests followed until 1545, and those in 1546, 1547 and 1548 were actually abundant, before three bad harvests followed in succession. The harvests in the 1550s produced average or good yields of grain, although with the notable exceptions of 1555 and 1556, which were very poor, resulting in high grain prices. But good harvest yields did not always translate into the ready availability of produce in London's markets and overall trends in the grain price were no sure guide to those charged in the city.

The summer of 1543 followed a good harvest in the previous year, judging from overall wheat prices, yet there was said to have been 'great dearth in the citie of London and the suburbes'. In the following year, after a harvest producing average yields of grain, 'wheate and other graine was very skant', and the Lord Mayor made a levy of £1,000 from the citizens to buy grain from Germany and Denmark. In 1545, too, London experienced a 'great dearth of corne and vitualles' and grain was bought from Denmark and the Baltic to supplement the city's stock, but after a good harvest in 1546 wheat and malt prices fell and brought the expectation that the 'great plentie therof in Englande ... shall cause itt to fall to lower prices'. In 1549 the alderman of Portsoken ward resigned his position and was fined £500, which was assigned towards buying wheat. That autumn its price rose again and imports were arranged, but the 'prices of fleshe waxed better cheape then yt had bene theise two yeares'. The harvest that year was deficient, but a timely delivery of grain in the following April, sold at Billingsgate, drew buyers from the counties around London 'so that yt was better cheap here then for the most part of all the shyres in England'. The practice of importing grain also worked well in 1551, when ten or twelve ships from Holland and several others from Brittany delivered grain to the port, 'which refreshed well the Cittie and the countrey neere London'.[13]

The prices charged for other foodstuffs and fuel did not necessarily follow the pattern of grain and flour prices because they were subject to other supply factors. In the winter of 1542/3 fuel prices were high 'by reason of the wett sommer, that wood could not be carryed for the high flowdes to the watter syde', with the price of coal rising as wood supplies dwindled until it was selling at almost twice the long-term average. That winter was cold and icy and 'vitalles ware excedinge dere, as saltfyshe with other salt meates, so that the mayre and aldermen ware fayne to ... see the people served at reasonable penyworthes'; a proclamation was issued permitting the eating of white meat during Lent, although not flesh. Meat prices rose that spring because of the unusually high mortality among cattle over the winter. In 1549 meat prices were said to be lower than they had been over the previous two years, but in 1551 they rose to such an extent that the Lord Mayor and Aldermen 'were greatlie exclamed of the people' because beef, veal and mutton were all expensive, 'for the grasiers sold their cattell at so high prices that the butcher could not sell it at meane prices'. Then, in 1552, 'all manner of victualles was exceedinge dere and at excessiue prices, both of fleshe and fishe, that the lyke hath not bene hard of'.[14]

The government became uneasy about the level of prices in London, and at the Guildhall on 8 June 1552 the Privy Councillors told the Lord Mayor, Aldermen and wardens of the livery companies of their concerns. The Lord Chancellor said that although prices elsewhere had fallen, they remained high in London, both of victuals and other wares. This he attributed to the fault of the Lord Mayor and aldermen for not pursuing and punishing those who were selling at high prices, despite having the authority to do so and having been instructed several times by the Privy Council to take action. He then issued the ultimate warning, that 'if they see not a speedy redresse and reformation shortly, that they should put all their liberties in daunger, to the great undoeinge of the Citie of London'. The threat to curtail the powers of the aldermen, perhaps even to withdraw the City's charter, indicated how seriously the government took the issue as a threat to social stability as well as having an impact on the wider economy. But its intervention was premature, for by the following February grain prices had fallen and the Lord Mayor, Sir George Barne, was able to increase the weight of the penny loaf, from twenty ounces to thirty-four ounces. He also set about remedying some abuses, for example by punishing coal sellers for selling sacks of short weight and he provided scales around the city, so that the weight of sacks could be easily checked. Despite those efforts, after Christmas 1553 both wood and coal prices rose because of shortages, and so the Lord Mayor ordered coals to be brought in by sea and sold at Billingsgate and Queenhithe, 'which greatlie helped tyll better provision might be fownde'. As well as trying to improve supplies, the City's officers continued to punish profiteers, such as a woodmonger in March 1554 who was condemned to stand in the pillory at Cheapside for selling wood at more than twice the price he had paid for it.[15]

The supervision of prices and the markets led to disputes, with the City's officers coming under attack from irate traders and consumers, on some occasions literally so. In 1545 a fishmonger was imprisoned 'for misusinge the mayor at the stockes and strykinge his officer in the open market' and in 1555 the Lord Mayor himself was struck by a baker while he was supervising the weighing of loaves in Holborn. This may have been a jurisdictional dispute, for the baker was indicted by the Middlesex justices and the Lord Mayor was outside the City boundary at the time, but 'all Mayors of London from time immemorial have been accustomed to weigh the loaves of bakers in Holburn'.[16]

Overall, the corporation's practice of importing grain for London's storehouses served the city well and the effects of the period of inflation may not have been as harsh as they were for those living outside the metropolis. Even so, wage-earners were unable to maintain their standard of living. Real wages fell by roughly 19 per cent between the 1490s and the 1530s, and then again by the same amount over the period of the debasements from 1542 to 1551, before recovering so that in the 1560s they were at roughly the same level as they had been in the 1530s. The wages of skilled workers were roughly 60 per cent higher than those of the unskilled, those with low wages or having only intermittent employment, who fell into the broad category of the poor. A survey taken in 1518 of those licensed to beg suggests that there were then 3,000 poor, and a list compiled in 1552 of 'every of the sorts of the poor' produced a figure of 6,900; both surveys excluded Southwark. The city's population had risen to 80,000 between the two dates, and when allowance is made for that increase and for the inhabitants of Southwark, it seems that those inhabitants who could, very roughly, be classified as 'poor' had risen from approximately 6 per cent to 11 per cent of the total over the first half of the century. A long period of stability ensued and, despite the increasing rate of population growth, the proportion regarded as poor did not rise appreciably. The poorest districts were around the fringe of the City and in some parishes along the riverside; the centre remained a predominantly wealthy area.[17]

Of course, the government bore much responsibility for the problems caused by inflation, especially through the debasement of the currency. But as well as helping to increase its revenue, devaluation of the currency made England's exports cheaper abroad. Woollen cloth remained the most valuable export, and Antwerp was still the chief port on the Continent for English trade. Cloth exports from London had risen through the early sixteenth century, albeit erratically, and more sharply from the mid-1530s. By the mid-1540s more than 90 per cent of cloth exports went through London – in only a few years did the proportion fall below that figure – and the city accounted for more than 85 per cent of wool exports in most years.[18] Provincial ports and some towns in the cloth-making areas of the Cotswolds, East Anglia and the West Riding of Yorkshire suffered economically from London's growing dominance. But while the increase in trade was profitable for London, it was also frustrating, because most cloth was sent to be finished and dyed in the Flemish cities, depriving London's artisans of the employment it would have provided had the cloth been finished before being shipped. It was alleged that the water of the Thames was not so suitable for dyeing cloth as that of the Scheldt or Elbe. That claim was refuted by William Cholmeley, a 'Londyner', in 1555 when he wrote a tract describing how, with the help of a workman from Antwerp who was 'verye expert in the feate of dyinge', he had succeeded in dyeing cloths in London of as good a quality as those produced abroad. Lacking adequate capital, Cholmeley had gone into business with a dyer in Southwark, and over three years they had made a clear profit from dyeing cloth 'after the maner of the dyinge in Fraunce and Flaunders'. He found the complaint about the water to be 'a foule slaunder upon the famouse river of Temys' by English dyers, and he also suspected that he would face 'a whole legion of merchauntis, dyars, and drapers of this realme ... bendyng them selves agaynst myne enterprise, who (no dought) wyll brynge in a whole sea of objections agaynst that which I have wrytten'.[19]

Cholmeley may have been correct in claiming that there were restrictive factors in the economy which limited the possible benefits from the cloth trade, but the interventionist policies under the first two Tudor kings had included revision of the City's freedom regulations. The livery companies could limit entry to a trade by charging apprentices fees that were beyond the means of some parents, thus imposing a social as well as an economic limitation on those entitled to the freedom. In 1529 Common Council had reduced the fees levied from apprentices in some companies, but in 1531 Parliament went much further. It condemned the policy of high fees generally on the grounds that they contravened an Act of 1504 that prohibited the companies from enacting ordinances which were 'agaynst the common profitte of the people'. Alleging that some had set the fees at up to £2, 'after their owne senester myndes and pleasure contrarie to the menyng of the Acte aforesayd and to the great hurte of the Kynges true Subjectes puttynge their Childe to be prentyse', the new legislation fixed the maximum fees that could be levied at 2s 6d for enrolling an apprentice and 3s 4d for admission to a company. In 1536 a further Act prohibited surcharges on entrance fees and also banned the custom of imposing an oath on men at the end of their apprenticeships, by which they undertook never to set up shops and so be competitors for the established figures in a trade. The eradication of these practices removed a restriction on the labour supply and the size of the livery companies, and so London's economy was able to respond when there was a boom.[20]

The increase in cloth prices and exports in the mid-century produced just such a boom and rising demand for labour; in the early 1550s the clothing trades accounted for 40 per cent of apprentices enrolled. When demand for cloth subsequently faltered, the labour supply was in any case affected by mortality during the epidemics of the sweat and plague. A severe outbreak of plague in 1563 caused 23,660 deaths in the City and surrounding parishes, 85 per cent of them attributed to plague, with an overall mortality rate of roughly 20 per cent of the population. This would be the worst epidemic of the Tudor era, although it proved to be only a temporary setback to London's steady growth, which soon resumed.

But the volume of cloth exports soon levelled out. Trade through Antwerp had been complicated by fluctuations in the exchange rate following the debasements of the coinage, until Thomas Gresham, son of Sir Richard Gresham, a former Lord Mayor, began to operate as the government's agent in the City. He managed to implement a procedure by which London's merchants exchanged their currency through him, rather than individually, which brought stability.

Diplomatic machinations led to closure of the trade between the Low Countries and England in 1563–4, drawing attention to the over-reliance on the Antwerp market, and with the deterioration of Anglo-Spanish relations the connection with the city grew increasingly fragile. From 1568 to 1573 there was an embargo on trade between England and ports under Spanish control. Antwerp also began to suffer economically as the Habsburgs attempted to suppress Protestantism, and the repressive tactic of using troops to quell disturbances in the Netherlands was to lead to the sack and firing of the city in 1576 by unpaid and mutinous soldiers, in an event that came to be known as the Spanish Fury, when thousands of its citizens were killed and perhaps one-third of its houses were destroyed. The city's recovery from the disaster was halted when it was surrendered to the Spanish in 1585. By the terms of the surrender any of its citizens who wished to leave could do so, provided they depart within a year. Many took advantage of the opportunity and went to the northern provinces, which emerged from the turmoil as the independent United Provinces. The Dutch cities benefited from those immigrants, their enterprise and skills, and textile industries developed in the region, marking a significant change in the economic geography of the Low Countries. Antwerp's troubles were compounded by the fact that the Dutch had control of the mouth of the Scheldt and charged very high rates for ships passing to and from the city, which was effectively ruined as a major international port. Bruges was surrendered by the same agreement and also lost specialist workers, and its access to the sea remained inadequate. That gave London an opportunity to surge ahead as the chief port of north-west Europe, although Amsterdam was soon to emerge as a serious challenger.

The Merchant Adventurers Company needed to change its 'mart' for English cloth as the political and military situation developed and at various times authorised its members to use other ports: Hamburg, Emden, Middelburg and Stade, on the Elbe, were all tried. A further change in the organisation of London's trade came following challenges to the privileges enjoyed by the Hanseatic merchants who, with Italian, Dutch and other foreign merchants, probably were responsible for over a half of the cloth shipped from London by the early 1540s. The non-Hanseatic merchants lost their short-term privileges in 1546, and the Merchant Adventurers lobbied persistently for the removal of the long-term ones enjoyed by traders accredited to the Hanse cities. They were so successful that the Duke of Northumberland withdrew these privileges in 1552. This was the beginning of a troubled period, with the privileges being successively restored, modified and withdrawn throughout the rest of the decade until a settlement was reached in 1560, albeit with the Hanse's advantages considerably reduced. By 1579 there were only four merchants based at the Steelyard. The economic power of the Hanse cities was, in any case, on the wane as direct Dutch and English trade with the Baltic undermined their earlier dominance. In 1598 Elizabeth finally both withdrew the merchants' privileges and expelled them from the Steelyard, in retaliation for the Emperor Rudolf II's expulsion of the Merchant Adventurers from Stade. But northern Europe's continued importance in London's trade was indicated by the Swiss visitor Thomas Platter's comment in 1599 that 'ships from France, the Netherlands, Germany and other countries land in this city, bringing goods with them and loading others in exchange for exportation'. His contemporary, Jacob Rathgeb, while noting that Londoners were trading 'in almost every corner of the world', specified France, the Netherlands, Sweden, Denmark and Hamburg as the countries from which ships came to London.[21]

The Venetian ambassador Giovanni Michiel wrote a summary of England in January 1557, having served in the post since May 1554. He described London as a city 'which maintains itself chiefly by trade' and anticipated difficulties for the Venetian merchants there, especially in the shipping of wool and cloth to Europe, who also imported especially wines, currants and other produce from the Levant. He attempted to give an impression of the wealth of London's merchants by saying that among the members of the Merchant Adventurers and the Merchants of the Staple 'there are many individuals possessed of from fifty to sixty thousand pounds sterling, all or the greater part in ready money ... besides an endless number of others of various companies, such as dealers in tin, in spices, and other grocery wares ... and, which will appear incredible, the company of those who deal in salt fish, they being extraordinarily rich, either to the amount aforesaid, or to a greater sum'.[22]

The English merchant community in London at the mid-century consisted of at least a hundred people, including both the 'greater' and the 'lesser' merchants, and perhaps as many as 300, if those operating on a smaller scale were included.[23] The established London merchants were said to maintain their position at the expense of newer members, partly by holding the senior posts in the Merchant Adevnturers Company themselves and partly by imposing charges that bore disproportionately on the 'new' adventurers. By a statute of 1497 the company's basic admission fee was set at £6 13s 4d; with the onset of inflation that became readily affordable for men attracted by the profits that seemed to be available, especially for those trading in cloth. They could raise the money themselves or take a loan, with the expectation of considerable profits to come. Of course, it was not that simple and success was not at all guaranteed for those without the necessary experience and contacts. As Thomas Gresham wrote, in 1553, 'How is it possible that a minstrel player, or a shoemaker, or any craftsman, or any other that hath not been brought up in the science [trade] to have the present understanding of the feat of the merchant adventurer?' But the senior figures came under pressure from within the company nevertheless, and in 1553 the dispute was heard by the Privy Council. Perhaps unsurprisingly, it found in favour of the 'old' merchants and concluded that those who had challenged the existing arrangements had done so without justification and 'gon abowt disordredly to stirre stryfe and contencion' to upset the merchants' privileges. Two of the leading challengers, John Tull and John Dimmock, were imprisoned, although probably only briefly. The established members of the company reacted to their victory by raising the admission fee tenfold, as a deterrent for those without sufficient capital and markedly reducing the opportunities for entry into the trade.[24]

The Merchant Adventurers' arrangements may have been maintained by that judgement, but were steadily eroded in the longer term as the London merchants diversified, both in terms of goods shipped and regions served. Joint-stock trading companies were formed for commerce with those new regions. The Muscovy Company was established in 1555, and its exploratory voyages lead to meetings with the czar and grants of trading privileges. The Eastland Company was formed for trade with Scandinavia and the Baltic in 1579, the Turkey Company was established in 1581 and the Venice Company in 1583 (they merged to become the Levant Company in 1592), the East India Company was formed in 1600 and the Virginia Company in 1609. Trade with Morocco began in 1551, but the Barbary Company, established in 1585, was dissolved twelve years later.

The new companies were dominated by Londoners; most of the initial investors in the Muscovy Company were London merchants, quickly buying up the 240 shares, at £25 per share, and all but three of the forty-two members of the Barbary Company listed in its charter came from the London merchant community. But there was also pressure for greater freedom in overseas trade and some traded outside the companies, challenging their monopoly rights. These individuals were known as 'interlopers', a term that came into use before the end of the century and included men such as Thomas Lowe and Henry Parvish who, in 1579, were alleged to be carrying on 'a stragglinge trade into Germany' by buying silk from Italian merchants in Nuremburg and Frankfurt. A few years later the writer of a pamphlet pointed out that members of the Merchant Adventurers Company were trading to Nuremburg 'and other parts of Germany, contrarie to the olde good orders of the Companie, especially that which forbiddeth trade out of the mart towns'.[25] Although the Privy Council backed the company when it complained of such interloping, as it had done earlier, the organisation of overseas commerce was becoming looser as trade expanded, in terms of the number of ships engaged and the variety and value of the merchandise traded. The range of goods imported steadily widened, with pepper, currants and raisins, oil, salt, spices, silk, cotton, indigo, calico, glass, dyes and sugar being brought in, and tobacco was shipped to Europe from the West Indies and Florida from the 1560s. In 1597 the French ambassador, André Hurault, Sieur de Maisse, observed that London's merchants dominated England's overseas trade: 'Everything that comes from the Levant and Venice is in their hands, and they no longer allow any stranger to carry merchandise, not that they forbid it, but they so harass them with taxes and seizures on their vessels that it is not possible to endure it.' They also traded with the French port of Rouen on a large scale, for example, and indeed with ports large and small around the coasts of northern Europe, from France to Scandinavia and the Baltic.[26] (But ports in Iberia were closed to English vessels during the war with Spain, which began in 1585.)

As well as regular trade, London's merchants obtained goods and profits through privateering, with marauding vessels seizing those of designated enemy countries and confiscating their cargoes, and perhaps the vessels as well. The activity was distinguished from piracy, which was of course injurious to a trading nation, by the issue of letters of marque by the government, licensing the setting out of ships to engage in such commercial raiding. Privateering became increasingly common from 1562 with Elizabeth's intervention in the wars in France; the privateering syndicates were authorised by the government, and the quest for plunder that would bring quick riches coincided with the military need to diminish the enemy's resources. The opportunities and the scale of investment in the operations greatly increased after the outbreak of war with Spain. Despite the numbers of vessels that were set out by the West Country ports in particular, London became dominant in English privateering. In 1589–91, seventy of the 236 privateers listed were from London; by 1598 a half of the eighty-six ships were from the capital.[27] Some twenty to thirty of its merchants financed the ventures and reaped the profits, combining trade with privateering, sometimes in partnership with senior figures at court. George Clifford, Earl of Cumberland, began a career as a privateer in 1586, perhaps in an attempt to recover his losses as a courtier and gambler. He organised at least one privateering voyage each year over the next ten years, mostly in conjunction with syndicates of London merchants. His reputation attracted partners: in December 1597 de Maisse noted that he was preparing to undertake a voyage with sixteen of the queen's ships 'and plenty of others belonging to individual merchants, who put themselves in his company to try their fortune'.[28]

Spices, luxury goods and other produce from the captured vessels that were brought into London might never have reached the city in such quantities in peacetime. Sugar was a staple of the Morocco trade: London imported sugar valued at £18,000 in 1565–6, the equivalent of 5,400 cwt, a figure that had almost doubled twenty years later to 9,000 cwt per annum. But in the three years spanning 1589–91 a haul of sugar valued at £100,000 was captured, equivalent to 10,000 cwt per annum. Much of the sugar landed from privateers in the West Country ports was shipped coastwise to London, and in the twelve-month period from Michaelmas 1595 to Michaelmas 1596, 7,250 cwt of sugar was imported into the capital. Some was re-exported, but most was refined in the city. Sugar had been refined in England from around 1544, but it had to compete with Antwerp sugar, which 'came thence better cheap than it could be afforded in London'. But with the improved supply and Antwerp's problems, sugar refining was expanded – there were three refineries in London by 1595. An important figure in the trade was Sir Thomas Myddleton, a member of the Grocers' Company who had served his apprenticeship with Ferdinando Poyntz, a sugar refiner, acting for him in Vlissingen and Middelburg. In the 1580s he developed his own business, trading with the Low Countries, Stade and Caen, as well as engaging in privateering. With his experience of the sugar business it was not surprising that he bought and operated a sugar refinery, in Mincing Lane. He also invested some of his growing wealth, from an increasing range of sources, in property in London, including Baynard's Castle, which he bought in 1602, and country estates in Denbighshire and Essex. Through privateering and the enterprise of its merchants, along with the expertise of immigrants, in the course of the late sixteenth century London became dominant in the European sugar supply. Some of it reached domestic consumers, as Paul Hentzner observed in 1598. When he watched the queen go to chapel at Greenwich one Sunday he noticed that her teeth were black, which was 'a defect the English seem subject to, from their too great use of sugar'.[29]

As well as the seagoing vessels in the Thames, there were many others that were engaged in coastal trade; the numbers impressed visitors such as de Maisse, who wrote that 'it is a magnificent sight to see the number of ships and boats which lie at anchor'.[30] London traded especially with the ports on the east and south coasts. Some of the goods shipped to London were imports that had been taken initially into a provincial port, such as soap at Plymouth and woad from Toulouse, which had been landed at the West Country harbours. A greater proportion of the coastwise trade to London was produce from within England and Wales. Wheat, rye, barley, beans and malt were brought from the east coast ports as far north as Hull, which could draw on its hinterland along the Ouse and Trent. King's Lynn was an especially prominent port for shipments of grain to London from Norfolk and the River Ouse and its tributaries. The Kentish ports, too, were significant providers of grain for the London markets: Sandwich, Rochester, Milton and Faversham were all engaged in the trade and they also sent hops and, with Rye and Winchelsea, firewood to the city in coasting vessels. Butter, cheese and fish were brought to London, with Norfolk, Essex and, above all, Suffolk sending cheese to the capital. The chief movement of fuel was coal from the rivers

Tyne and Wear, which was an expanding trade in the period, with 37,950 tons reaching London in 1585–6 and 54,742 tons by 1591–2. This reflected the city's growing population and also coal's steady replacement of wood as the chief domestic fuel.

Goods sent from London to the provincial ports included manufactured goods from haberdashers, ironmongers, upholsterers and braziers, as well as from brewers, for not all beer was brewed locally and quantities were shipped from the capital to some two-dozen ports around the coast, as far as Berwick in the north-east and Helston in Cornwall in the south-west. More specialised was the malmsey wine freighted from London to Newcastle and then carried overland to Keswick. There was, too, a whole miscellany of items sent from London as return cargoes in the coasting vessels supplying its needs. In 1580 Milton, in Kent, received, among many other things, two hampers of shoes and a consignment of 'made ware for maryners apparell'; in 1586 Great Yarmouth took delivery of frieze gowns and seven dozen 'dobletts and breeches'; and in 1595 '9 doz. petycotes' were received in Lyme Regis from London. Some of the items had been imported, such as stone pots that had been made in Germany and frying pans from Amsterdam, and others probably had been shipped coastwise to London from another port, with London acting as an exchange. Cloth was both taken to London and sent out from it, in some cases to a port which was itself a supplier of cloth, reflecting the variety of grades and uses of the fabrics as well as their prominent place in the economy.[31]

The smaller vessels in the Thames transported goods along the river network. The Thames was navigable as far upstream as Burcot, and goods from London for Oxford, for example, were taken there by boat and then overland by carriers. The goods sent from London by river were as varied as those moved in the coastal trade, including grocery, haberdashery and mercery wares, and foodstuffs, too, such as the 100 salt fish sent to Magdalen College, Oxford, in 1588. Supplies of grain and malt were taken to London along the rivers. In 1571 an Act of Parliament was passed 'for the bringing of the Ryver of Lee to the northside of the citie of London'. This involved a new cut at the expense of the corporation, and the cleansing and improvement of the River Lea.

The work cost perhaps as much as £80,000, but when completed it was both easier and significantly cheaper to freight agricultural produce to the city from Hertfordshire by river than overland. The improvement made Ware a river port of some significance, one of several market towns on the river network of south-east England that owed their prosperity to the trade with London. Henley-on-Thames was said to be inhabited by watermen 'who make their chiefest gaine by carrying downe in their barges wood and corne to London'.[32]

London's connections with the provinces were also maintained by a network of carriers with packhorses and vehicles. They took commodities to and from the coastal and river ports and also travelled directly to London. Some maintained regular services, such as those used by the Worcester clothiers to take their cloth to London; one carrier was owed money by three clothiers when he died, due to him for carriage of their cloth.[33] By 1580 there was a carrier service between York and London; combined with the coastal trade, London was more important to York's trade than anywhere else outside its own county. When a York draper died in 1585 he owed more than £1,700 to four London merchant-tailors for cloths, £727 of which was due to just one of them.[34] In 1599 two carriers regularly made the journey between Ipswich and the capital, and in 1580 'the carryers of Chester come weekly to Bosomes Inne in St Lorance Lane' (Blossoms Inn, on the north side of Cheapside). Much of the cloth taken to London from the producing areas was carried overland, while groceries, mercery ware and iron goods provided return loads. The carriers' varied consignments included six puddings weighing 16 lbs, sent to London from Smithills near Bolton. Another load included six Dutch chairs taken from London to Keswick, a centre of the cloth trade and of mining, where the local mining company bought wine, candles and, perhaps more surprisingly, oranges and artichokes from the capital.[35]

Food prices generally were steady during the third quarter of the century, and harvests in the 1580s and early 1590s were good, with the exception of 1586. But these were followed by four successive poor harvests from 1594. Grain prices rose by roughly a third, and in January 1594 the aldermen asked for a ban on grain exports.

By September 1595 the city's granaries were empty and wheat and
rye were imported from the Baltic, but rains across northern and
central Europe made that a year of widespread shortages and high
prices. Disturbances that summer probably constituted the first
food riots in the capital since the 1520s. In October twenty ships
with cargoes of grain arrived from the Baltic, but there was no
respite in 1596, which saw a desperately bad harvest, with prices
more than 80 per cent higher than in the early years of the decade,
and a penny loaf in London weighing just a quarter of what it had
done in 1560. The corporation distributed 4,000 loaves weekly to
the poorest households in what proved to be the most expensive
year for bread in London during the entire century. The prices of
a range of consumables also reached a new peak. But this parlous
trend did not continue, for after a bad harvest in 1597 crop yields
improved over the next few years and into the early seventeenth
century, and so prices fell.

The Londoners' diet continued to include oysters and a range of
fish, including 'cod, plaice, small white river fish, pike, carp, trout,
lobster and crawfish, and in fine all kinds of sea fish, which are sold
like meat in other parts, both fresh and salted', according to Jacob
Rathgeb, in 1592.[36] By 1569 abundance of pears, plums, damsons
'and other like fruit' was taken daily in season to the city to be
sold.[37] Other foodstuffs reached London from the provinces. Cattle
and sheep were driven on the hoof from an expanding area across
the pastoral regions of England and Wales to be fattened on the
pastures around the city, before being taken to market. A French
visitor in 1578, L. Grenade, practically drooled over the 'beauty
and excellence' of the meat for sale at the shambles in Eastcheap,
which was 'not only overflowing with agreeable qualities and at
the same time tender and of a delicate taste, but clean and also
extremely well dressed'. Fresh meat was also provided by the
Londoners themselves from the poultry and rabbits raised on
their premises. Rabbits were bred in yards and within buildings,
for their pelts, some of which were exported from at least the
fourteenth century, and for meat, a delicacy for the well-to-do and
a staple for the poor.[38] Root crops were brought from the market
gardens at Norwich, where market gardening was begun by Dutch
immigrants, who introduced carrots, turnips and parsnips. In

1593–4, 280 tons of roots were shipped from Great Yarmouth to London; in 1597–8 the figure was 812 tons. Root crops were also imported. In November 1596 vessels from Holland unloaded at London 12,600 cabbages and onions in sixty-five barrels and on 10,400 'ropes'. By the end of the century Londoners could buy peas, beans, cabbages, turnips, radishes, artichokes and onions, and carrots and parsnips were said to be 'common meate among the common people, all the time of autumne, and chiefly upon fish daies'. Salad stuff and soft fruits were available in summer, and the strawberries grown in the Bishop of Ely's gardens in Holborn were famous enough to be mentioned by Shakespeare, in *Richard III*.[39] Around the turn of the century London's own market gardens were being developed at Hackney, Shoreditch, Chelsea, Kensington and Fulham. The crops were valuable enough to be worth stealing; in July 1596 Henry Hunt of Shoreditch, gardener, was bound over by the Middlesex magistrates for £10 on a charge of 'stealinge of artichokes'.[40] As the market gardens around London were developed, the need to import vegetables was reduced. But at the same time the gardens within the city that are shown on plan-views of the mid-century were being diminished, as the ground was built upon.

Finally, ships brought travellers to London from abroad and around the coasts, and the carriers, too, conveyed passengers. A carrier took the Hochstetter family from London to Keswick; they were members of a prominent banking and mining dynasty in Augsburg. Carriers provided transport for innumerable young men who were setting out to the capital to enrol as apprentices. In 1581 the city of York gave a donation for William Yong, a boy, to help him find a master in the city, and if he could not do so then he was to be newly clothed and sent to London with the carrier.[41] Like so many others, William would then face, for the first time, the enormous size and bewildering bustle of the great city.

9

Cheerful Givers

The wealth generated by London's expanding trade was shared among its citizens, through the economic activity and employment generated, and the charity of those who profited from that trade. As the wealthiest group in London, the merchants were prominent in continuing the tradition of philanthropy in the metropolis and in other places with which they had connections. Those who had grown up after the Reformation were aware of the need to demonstrate that England could provide poor relief as capably as its Roman Catholic neighbours, and to refute allegations that charitable giving had been adversely affected by the religious upheavals. Their response was to direct charity to those in actual need, the poor, children, the disabled and the elderly, rather than channel it through the Church. They would do so without needing to be pressured; the outlook stated in Paul's second letter to the Corinthians was to the point, that 'god loveth a chearfull gever'.[1]

Not all of the charities that had ceased to exist had been lost because of the dissolution of the monasteries and chantries. John Stow mentioned an example at Houndsditch, where, on the edge of a field 'towards the street were some small cottages, of two stories high, and little garden-plots backward, for poor bed-rid people, for in that street dwelt none other, built by some prior of the Holy Trinity'. Stow described the practice by which they received alms, recalling that when he was a youth (he was born in 1525) 'devout people, as well men as women of this city, were accustomed to walk that way purposely to bestow their charitable alms; every poor man or woman lying in their bed within their window, and a pair of beads, to show that there lay a bed-rid body, unable but to pray only'. But in the mid-1540s some gunfounders acquired land nearby and established a foundry for making brass ordnance, and then 'in a short time divers others also built there, so that the poor bed-rid people were worn out, and, in place of their homely cottages, such houses built as do rather want room than rent'. And so the almspeople were forced out by the pressure of development as the city grew.[2]

The foundation of almshouses spanned the pre- and post-Reformation periods, and they were established in increasing numbers. Andrew Judd, a skinner, who was Lord Mayor in 1550–1, established almshouses at St Helen's, Bishopsgate for six poor people, and gave his company property to provide funds for weekly pensions of 8*d* each, with £1 5*s* 4*d* annually for coal. His daughter augmented the endowment with land worth £15 per year. An endowment that would generate enough to pay the almspeople's pensions and other benefits was essential, as well as providing the site and the cost of the buildings. Shakespeare referred to 'alms-houses right well supplied' which were 'to relief of lazars [lepers] and weak age, Of indigent faint souls, past corporal toil'. He set the comment in the early stages of Henry V's reign, but it was equally applicable to the late 1590s when he wrote the text, or indeed to any period.[3] On the east side of Monkwell Street, just inside the city wall near Cripplegate, almshouses for twelve 'poor and aged people' were founded by Sir Ambrose Nicholas, salter, Lord Mayor in 1575–6. After his death they became the responsibility of his company. John Stow described them as 'proper alms houses' and gave the almspeople's benefits as 7*d* per week, and five sacks of charcoal and twenty-five bundles of firewood annually. Richard Hills, a merchant-tailor, gave 'some small cottages' on Tower Hill as a site for almshouses, which were built by the Merchant Taylors' Company in 1593. They were 'fair alms houses, strongly built of brick and timber, and covered with slate', housing fourteen single women, who received 1*s* 4*d* per week 'or better' and £8 15*s* annually for fuel. An even larger gift had been made earlier in the century by Avise Gibson, who founded a school for sixty poor children and an almshouse for fourteen elderly people at Radcliffe, with a chapel. On her instructions they were to be administered by the Coopers' Company, and by the 1590s the company had placed its own coat-of-arms on the building, replacing those of the Grocers' Company, her first husband's livery company.[4] It seems there was a competitive edge when credit could be claimed from a connection with the more substantial philanthropic donations.

By the end of the century London's livery companies were responsible for overseeing 200 places in almshouses, and the value of endowments for residents had risen from £400 per annum in 1570–3, to £676 per annum in 1594–7. Benefactors did not restrict their munificence to London but also established schools, almshouses and other charities across the country, in their place or county of origin, or where they had invested in a landed estate. Of those whose disposable wealth was £1,500 or more at death, 18 per cent of them in the 1550s and 24 per cent in the 1590s left money to the poor outside London.[5] In 1574 William Frankland bequeathed two tenements to the Clothworkers' Company, with the rental income to provide coal for the poor of All Hallows the Great and Skipton, in Yorkshire, and his contemporary William Lambe, also a member of the company, gave the funds for an almshouse and a free grammar school at Sutton Valence, in Kent.[6]

Sir Thomas White was the largest benefactor in the mid-century period, and he was a Roman Catholic. He was Master of the Merchant Taylors' Company in 1536. He gave funds to provide interest-free loans for young clothiers in cities and towns across England, most of them involved in the cloth trade. The earliest scheme began in 1542, providing £10 for four men for nine years each, which became the model for two similar programmes, the more elaborate of which supplied loans of £104 for men in twenty-three cities and the Merchant Taylors' Company; it became fully operative from 1577.[7]

White was also involved in the establishment of the Merchant Taylors' School in Suffolk Lane, in 1561. This was a new foundation, designed to benefit Londoners. The first boys were the sons of a cross-section of London tradesmen: merchant-tailors, a clergyman, plumber, leatherseller, carpenter, upholsterer, clothworker, salter, vintner, grocer, dyer, draper and wax chandler. Of the 250 pupils, 100 who were 'poor men's sons' were to have their education free, fifty more, also categorised as 'poor', were to pay 2*s* 6*d* per quarter, while the remaining 100 boys were 'rich or mean men's children' and paid 5*s* 0*d* quarterly.[8] A connection was established between the school and White's foundation of St John's College, Oxford, which was established in 1555. He intended that the college should train Roman Catholic clergy, but the religious swing after Mary's death in 1558 confounded that intention; he died in 1567.

Later merchants had wider commercial interests and continued the tradition of charitable giving. Richard Staper was particularly successful in business and traded with a variety of markets, whereas White's wealth had come chiefly from the traditional trade in cloth. Staper was one of the two leading figures in the opening of the trade to the eastern Mediterranean and a member of the Levant companies and the East India Company. He also traded with Morocco, as well as with Genoa and Livorno, and was a member of the Eastland Company, trading to the Baltic and Germany, and he imported goods from Amsterdam, the rising star of north European trade. Staper was born around 1540 and died in 1608, so his career spanned the period of widening trade in the late sixteenth century. His monument in the church of St Mary Outwich was appropriately surmounted by a galleon, and the inscription proudly describes him as 'the greatest merchant in his Tyme, the chiefest actor in discoveri of The trades of Turkey and East India'. Staper was a member of the Clothworkers' Company although he did not engage in civic life at the highest level; despite being chosen as an alderman in 1594 he was discharged within three days. But he did make the charitable donations expected of such a successful man and was described as 'bountiful to the Poor'. Following the customary practice, poor men were to follow his coffin and attend his funeral. He specified that forty of the sixty-four men were to be from the Clothworkers' Company, and all were to be provided with gowns. The company was to administer £110, which would generate income to be distributed annually to five poor men, and his parish was bequeathed £20 towards the cost of building shops at the east end of the church, to provide rental income. His apprentices and maid servants each received £2 and a black gown. His will included bequests to Christ's Hospital, St Thomas's Hospital, Bridewell and ten prisons. The legacies totalled at least

£800 and the residue of his estate went to his three sons, the eldest of whom, Hewitt, was to inherit the 'greate house' with £200 for improvements to it. Hewitt also operated as a merchant, as a member of the East India Company and trader with the Levant.[9]

Staper's contemporary Edward Holmden was a member of the Grocers' Company and served as its Master in 1596. He traded on a large scale to Venice, the Levant and Zante, in the Ionian Islands, was also a member of the Morocco Company and a senior figure in the East India Company. Holmden married a niece of Sir Thomas Ramsey, also a member of the Grocers' Company and Lord Mayor in 1577–8. At Ramsey's death in 1590 his bequests included gifts to the hospitals, prisons and the poor, with £200 for a loan stock for four young members of his company. His wife Mary furthered the philanthropic projects they had developed, with Christ's Hospital a prominent beneficiary as well as loan stocks of £200 granted to each of five livery companies to support their poor, a stock of £500 to assist debtors, and an endowment that produced £100 per annum, shared between exhibitions for university students, wounded soldiers, sermons, and clothing and other support for the poor. She also made provision for a grammar school at Halstead, in Essex, and gave £1,000 to her native city of Bristol. The Ramseys' charitable donations between 1583 and Mary's death in 1601 were £14,318.[10]

Staper's monument is now in St Helen's, Bishopsgate, as are those of Sir Thomas Gresham and Sir John Spencer. Gresham died in 1579 and was commemorated by 'a fair monument, by him prepared in his life', according to John Stow.[11] As well as his efforts in managing the exchange rate, Gresham had an important role in London's commercial life. He attended Gonville Hall, Cambridge, and was then apprenticed to his uncle, John Gresham, and in 1543 was made a freeman of the Mercers' Company. He was engaged in the family's business, selling English cloth and buying mercery ware, chiefly through Antwerp. Thomas also did some business on the government's behalf and in the winter of 1551–2 was appointed King's Merchant, or royal agent, in the Netherlands, which involved raising loans for the English Crown on the Antwerp money market and also acquiring military supplies. He held the post until 1564 and acted in a diplomatic capacity, as well as advising both Mary and Elizabeth on commercial policy, including the recoinage of 1561 and the reform of the custom house. He was knighted in 1559. The family business continued to trade in Antwerp and he visited the city intermittently until 1567.

By the 1560s Sir Thomas was a wealthy man and had built a town house off Broad Street, consisting of two-storey buildings arranged around a courtyard, while along the frontage was a range of eight almshouses. The house was lavishly furnished, with the furniture alone costing £1,127. His plans for the future were changed after the death of his only son, Richard, in 1564. He decided that an appropriate legacy to his city would be the erection of a bourse where the merchants could meet to trade, rather than in the open in Lombard Street. The bourse at Antwerp had been completed in 1531, and in 1534 Henry VIII had suggested that Leadenhall could serve a similar purpose in London, but the City had not acted on this. Three years later Gresham's father had proposed to Thomas Cromwell that a bourse should be erected in London, but that proposal, too, was not followed up before his death in 1549. Sir Thomas was, therefore, reviving an old idea when in January 1565 he proposed to the City that he would pay the costs of the building if it obtained the site. The City agreed and acquired a large plot between Cornhill and Threadneedle Street, where Sir Thomas laid the foundation stone in June 1565. The building was completed in December 1568. Gresham's aim was to provide a building 'more fair and costly builded in all points than the burse of Antwerp' and he appointed the Antwerp mason Hendryck van Paesschen to undertake the work. Van Paesschen produced a building that was indeed very similar to that in Antwerp in appearance and layout. In January 1571 the queen visited Sir Thomas at his house before going on to the bourse, where, according to John Stow, 'shee caused the same Bursse by an Herauld and a Trumpet, to be proclamed the Royal Exchange, and so to be called from thenceforth, and not otherwise'.[12]

Among the building's many admirers was L. Grenade, who wrote that 'it is scarcely possible to find in the whole of Europe such a lavish edifice which serves the same purpose'.[13] The merchants met in the courtyard in groups according to the region or city with which they were trading, and it became a centre for the exchange of news and gossip as well as for the transaction of business. The gallery and the storey above it, known as the Pawn and the Upper Pawn, contained 120 shops, occupied by haberdashers and mercers especially, with painter-stainers, merchant-tailors, clothworkers, grocers, leather-sellers and stationers the other most numerous tenants.

The revenue from the shops and vaults in the Royal Exchange was intended by Gresham to maintain his other endowments, the almshouses in Broad Street and Gresham College. But his widow was opposed to the use of part of his legacy for the college, and so it was not until after her death in 1596, seventeen years after her husband's, that the Joint Grand Gresham Committee of the Mercers' Company and the City could meet to arrange its establishment. There were to be professorships in seven subjects, with the lectures delivered successively, one on each day of the week. The lectures began in 1597 in the subjects chosen by Gresham: divinity, astronomy, geometry, music, law, physic and rhetoric. By the terms of his will 'none shall be chosen to read any of the said lectures so long as he shall be married, or be suffered to read any of the said lectures after that he shall be married'. The college was established at Gresham's mansion in Broad Street, where the lectures were delivered and the professors kept lodgings. Gresham's gifts to his city were bounty indeed, yet the parishioners of St Helen's may have been a little disappointed that he had not paid for a steeple for their church, as he had promised to do in order to compensate for the space taken by his monument.[14]

Gresham's charity followed the pattern expected of a wealthy merchant, albeit on a munificent scale. But Sir John Spencer failed in that respect, not having secured his fortune for posterity. He had accumulated wealth through trade in his early years as an importer of raisins, oil, iron and wine from Spain. He then cast his net wider and began trading with the Levant, exchanging cloth and tin for spices, cotton wool and silks, which could fetch high prices in London, from the courtiers, the aristocracy and its own increasingly wealthy citizens. When the East India Company was founded in 1599, Spencer was one of the leading investors. He married a rich widow, whose previous husbands had been a wealthy brewer in

Southwark and a London haberdasher, and in later life moved into money lending, with members of the aristocracy among his clients. Spencer played the part in public affairs that was expected of a successful citizen. He was a common councillor from 1576 until he was elected an alderman in 1583, and he served as Lord Mayor in 1594–5. In 1594 he bought Crosby Place in Bishopsgate, where he is said to have 'made great reparations'. He kept his mayoralty there and in 1603 'lodged and splendidly entertained' the French ambassador; he also maintained a country house at Canonbury in Islington.

Spencer was a difficult man who was often at odds with his fellow aldermen and attracted public criticism, especially over his handling, or as some saw it mishandling, of riots over high food prices during his time as Lord Mayor. The pillories in Cheapside and at Leadenhall were pulled down and there was a clash between a large crowd of apprentices and the City's officers on Tower Hill. Spencer's unpopularity was such that a crowd erected a gallows outside his house and the rioters threatened that he 'should not have his head on his shoulders within one hour after'. There were, too, rumours of corruption while he held office, and he acquired a reputation as a miser, being said to have 'spent by the dramme and laid up by the pound'. Yet he survived such popular opprobrium and, as had become customary, was knighted for his service as Lord Mayor.[15] His only surviving offspring was his daughter Elizabeth, who was courted by William, Lord Compton, a Warwickshire gentleman, in 1598. Spencer did all that he could to prevent the match, but Compton used his influence to have him imprisoned in the Fleet prison for his ill-treatment of his daughter. In March 1599 Compton and Elizabeth married, yet Spencer refused to be reconciled with them. As he grew older it was speculated that he intended to give £20,000 to 'his poor kindred' and the same sum for charity. But he had not in fact made any provisions along those lines, and after his death, in March 1610, no will could be found. Perhaps he had simply died without drawing up the document, which is rather improbable for someone so greatly concerned about the fate of his fortune, or, as gossip had it, Compton 'hath suppressed a will of the deceased's'.[16] Whatever the truth, Compton gained possession of Spencer's wealth and so could fund a new aristocratic dynasty.

In contrast, John Isham made the transition from London merchant to landed magnate himself. His family traded in woollen cloth, especially broad-cloths from the West Country and kerseys from Yorkshire, and imported Italian silks and other luxury textiles. John became free of the Mercers' Company in 1551 and shortly afterwards married the widow of a member of the Merchant Adventurers' company. Isham's business suffered from the disruption of the trade with Antwerp and in 1560 he bought an estate at Lamport in Northamptonshire, which he then developed by enclosing the common fields. He died in 1596 and was buried in Lamport church, having directed that his tomb slab should have brass plates at the corners carrying the coats-of-arms of the City of London, the Merchant Adventurers' Company, the Mercers' Company, and his family, to 'testifie to posteritie of what house I discend bothe of my father and my mothers side, that I was a Merchaunt Adventurer of the Cittie of London and free of the Company of Mercers and by that meanes with the blessing of God received my preferrement and was enhabled to purchase the mannor of Langporte and patronage of the churche therof'. Despite the acknowledgement of the source of his wealth, he was not a direct benefactor to London and its citizens.[17]

Spencer and Isham were, for very different reasons, unusual among London's merchants in not assigning part of their wealth for charity. The merchants made the greatest contribution to the philanthropic effort in the years after the Reformation, and the largest group of women donors were wives, widows or daughters of merchants. There were fifty-one merchants among the eighty-eight donors in four central parishes between 1540 and 1600, and over the same period more than 800 London merchants made charitable donations or bequests.[18] Attitudes to their riches were changing when Thomas Churchyard wrote approvingly in 1579 of 'Merchaunts that sails [to] forrain countreys, and brynges home commodities and … doe utter their ware with regard of conscience and profite to the publike estate'.[19] He was one of those writers who had come to appreciate the beneficial role played by the merchants, rather than to criticise them for operating selfishly outside the framework of the guild system.

Beyond the large-scale endowments that naturally attracted most attention there were many other donations and bequests, setting up bread doles, often distributed annually, and other periodic payments targeted at specific groups, commonly members of a trade or residents in a parish. Doles attracted some criticism if they did not target the needy or specified groups, and so drew large numbers at the distribution. When this was the case the process could not be orderly or seen to be fair. At St Botolph, Bishopsgate in 1592 a 'multitude of other straundge disordered poore people' appeared at a dole, according to the parish clerk.[20] There was a tragic outcome to the distribution after Lady Mary Ramsey's funeral in 1601, because 'at her sixepeny dole kept at Leaden Hall, the number of beggers was so excessive and unreasonable that seventeen of them were thronged and trampled to death in the place, and divers sore hurt and bruised'.[21] Despite such reservations, it seems that in the latter part of the century immediate donations to the poor were coming to be more favoured than large-scale endowments; direct donations increased by 70 per cent in real terms between 1573 and 1597, while endowments rose by only a half of that rate.[22]

Occasional donations included collections taken after church services. At Holy Trinity, Minories an average of £28 annually was received over the period 1568–76 from such collections.[23] Gifts were also made to supplicant beggars at the church door or in another approved context. Licences were granted to authorise begging – a practice that could be profitable, for in September 1562 a man was put in the pillory for 'conterfeytyng a false wrytyng to bege in dyvers places in London, and puttyng in mony honest men's hands to gyff ym lysens to bege, butt yt was false'. (That is, he had bribed those who issued such licences, or rather who could make convincing copies, to make him a false licence; he would scarcely have done so had he not expected to raise enough by begging to pay them and have money for himself besides.)[24] The Earl of Leicester's accounts for December 1584 include *6d* paid to 'a poore man in Fletestrete', *8s 0d* allocated 'to geve to the poore in small money' during the first nine days of the month, *5s 0d* to the doorkeeper 'at the Parlyment House', with *2s 0d* more 'to another olde man theire at the same tyme', and on another occasion 6*d* to 'two poore folk at the Parlyment House' and 5*s* 0*d* to 'a poore woman at Ratlief'. There are similar entries throughout his accounts, recording occasional donations to those who were fortunate enough to attract the earl's attention.[25] Some places were more advantageous than others for receiving casual donations, and there was the possibility of door-to-door collections; one donor noted for his charity was said to have given 'to the poor at his door and abroad'.[26]

Victims of fires, floods or other disasters could apply for letters patent authorising the issue of a charitable brief, used as the basis for collections. Those organising such collections would ask that London be included in the areas in which they were authorised, because Londoners were so generous. A nationwide appeal after a destructive fire at Nantwich in 1583 raised £3,142, of which the queen donated £1,000 and collections in London and Middlesex contributed £717; the treasurer of the appeal fund was a senior figure in the Haberdashers' Company.[27] And, of course, money was available to assist Londoners. An explosion in April 1544 in a gunpowder house in East Smithfield killed seven people and in April 1552 powder in a building on Tower Hill detonated, killing all fifteen of those working there.[28] Sheer carelessness caused a similar tragedy in July 1560, when 'through shooting of a gunne which brake in the house of one Adrian Arten, a Dutchman in Crooked lane, and setting fire on a firken and barell of gunpowder, four houses were blown up, and divers other sore scattered'. In that disaster eleven people were killed and sixteen were injured, which prompted an order by the Lord Mayor 'that no man shuld have no gone-powder in ther howses nor sellers [cellars]'.[29] Evidently this was disregarded, for in April 1583 an explosion in Fetter Lane 'blew up all the gunpowder house, and other tenements in Fetter Lane, to the destruction of many houses, and spoil of much goods thereabouts'. The church of St Andrew's, Holborn was 150 yards from the closest part of Fetter Lane, yet its windows were 'pitifully shaken, rent, and broken down, as all the houses round about that part of the parish almost were, with the monstrous and huge blast of the gunpowder'. Windows in Lincoln's Inn Chapel, west of Chancery Lane, the side further away from Fetter Lane, were also damaged – and that was a quarter of a mile from St Andrew's. Surprisingly, given the scale of the disaster, only two men and one woman were killed, although others were 'sore hurt, some blasted with the flames, some bruised with timber that fell upon them: and a child lying in the house escaped untouched'.[30] Such accidents, causing varying degrees of damage and distress, drew upon the resources of the owners and tenants to rebuild and restock the premises, and also attracted charitable collections. But some requests for a collection were coolly received. A recommendation to the Court of Aldermen in 1592 on behalf of Peter Clemens, a tallow chandler, after a fire on his property was particularly exasperating, for he was not a freeman and so should not have been practising his trade within the City 'and thereby firing his own house, and greatly imperilling his neighbours'. Moreover, it was suspected that he would use the funds collected to pay his creditors for his own business purposes, not to restore the property.[31]

The resources of the leading parishioners were drawn upon when a church was burned. In September 1545 St Giles, Cripplegate church was destroyed by fire, and in November 1548 the church of St Anne-in-the-Willows was also burned down.[32] Both were rebuilt. During a thunderstorm in the afternoon of 4 June 1561, the tower of St Martin Ludgate was struck by lightning, beginning a fire that destroyed the building. It, too, was rebuilt and at the end of the century was described by Stow as 'a proper church, and lately new built'.[33]

The storm that began the fire which destroyed St Martin Ludgate caused a more spectacular disaster, for lightning also started a blaze in the steeple of St Paul's Cathedral. The steeple was of oak, covered with lead, and was a replacement for the steeple destroyed by lightning in 1444 and replaced in 1462. The slender structure was topped with a ball containing relics, a cross and a weathercock in the form of an eagle; the weathercock had been replaced after being blown down in 1506, and the whole ensemble had been taken down and repaired in 1553. According to eyewitnesses the lightning struck about six to nine feet below the base of the cross, and by the late afternoon the steeple was seen to be on fire, below the ball. Its timber frame probably caught fire because of holes left in the lead for fixing scaffolding, presumably a legacy of the repairs eight years earlier. Within a short time the cross and the eagle fell onto the roof of the south transept, and, as the steeple burned downwards, molten lead and burning timbers fell from it and started fires on the cathedral's four roofs over the choir, nave and two transepts. A crowd quickly gathered and it was debated how the blaze could be checked. Given the height of the roofs and the area they covered, there was no way of halting the flames, and the possibility of using artillery fire to knock away the steeple was quickly overtaken by events as the steeple crumpled up – if it had been a practicable idea at all. Sensibly, efforts were concentrated in preventing the flames spreading to the bishop's palace on the cathedral's north side, from where they could have broken into the crowded buildings in Paternoster Row beyond. More than 500 people joined in the effort, carrying buckets of water to stem the flames and save the palace. They were successful, and during the evening the winds that had followed the storm died down and the fires could be extinguished. But the damage was extensive, for the steeple and all four roofs had been destroyed, while within the cathedral the communion table had been burned.[34]

The immediate need was to re-roof the building to protect it from the weather. A commission was appointed to oversee the work, consisting of six citizens and two petty canons of the cathedral, which first met on 16 June. The work of covering the roofs with a temporary layer of boards swiftly went ahead; Stow wrote that the work was completed within a month, and, although this may have been an exaggeration, it was done by the autumn. The cost of repairs had to be met, and on 24 June the queen instructed the Lord Mayor to impose levies on the capital's citizens and for the archbishop to place a charge on the clergy in the province of Canterbury. The citizens were to pay three levies, one immediately, the second within six months and the third within a year. But the yield was less than expected, for the first two combined produced only £813 18s 10d, which was £520 14s 6d less than anticipated. On the other hand, the Londoners had collected a further £1,045 7s 2d in voluntary donations, which when combined with the third levy and arrears, totalling £1,388 10s 0d, eventually produced a contribution of £3,247 16s 2d from the city.[35] The clergy raised £1,461 13s 11d, of which £297 1s 1d was contributed by the diocese of London. Edmund Grindal, the bishop, gave £284 13s 11d, the dean and chapter £136 13s 4d and the courts of Common Pleas and King's Bench together donated £52 1s 8d. The queen promised £666 13s 4d and 1,000 loads of timber from the Crown forests, although the accounts include only £266 actually received from the royal purse. But these sums were nowhere near enough to cover the estimated cost of restoration, which was put at £17,738, not including labour costs, and just £6,702 had been spent when the account was closed in December 1564.[36]

The estimate for restoration was prepared by John Revell, the queen's surveyor and a former Master of the Carpenters' Company. He had a role through her donation of timber, and he oversaw the preparation of the timber trusses for the replacement roofs. These were made under his direction on the royal manors of Welbeck in Nottinghamshire and Guisborough in Yorkshire and were shipped to London. They began to arrive at the cathedral in the summer of 1562, with the number of carpenters on site increased from three to over forty in September and October. It is probable that little work was carried out during the winter, but there was a further increase in activity in March and April 1563. Sir William Dugdale later wrote that the work 'was prosecuted with such diligence, that before the month of Aprill Anno [1563] all the Roofs of timber ... were perfectly finished and covered with lead'.[37] The plague epidemic that summer and autumn probably curtailed the work, and Revell died in December 1563. The roofs over the choir and nave had been completed by then, but there is no evidence in the accounts that those over the transepts were erected. It may be that £720 laid out by Grindal for timber, lead and labour was for those roofs, but it is also possible that those expenses were contributions to the main roofs and other repairs and that the temporary coverings of boards on the transepts remained in place. This is suggested by a letter from Grindal in 1582, in which he wrote that the work needed to be 'perfectly finished, the want of which was the cause of the present decay'.[38] The fabric deteriorated further, and in 1581 John Aylmer, who had been appointed bishop in 1577, admitted to the Lord Mayor that a surveyors' report showed that 'the ruin was very great; more, he supposed, than they estimated'; the walls 'were laid open and greatly spoiled with rain, the gutter leads cut off, and other defaults permitted, whereby great ruin had ensued, and more would follow'.[39] This was dramatically demonstrated in 1600, when 'a peece of the south battlements of Powles fell downe lately and kild a carmans horse'.[40]

While the roofs were being restored a debate raged over the cause of the fire. James Pilkington, Bishop of Durham, preached at Paul's Cross four days after the blaze, and a riposte to his interpretation was issued by John Morwen, who had been a chaplain to Edmund Bonner and a Marian prebendary of the cathedral. Both parties could claim some moral high ground: the Roman Catholic relics in the ball had not saved the steeple and roofs and had been destroyed, and the Elizabethan communion table had been burned. There was agreement by both parties that the disaster was a punishment by God, either for the city's sins or, more specifically, because of the way that the cathedral had come to be used – the clergy would say misused – by the laity. The question was posed whether the building should be repaired at all 'considering howe yt was destroyed by the finger of god because it was abused'.[41]

Pilkington's reply to Morwen showed some similarity in their positions, for he wrote that 'we both do agree the church of Pauls is abused, and therefore justly plagued'. It served as a thoroughfare for pedestrians and for porters who were carrying their loads from Cheapside to Ludgate Hill, and they even led their horses and mules through the building, burdened with 'great vessels of ale or beer, great baskets full of bread, fish, flesh and fruit' and other goods. Pilkington described how the south aisle was for 'usury and popery, the north for simony, and the horse fair in the midst for all kinds of bargains, meetings, brawlings, murders, conspiracies, and the font for ordinary payments of money'. One pillar served as where servants were hired, another was the place for engaging lawyers, and at a door in the north aisle clergymen on the lookout for a benefice or lectureship advertised their availability and searched for vacancies. The long nave was a general meeting place, where news was exchanged, business transacted, and gallants paraded hoping to catch the eye of a potential patron, and visitors from the country wandered, gazing in awe at the scale of the building. The Court of the Clothworkers' Company was told in 1580 that the meetings of its journeymen on Sunday mornings were so near the choir that they were 'both troublesome to the divine service and disquieting of such well disposed as repair to the same'.[42]

Such practices were of long standing and ingrained social habits were not to be changed by the clergy's plaintive response to the fire, or by any other pressures. In any case, the cathedral served both as an ecclesiastical centre and a place where theological notions could be expressed in sermons, as well as having the secular role of a hub for information and ideas disseminated by booksellers and printers selling their pamphlets and books in stalls in the churchyard, which became a centre of publishing in London.[43] Somewhat ironically, it was also a place where fire-fighting equipment could be obtained, and in 1583 the churchwardens of St Mary Woolchurch Haw bought a dozen leather fire-buckets from John Franklin in St Paul's churchyard for £1 10s 0d, paying a further 2s 6d to have the name of the parish and their own names painted on them.[44]

While attention was focused on the restoration of the roofs, there was also the intention to rebuild the steeple. For a New Year's gift in 1562 Revell presented the queen with 'a marchpane [sweetmeat] with a model of Powle's Church and steeple in paste'. A design for a new steeple drawn in 1562 may have been by him, and his death perhaps reduced the momentum behind the project.[45] But finance was the chief problem. Stow reported in his *Survey of London* in 1598 that 'it was said that the money appointed for new building of the steeple was collected and brought to the hands of Edmond Grindal', although in the second edition, issued five years later, the clause referring to Grindal was removed and there is no other evidence that such funds had been raised.[46]

In 1576 the queen was said to be 'very urgent about the rebuilding of the Spire', and in 1580 the Privy Council wrote to the Lord Mayor and Aldermen complaining that 'although Her Majesty's pleasure had several times been made known to them touching the re-edifying of St Paul's steeple, nothing had been done'; they asked that some aldermen should attend the Council to explain matters. The Lord Mayor informed Aylmer, who denied that it was the bishop's responsibility to pay for a new steeple and pointed out that the whole revenues of the diocese would be insufficient for the purpose. In his opinion, 'it was a public work, at the alms of the whole realm', and in this he was supported by Grindal, now

Archbishop of Canterbury, who also thought that the work should be carried out at the public charge. In 1582 Sir Christopher Hatton was appointed by the queen to look into the matter: according to his report £9,000 would be needed to complete the steeple in stone and a further £2,490 for other repairs to the building.[47] The City probably felt that the steeple was an adornment and not essential work, and so not its responsibility, and it was heavily committed in maintaining Christ's Hospital, Bridewell and the hospitals. The queen's insistence and a general acceptance of the desirability of replacing such a prominent and prestigious feature were not enough to compensate for the unwillingness to provide the necessary funds. Londoners donated more than half of the sums collected for the re-roofing and other repairs, but even their benevolence had its limits and the steeple was not rebuilt.

10

Growing Pains

London experienced unprecedented population growth in the second half of the sixteenth century. As it grew, so its administration became increasingly complex and difficult, at times even dangerous, such as during outbreaks of epidemic disease. Those who were chosen as aldermen and common councillors were predominantly wealthy men, and some of them either resented the time and attention required by the office or perhaps regarded certain of the duties as distasteful. The City's officers and the justices had to oversee its own regulations administering the metropolitan community and urban environment, as well as implementing those imposed by the government, which was eager to maintain law and order and achieve the conditions that would prevent epidemics.

Some men preferred to pay a fine rather than take up the office of alderman, with its expense, time and trouble. In 1542 a haberdasher who had been chosen as the alderman of Bishopsgate Ward was fined £265, and in the previous year John Richmond's fine for refusing to serve as sheriff was set at £200. This became the fixed levy from those declining the office, and the chamberlain's account for 1584–5 includes receipts of £1,600 from eight men for not serving as sheriff, a not inconsiderable addition to the City's revenues.[1] The cost of holding high office was accepted as being a disincentive and in 1555 it was said that the expenditure incurred by a Lord Mayor or sheriff was so high that 'almost all good citizens fly and refuse to serve'. An attempt was made to reduce the costs and an annual grant of £100 from the chamber was made towards the charge of the annual Lord Mayor's feast.[2]

The City's officials had to deal with disbanded soldiers who drifted to London and were frowned upon as vagabonds, or masterless men, who were liable to foment disorder. In the autumn of 1545 the alderman of Bridge Ward and 'certeyne substancyal men dwelling uppon the Bridge' faced an example of the kind of threatening incident that occasionally occurred, and they drew the Privy Council's attention to the affray. They described how 'certeyne lewde fellowes in the night passing upon the Bridge hewed downe lantrenes and signes, and with lewde wordes wold have provoked thonest men to have issued out of their houses', while apprentices and 'men of the country passing by' were slapped in the face with fish that the miscreants had on the ends of their swords. This could merely have been regarded as a rowdy escapade, but two men who were arrested as suspects were also thought to have been involved in an earlier commotion at the Bell Inn in Fish Street in which a servant of Sir Thomas Heneage was killed.[3] Rumbustious pranks and unruly behaviour by young gentlemen of the Inns of Court, or who were connected to the royal court, and their servants provided vexatious problems for the justices and a threat to the members of the watch patrolling the streets. An indication of the dangers faced by the junior officers in the city came in 1554 when a baker stabbed a constable who was keeping an eye on an alehouse in Westminster 'for its disorderly rule' and the constable died of the wound.[4] An officer was killed in 1580 by a man who he had arrested; the murderer was executed in Cheapside.[5]

In *Touchstone for the Time* (1585) George Whetstone described the various types of ordinaries, or common drinking houses. In the better kind gentlemen were carefully groomed before being steadily cheated, perhaps over a number of days; then there were those patronised by the citizens, where they played at dice and cards. But it was the third sort of ordinary which really caused concern, for they were 'in Allies, gardens, and other obscure corners out of the common walks of the Magistrate. The dayly guests of these priuie houses, are maisterless men, needy shifters, theeues, cutpurses, unthriftie seruants, both seruing men, and prentises.' How many such dark corners there were in the growing city was of concern to the government. In June 1571 the Privy Council instructed the aldermen to 'cause a straight serch and good stronge watche ... in every parishe and warde ... and the suburbes'. The objective was to 'apprehend all vacabonds, sturdy beggers comonlie called Roges, or Egiptians [gypsies], and all other idle vagrant personnes having no masters nor any certaintie howe or wherby to lyve'. Some of those found would probably 'counterfait them selfes as impotent beggars', and so care was to be taken to distinguish those who were genuinely 'impotent by age, sycknes, or otherwise' from the vagrants. Those who were classed as vagabonds were to be placed in the stocks and 'may bee by punishment forced to labor for theire lyvinge'. The search was to be repeated monthly until at least the beginning of November and was to include places where unlawful games were played, 'and speciallie of bowlinge (a disorder verey muche vsed at this daye throughoute the realme)'.[6]

Bowling alleys were long-term targets of the authorities. The districts close to Paul's Wharf and Aldgate had developed as centres of bowling alleys and gaming-houses, and the Lord Mayor led a raid on them in 1550, when sixty 'simple persons and vagabondes playinge at tables and bowles' were arrested; the officers 'brake theyr playinge tables in peeces, and bound diuers of them by recognisance that they should neuer more haunt such places'. Bowling alleys were again the focus in December 1553, when the Lord Mayor and sheriffs went with their officers to three alleys, near Aldgate, at St Nicolas shambles and in the Old Bailey, 'and with mattockes did breake and digge up all the said alleys'. The phrase is explained by the fact that in bowling alleys of the period the surfaces consisted of soap ashes combined with house ashes and founders' earth.[7] But with time problems developed for the City; it seems that bowling alleys, so long a bane of the justices, were becoming acceptable, albeit not yet respectable. When the Lord Mayor prevented the construction of a 'close alley' in 1580 he was informed by the Comptroller of the Queen's Household that it was one of his servants who was building it 'for the recreation of honest citizens to bowl in, in foul weather' and with the queen's licence. Faced with such a powerful protector the Lord Mayor clearly was going to have difficulty enforcing the City's policy in the case, although he justified his actions by stating that there were already two such alleys in the neighbourhood, so that if the new one should be completed there would be three on just half an acre of ground. He also objected that the builder was permitting 'dicing, carding, and table-play, which was resorted to by the worst and meanest persons, who spent their time and money in unlawful play and betting' and so neglecting their families, and that the gathering of people at such places risked 'infections, quarrels, and other disorders'. For these reasons the City thought it necessary to prevent further building and also to question the licences already granted.[8] But as the population increased, so did the demand for places of amusement.

William Fleetwood, the Recorder of London from 1571 to 1591, was assiduous in searching for vagabonds. In 1585 he chanced upon what he described as a school 'to learne young boyes to cut purses' and he was able to make a list of forty-five 'masterless men' and cutpurses, as well as eighteen places described as 'Harboring-howses for maisterles-men, and for such as lyve by thefte and other such like shifts.'[9] One evening in 1581 the queen was at Islington in her coach when she was 'environed with a nosmber of Rooges', so that the Lord Mayor had to be called to disperse them. Over the following few days Fleetwood organised several sweeps across the city to apprehend those who fell into the broad category of vagabond. He obtained permission to investigate the sanctuaries, former monastic precincts that had retained their exemption from the jurisdiction of the City and the justices, which included Westminster, the Savoy, Whitefriars and St Martin-le-Grand. These were refuges for those evading the law, such as debtors, and in them Fleetwood detained forty 'rooggs, men and women', while at St Paul's he arrested a further twenty 'cloked roogs that there use to kepe standing'. All were taken to Bridewell for questioning and to be categorised. What emerged from this search, which seems to have been a thorough one, was that of the approximately 250 who were apprehended, only twelve in Fleetwood's estimation were from London, Westminster and Southwark; the remainder were from the provinces and Wales, and 'fewe or none of thaym had ben abowt London above iij. or iiij. mownthes'. Moreover, none had been previously detained as vagabonds. In fact, it is likely that the majority of those who were hanging around the city were the unemployed and under-employed who had arrived in London hoping to find work, and not the unrepentant layabouts and villains described in the legislation directed against them. The strongest were set to work at Bridewell and the others were sent to their place of origin.[10] The numbers tracked down by Fleetwood and the justices in this and other investigations were not large in terms of the city's population, and the fear of those operating outside the orderly rules of society may have exaggerated the scale of the problem.

Despite this, occasional and opportunist crime seems to have been a characteristic of late-sixteenth-century London. William Smith was a freeman of the Haberdashers' Company, who acted also as a herald and chronicler of London and author of 'A breffe discription of the royall citie of London', written in 1575. In it, he recorded that sessions were held every four to six weeks, with as many as sixty persons convicted at each sitting. At the October sessions in 1578 more than 200 people were tried, most of them for petty theft. Shortly after completing 'A breffe description ...' Smith moved to Nuremberg and settled there as an innkeeper, where he praised the resident Nurembergers in terms which censured Londoners: 'So trew and Just are they that if you lose a purse with money in the street, Ring, bracelet or such Lyke, you shal be sure to have it again. I would it were so in London.'[11]

The penalties could be humiliating and savage. In 1543 the Mayor 'punished many harlots of the stewes by dobbinge [ducking] in the Thames on a cookinge stoole at the Thre Cranes in the Vintre'. Those condemned as vagabonds included seven women, who in January 1552 were 'whyppyd ... at the carttes arse, iiij. at one end iij. at another, for vacobondes that wold not labor, but play the unthryftes'. Also in that mayoral year the officers 'punished bawds and whores by rydinge in cartes, and whipped vagabondes out of the city'. Those trading with false measures were also harshly dealt with. At a court held in June 1552 an upholsterer of Cornhill was convicted for using 'a yarde of false measure which lacked a good ynche ... [he was] sett in the stockes, and the yardes hanged ouer his head, with a paper written for false measure, and so satt from a quarter of an hour before xii of the clocke till ii of the clocke in the sayd stockes'. In the same month 'one Thomas Harvie, a baker in Southwarke, was set on the pillory in Southwarke for lackinge six ounces waight in a penny loafe'.[12] Other common punishments meted out were whipping, nailing the prisoner's ear to the pillory, and mutilation by having an ear or hand cut off. In 1602 a barrister stood in the pillory near the gate of the Temple and lost both his ears for plotting the murder of a fellow lawyer. Stow mentioned a case where three men were convicted of producing a libel and condemned to have their right hands severed; one was reprieved but the other two 'lost their hands by chopping off'.[13] Prostitutes were frequently targeted, prompting John Howes, of the Grocers' Company, to make a critical comment on the misuse of resources, when he wrote, in 1587, that 'suerly god can not but be angrie with vs, that will suffer our Christian Brethren to die in the streates for wante of relyefe, and wee spende and consume our wealthe and our wytte in searching out of Harlotts, and leave the worckes of faythe and mercie vndone'. The approach to prostitution was maintained despite his and other objections. Thomas Platter described it in 1599, seemingly to approve, commenting, 'Good order is also kept in the city in the matter of prostitution, for which special commissions are set up, and when they meet with a case, they punish the man with imprisonment and a fine. The woman is taken to Bridewell ... where the executioner scourges her naked before the populace.' He tacitly admitted that the policy was not a success, though, for he added that 'although close watch is kept on them, great swarms of these women haunt the town in taverns and playhouses'.[14]

Crimes that attracted harsh treatment or the death penalty included premeditated thefts, such as those from churches and the houses of the aristocracy and gentry, brawling and killings, often it seems as result of disagreements in a society in which it was customary to carry a weapon. Smith's figures for executions were 'in one day 20 or 30, & I have knowne 36 at a tyme to suffer'. In December 1577 Fleetwood mentioned that at the recent sessions at Newgate twenty-three prisoners were condemned to death, and in the following October nine were hanged after being convicted of a specialist crime, for they were 'horse-stealers, being old thieves. There was not one reprieved by any suit from the Court.'[15] In his account of London, written in 1578, L. Grenade mentioned that 'there will be some occasions when they hang 25 or 30 in one day', and according to Paul Hentzner, visiting from Brandenburg in 1598, 'Above three hundred are said to be hanged annually in London.' That would equate to twenty-five to thirty each sessions, which agrees with Grenade's figure and roughly matches that supplied by Smith.[16] Visitors' attention was drawn to the executions partly through the practice of displaying the heads of executed traitors and others who were prominent enough, or whose offence was heinous enough, on poles on the City's gates, including the Great Stone Gate of London Bridge. Visitors could count more than thirty heads displayed in this way as a deterrent to others.

Another anxiety which prompted enumerations was the influx of people to London from abroad. Immigration was approved of for bringing in skills which would create new trades and so reduce imports, yet was also a cause of concern due to the Londoners' reactions. These included resentment of those who seemingly were breaching privileges and regulations, and taking work away from them, expressed in fliers and pamphlets distributed around the streets, and probably in innumerable discontented mutterings in alehouses. Yet many of the immigrants were Protestant refugees, fleeing from the Wars of Religion in France and the repressive attempts by the Spanish government to defeat the growing revolt in the Low Countries. Grenade expressed his appreciation of the Londoners' hospitality to religious refugees and 'the benefits they received from the citizens of London at their time of dire need'.[17]

The incomers centred on the French and Dutch churches, revived after Elizabeth's succession. In 1571 Dutch or German speakers comprised 61 per cent of aliens in London and 20 per cent were French speaking, from both France and the French-speaking regions of the southern Netherlands. Even during the period of maximum repression, from the late 1560s until the 1590s, not all incomers were refugees, for roughly a third of those recorded in 1573 admitted 'that their coming hither was onlie to seeke woorke for their livinge'. The numbers of aliens recorded in enumerations fluctuated and none of the returns can have been entirely accurate, probably under-recording the true numbers. In 1563 they gave a figure of 4,534, which had risen to 6,704 in 1568 and 7,143 in 1573, before two suspiciously lower figures of 4,047 in 1581 and 4,141 in 1583, from enumerations which might have been taken on a different basis, and then 7,113 in 1593.[18] The figure for 1593 did not include Westminster, and the true number may have been around 10,000. It showed that twice as many immigrants had come from the Low Countries as from France, and fewer still from Germany. The count in 1573 suggested that the strangers composed about 10 per cent of the population, and that taken twenty years later indicates that the proportion had fallen to 5 or 6 per cent, as the population of the metropolis had increased, and also reflecting the movement of people out as well as in. London's stranger population probably peaked in the mid-1590s, for the flow of refugees from France was reduced after the Edict of Nantes was issued in 1598, which then allowed French Protestants freedom of worship, and that from the Low Countries by the gradual establishment of the security of the northern provinces as the Spanish military effort flagged from the mid-1580s.

The livery companies kept a keen eye on specialist workers practising new or growing trades and operating outside established control, whether migrants or not. The growth of such trades reflected the city's increasingly diversified economy and although measures could be taken, the process could not be halted. The Cutlers' Company's chief rival in jurisdictional matters during the early sixteenth century was the Armourers' Company, but the two subsequently found common ground in the search for interlopers in the trade. In 1589 they combined to investigate 'naughty and deceitful sword blades' that were being sold in the city. Then in 1592 the cutlers submitted a petition to the Lord Mayor complaining of the 'multitude of strangers using their Art and occupation'. They knew of twenty denizens in and around the city and another fifty-seven who were not denizens, of whom seventeen were householders. Such precise figures suggest a close investigation of the working of the trade, even though the strangers were said to work in 'secret places'. The context for these numbers was that in 1593 fifteen members of the company set up in business and there were fifty-five registered apprentices. The haberdashers also acted against those who were not members of their company; in 1571 at least seventy-eight strangers' households were making hats and caps in the city. In 1581 the company promoted a measure that would ban aliens from working in the trade, even though some workers had been successfully integrated. Robert Bonfoire had come from Normandy roughly at the time of Elizabeth's accession and by 1593 had two English apprentices and employed ten journeymen, so was running a fair-sized business within the company's remit. Perhaps a greater threat to the existing arrangements were those Englishmen who had been trained outside the company and then operated beyond both the company's and the City's jurisdictions. This applied to feltmakers who were located in the suburbs, where the necessary quantities of water were readily obtainable and there was adequate space for drying the wools.[19] The immigrants were perceived as a threat to the organisation of the trades, but the livery companies faced various other pressures in maintaining their hegemony.

The College of Physicians had a keen interest in those who had arrived in London and practised medicine. Between *c*.1555 and *c*.1572 at least seventeen or eighteen out of a total of seventy to eighty members had come from abroad: France, Italy, Spain, the Low Countries and Scotland. The college was resolute in pursuing those who resisted their authority. Charles Cornet, from Flanders, who was described in no uncertain terms as 'an ignorant Fleming and a most shameless buffoon', was condemned in 1555 and made to put up 'bills of his condemnation ... on all the corners of the City' stating the fact, and he was imprisoned. But he persisted in his practice and gained some powerful allies, including the Dean of Westminster. The college likewise enlisted its supporters, including Drs Roper and Vaughan from among the royal physicians, and took the case to the Court of Chancery, where it was successful. Cornet's 'feigned and unwholesome remedies having been burned in the open market-place of Westminster', he took refuge, at first in St Martin-le-Grand and then in Westminster Abbey. The college had him rooted out, despite the dean's efforts, and pursued not only Cornet but those who had maintained him at St Martin's, whom they imprisoned. More amenable was Gerard Gossenius, from Brabant, who said that he had been a doctor in Louvain but that 'his letters testimonial with other evidence had been lost in a storm at sea' when he fled from the Duke of Alva's forces. The explanation was plausible, and he agreed not to practise medicine while he stayed in England; in any case 'it was decided that he should return to his own country within a few days'.[20]

The most prominent figure at the college during the third quarter of the century was Dr John Caius, who trained at Padua, before returning to Cambridge and then moving to London in 1547, giving anatomical lectures to the members of the Barber-Surgeons Company. He became a fellow of the college in 1547 and served as president from 1555 until 1564, with the break of a year in 1561–2, and again in 1571. He died in 1574. He wrote an account of the sweat, based on observations made during the outbreak of the disease in 1551. The disease reached London on 7 July and lasted until 16 July, abating for a period before reappearing briefly on 30 July. His figures suggest a death toll of almost 1,100. The book was published in Latin in that year and in English in 1552 as *A Boke or Counseill Against the Disease Commonly Called the Sweate, or Sweatyng Sicknesse*. It summarises the earlier outbreaks from 1485, and contains detailed descriptions of the symptoms and the spread of the disease, with advice on how it could be avoided and how the victims should be treated. Essentially, Caius's advice was to get them so warm that they would sweat the disease out, while ensuring that they were not exposed to the least cold. Caius's work was the first account of a single disease to be written and published in English and was very influential; it was drawn upon by Francis Bacon to describe the epidemic of 1485 in his *The History of the Reign of Henry VII* (1622). But Caius's observations could not be tested during another outbreak, for the outbreak in 1551 was the final eruption of the disease in England.[21]

The college was consulted by the government as it developed a plague policy during the second half of the century. In 1578 it was asked for advice on preventative medicines, cures for those who had the disease, how long infected houses should be kept closed, and how the houses and clothing of the victims should be cleansed.[22] The consultation was part of the preparations for the national set of orders that was issued in that year, from which London was exempt. The corporation's representatives had met with the Privy Council to consider a set of twenty-two articles. It disliked the proposals for the appointment of overseers and paid physicians, apothecaries and clergymen, who were to care for the sick, with a compulsory levy to pay the expenses, preferring the existing arrangements whereby the aldermen and parish officers implemented the necessary measures and funds were raised by contributions as the need arose. Its preference was accepted, although with the proviso that the aldermen, ward and parish officials were to be assisted by two general overseers appointed monthly in each ward by the aldermen and overseen by them, with a weekly inspection of the ward. Those arrangements were duly approved by the Common Council and issued as a set of orders.[23]

The Privy Council was sceptical of the effectiveness with which its plague orders were being implemented in London and it periodically admonished the Lord Mayor, especially for not ensuring 'the severing of the sounde from the diseased' by closing infected houses. In 1577 the Council instructed him that there should be a 'diligent enquiry' to ascertain which houses were infected and ordering that they should be closed, regardless of the standing of the occupants, 'be they persons of what degree or quality soever'. It requested information on breaches of the orders, such as the concealment of infected houses by parish officers 'either for corruption or friendship', so that the healthy unwittingly mixed with plague victims in the streets and at the shops and markets. It returned to the issue of social partiality 'either in restraining the poor upon infection of plague more than the rich, or in sparing the rich transgressing the good orders taken for the stay of the infection, and punishing the poorer sort'. Another concern was the falsification of the weekly returns of the causes of death, with the numbers understated 'by the corruption and indirect dealing of some inferior minister'.[24] The Lord Mayor's response was to point to the scale of the problem in such a populous city, as well as the reaction of the citizens themselves 'either in the inferior officers who seek not so carefully to discharge their duty, or in the people, who will hardly conceive what is for their good provided'.[25]

Fear of contracting the disease understandably deterred officials from looking too closely into properties where the occupants may have been infected. Their task was made all the more difficult by inhabitants who were uncooperative, not wishing their houses or those of their neighbours to be closed, thereby risking disruption of the local community and economy. Yet some officials were conscientious; the Bills of Mortality were compiled throughout the epidemic in 1563 by the parish officers who remained and fulfilled their duties. The City repeated its orders, that notification of a case of plague was to be sent in writing to the alderman of the ward within three hours, that the streets were to be washed down daily, rubbish was to be carried away regularly by the scavengers, no lodgers were to be accommodated, an infected house was to be marked on its door, and anyone who emerged from an infected house was to carry a rod at least two feet long 'without hiding or carringe the same close from open sight', so that others would be aware that they should avoid them.[26] In 1578 there were 3,500 deaths from plague within the City and liberties and more than double the average number of burials. During the epidemic Fleetwood continued to attend to his duties, even to the extent of allowing people with plague sores to come to him daily and going around the City himself to look for 'lewd persons', but the shock of finding 'dead corses under the table' in the houses he entered 'did greatly amaze him' and so he retreated to Buckinghamshire for a respite.[27]

Despite the doubts about the implementation of the Council's measures in London, the plague orders for the city were not issued until May 1583, towards the end of a period during which plague had struck often. The Michaelmas law term was adjourned from Westminster in every year between 1574 and 1582, with the sole exception of 1580, and even in that year there were 128 plague deaths. There were more than 1,000 deaths from the disease in 1581 and in 1582 plague caused 2,976 of the 6,762 recorded deaths. The orders issued in 1583 codified existing practices. Household quarantine was retained and the period for which an infected house was to be closed was set at twenty-eight days, having been reduced to twenty days in 1570. Anyone who entered an infected house was not to be allowed out. The problem of supplying the closed houses with provisions was addressed, with two women in each parish appointed for that task, and one person was to be permitted to leave a house for the same purpose, carrying a red rod, now specified to be three feet long. But if someone from an infected house chose to leave the city, they would be allowed to do so, provided that they did not return within twenty-eight days. That was a clear attempt to reduce the problem of supplying the closed houses and shifting it to the surrounding areas, but their residents were understandably hostile to those coming from the city at such a time. Most places would not admit travellers who did not have a health certificate stating that they had not been in contact with anyone with the disease. Infected houses were to be marked, as before, with the words 'Lord Have Mercy Upon Us', which were to be displayed 'in a place notorious & plaine for them that passe by to see it'.[28] The general plague orders were issued again in 1592 and included the advice that a fragrant fume should be used within doors, including dried rosemary, juniper, bayleaves or frankincense, burnt in a chafing-dish and carried from room to room – unpleasant smells were associated with plague and pleasant ones were thought to ward off the disease. Individuals carried pomanders stuffed with a concoction of herbs: rosemary, rue, lavender, sage, mint and wormwood were especially favoured. Householders who could afford the herbs placed them on their window-ledges and strewed them on the floors and in doorways, so that pleasant air wafted into their houses.

Parallel with the regulations concerning the plague and its effects were policies aimed at improving the urban environment. The opinion that foul and tainted air provided the conditions in which plague flourished led to a concerted effort to improve them, both in the streets and in buildings. During an epidemic, fires were to be lit in the streets in the evenings on at least three days a week to prevent the air from stagnating. The Privy Council was insistent upon this, although the City's officers seemed to doubt its effectiveness. Pavements were to be kept in good repair and without any holes where dirt or filth could accumulate, and dung was not to be thrown into the streets. At least ten buckets of well-water were to be cast into every street each day before six o'clock in the morning, to wash them and the channels that ran down their middle, and they were also to be swept clean each morning before six o'clock and every evening after six o'clock. Special risks were not forgotten, so that the makers of puddings and tripe were to take their waste water directly to the Thames and not throw it into the street.[29] Dogs were still regarded as a possible means by which the disease was transmitted and they were killed in large numbers, although there were other reasons for disposing of them, particularly strays, for the barking of 'the great multitude of dogges' caused 'a grete disquietnes and troble' for the citizens during the nights, when they should have been sleeping, and were also the cause of quarrels and disturbances. In 1584 it was noted that 'a verie greate nomber of dogges are kepte within this Citie' and those not fit for 'anie good use' were to be destroyed.[30] Even during years with few plague deaths, the City's dog catcher was paid for killing hundreds, and in some years more than a thousand, of the animals; they were to be buried at least four feet deep, as were the corpses of plague victims.

Overcrowding became an almost constant concern as the population increased and more buildings were erected or adapted as accommodation. In 1574 the Privy Council instructed the City to carry out a search for 'strangers', who should be removed to reduce the risk of infection by 'over pestering of houses'.[31] Among those who were regarded as undesirables were lodgers, who were not regarded as members of the household.

The connection between overcrowding, plague and the growth of the city was made explicit in a royal proclamation issued in 1580. This introduced the policy of curbing London's growth by prohibiting new buildings. It stated that because of the increase in population the good government of the city could 'hardly be done without device of more new jurisdictions and officers for that purpose', the supply of 'victual, food, and other like necessaries' would be difficult to sustain and the health of the people 'may seem impossible to continue'. These problems were attributed to 'such great multitudes of people brought to inhabit in small rooms, whereof a great part are seen very poor, yea, such as must live of begging or by worse means, and they heaped up together, and in a sort smothered with many families of children and servants in one house or small tenement'. The conditions presented a danger that if 'any plague or popular sickness' should break out, it would spread through the city and suburbs, and then across the country because of the numbers of people who came to London. And so the proclamation, which had the support of the City, ordered that everyone 'of what quality soever they may be, to desist and forbear from any new buildings of any house or tenement, within three miles from any of the gates of the said City of London, to serve for habitation or lodging for any person, where no former house hath bene known to have bene, in the memory of such as are now living'. The proclamation went on to reiterate the policy on occupation by ordering that only one family should reside in any house. Those who continued to build after having been warned were to be imprisoned and released only when sureties had entered into bonds that they would not attempt to continue with the buildings. The City was instructed to take action against those who had allowed an increase in the number of 'indwellers, inmates or undersitters' within the previous seven years.[32]

The regulations of 1580 indicate what the government aspired to but could not enforce in the face of strong demand for labour and a ready supply of it. Those who owned suitable properties could profit by subdividing them and landowners could make money by building. Such commercial pressures were far stronger than the resources, and perhaps the will, of the corporation or the county justices. Yet attempts were made to uphold the policy. Three years after the proclamation the Privy Council complained that the number of buildings had greatly increased, and on its direction the City made a survey of the offending properties. The Council ordered that those responsible should be bound over to appear before the Star Chamber court, or imprisoned if they refused. In 1585 St Olave's, Southwark appointed surveyors of inmates, whose duties were 'to vewe that none kepe no Inmates nor suffer none with childe nor no other poore to come out of other parishes to the burden of this parishe'. St Saviour's made similar appointments in 1593.[33] Intermittent efforts were made thereafter to enforce the terms of the proclamation, by imposing fines, pulling down new buildings and removing inmates. In 1602 John Chamberlain told his friend Dudley Carleton that the Privy Council had 'lately spied great inconvenience of the increase of housing within and without London, by building over stables, in gardens, and other od corners' and had begun to pull down such structures, 'almost in every parish to light on the unluckiest, here and there one'. As Chamberlain wryly commented, that approach was not going to solve the problem.[34]

In 1587 John Howes wrote a criticism of 'the Governemente of the Poore within this Cittie', perhaps prompted by the effects of the bad harvest in the previous year. One of his themes was housing and he condemned the 'lowsie and fylthie cottages, to[o] bad and to[o] beastely for dogs to lye in' and cited the example of landlords who accommodated three or four inmates in one room without a chimney or privy. These conditions he blamed on 'the myserable covetousnes of the Landlords of Alleyes in London, whoe ar not only carelesse in receaving of Tenaunts into theire fylthie houses, but allso gredely exacting and raysing of greate rents upon the poore'. Many were victuallers who compelled their tenants to buy their provisions and fuel from them, rather than shopping around for the cheapest prices, and expelled them if they defaulted on their weekly rents. Their greed and carelessness in admitting tenants and then ejecting them was one cause of the numbers of beggars in the streets. His solution was intervention by the corporation, who should erect tenements for the poor and then 'remove the poore people out of those filthy Allies, and let the Allies be raised downe to the grounde and converted to open Yardes or gardens, and so the Citye shalbe kepte swete and delivered of a thowsand contagious disseases'.[35]

Howes also proposed a scheme for model housing, carried out by the corporation and based upon the Fuggerei in Augsburg, a housing development built for the poor by Jakob Fugger, begun in 1514. He proposed that the corporation, its Bridgehouse committee or the livery companies should 'buye in those Alleyes and make of them convenyent and necessarie lodgings for poore people, and set a reasonable rent vpon them that the poore maie lyve without oppression ... and have swete and convenyent roomes to dwell yn'. One justification that Howes ventured for such a development was that the city would then be 'clensed from many fylthie contageous plagues and disseases, which wee ar nowe yerely subiecte vnto by reason of these covetous carelesse Landlords, who pester their houses with people, having no necessarie easements [privies] for them'. It was a bold and far-sighted scheme, but without the political will and the necessary finance it could not go ahead. He also advocated the erection of pesthouses, where the victims of plague or other diseases could be isolated. They were to be staffed by physicians, apothecaries, surgeons, preachers and keepers, or nurses. Having such pesthouses would remove the sick from the streets during epidemics, and because they would be well supplied with provisions they might be the means to save some who died of neglect during epidemics 'that otherwise might lyve'. The proposal followed Continental models, but the pesthouses were not built.[36]

Not all of Howes's observations were condemnatory and he drew attention to the 'freshe water' at Cornhill, with the comment that if such water ran through every street in the city 'this wilbe the sweetest City in Christendomme'.[37] He was referring to a recent development, in 1582, when the Dutchman Peter Morris constructed a wheel that used the pressure of the flow through the arches at the north end of London Bridge to raise water to a new conduit in Cornhill, near the junction with Leadenhall Street. This had four spouts, one on each side, from which river water flowed at every high tide. In the mid-1590s Bevis Bulmar, a mining engineer, constructed within a derelict building at Broken Wharf, west of Queenhithe, a substantial rectangular tower for raising river water to supply the City. Clear water was regarded as healthy, while foul and stagnant water in ponds or ditches could create the miasmic air that harboured diseases.

From 1582 there was a respite from plague until the beginnings of an outbreak in the summer of 1592. By early September that year plague was said to be 'nowe greatly increased' in London, and the Privy Council became so concerned that it reissued the plague orders. It blamed the 'carelessness of the people' and the failure to isolate the sick. Starch making was thought to be an especial danger because of the number of hogs used in the process, which were 'a noysome kind of cattle ... verie apte to drawe on the infection', and the Council ordered that it should cease for the time being. It also suggested that the feast and ceremonies at the swearing in of the new Lord Mayor should not be held and that Londoners should be told that this was done not to save money but because of the dangers of 'drawinge of assemblie of people togeather'. The money saved was to be put towards the cost of maintaining those quarantined in their houses, perhaps making plague victims more willing to observe the quarantine. By January 1593 the Council was sufficiently alarmed to reiterate its order that the policy of household quarantine should be rigorously implemented, and it summoned six aldermen to appear before it to explain what was being done. The gathering of people at plays, in the animal baiting arenas, at bowls and anywhere that they met together in groups was prohibited, 'preacheing and Devyne service at churches excepted'. The livery companies' feasts were banned and their necessary meetings were to be attended by as small a number of people as possible. By July 1593 a red cross, rather than a printed paper, was used to identify an infected house; the Council ordered that it should be nailed to the door, as a painted one could be wiped off.[38]

The vestry at St Margaret Lothbury responded to the crisis by appointing two men as surveyors and three women as searchers of the bodies, and ordering that 'all people kepe the orders sett downe'. Those who were quarantined were to have 'so much as yt shalbe thought meete and sufficient for them', with the costs covered by a monthly levy from seventy-four householders. At one collection there were sixteen defaulters and at another the number was twenty-three, perhaps because they had gone away to avoid the plague, and almost a fifth of the amount due was not received. Voluntary donations were therefore vital and the parish received £2 13s 10d from 'sondry persons', £2 of which was generously donated by Mistress Killigrew. The difficulty of taking decisions during an epidemic was highlighted when the question of inmates was raised at the vestry held in the spring of 1593, for nothing was done because 'foulkes would not tary'.[39]

The problems of the vestry at St Margaret's were repeated across the city in what was the worst epidemic since 1563. Burial rates were 4.25 times higher than in a normal year, although the central parishes escaped relatively lightly, while those on the fringe of the City experienced the heaviest mortality. The experience of the richer central parishes in 1593 may reflect the comparatively high proportion of parishioners who could leave during the epidemic, and perhaps more effective enforcement of the regulations in those small parishes than in the larger and increasingly populous ones around the City. Among these outlying parishes, St James's, Clerkenwell saw a fourfold increase in burials compared with the early years of the decade, and at St Martin-in-the-Fields there was a threefold increase. In the crowded north-east parishes of St Botolph-without-Aldgate and St Botolph-without-Bishopsgate the numbers of burials were six times higher than normal, and St Katherine's-by-the-Tower suffered even more heavily. Within the City and the Liberties the number of deaths between 21 December 1592 and 20 December 1593 was 17,844, with 10,662 of them attributed to plague, while for the whole of the city the figures were 25,886 deaths, 15,003 from plague – roughly 13 per cent of the population. The danger then receded and over the next four years the average number of plague deaths was just eight.[40]

The epidemic had once again demonstrated the problems of enforcing household quarantine and the collection of funds to provide for those confined to their houses. It did not lead to a reconsideration of the plague orders, but the connection between overcrowding and plague was reiterated. Active concerns for cleanliness and the urban environment, with a reduction in pollution, continued to be part of the measures to reduce epidemic diseases. Since the early sixteenth century a coherent policy to combat plague had been developed, and the government's main efforts were directed to ensuring that the orders were applied rigorously by the Lord Mayor and Aldermen and, as the population beyond their jurisdiction expanded, the Justices of the Peace for Middlesex and Surrey.

11

Recreation and Show

The growing numbers of Londoners had a range of recreational activities to choose from. Although nostalgic observers claimed that sporting activities such as archery were in decline and that sedentary ways to pass the time had become popular – activities frowned on by disapproving moralisers – plenty of attractive entertainments were available. This was the period when the Lord Mayor's Show developed into a truly impressive day-long spectacle, with hundreds taking part, and plays emerged from the court and aristocratic mansions onto a genuinely public stage, where a wide-ranging and constantly expanding repertoire could be enjoyed by everyone for a small charge.

Londoners could visit the royal menagerie in the Tower, with its lions and lionesses, a lynx, a wolf, an eagle and a large porcupine. There seems to have been no restriction on visitors wandering in to gaze at the animals, and even go further into the fortress. When two men planned to make surreptitious contact with one of the prisoners, they dressed as 'simple London citizens' who wanted to look at the lions and other animals 'which curious people come to see'.[1] Animals could be seen fighting on Thursdays and Sundays in two arenas on Bankside, described by John Stow as 'two bear gardens, the old and new places, wherein be kept bears, bulls, and other beasts, to be baited; as also mastiffs in several kennels, nourished to bait them. These bears and other beasts are there baited in plots of ground, scaffolded about for the beholders to stand safe.' Visitors to London were fascinated by the spectacle, although Thomas Platter, who was there in 1599, did complain of the stench that pervaded the area. One of the worst accidents in London during Elizabeth's reign occurred on a Sunday afternoon in January 1583, when, according to Stow, 'the old and underpropped scaffolds round about the Bear Garden, commonly called Paris Garden ... overcharged with people, fell suddenly down, whereby to the number of eight persons, men and women, were slain, and many others sore hurt and bruised to the shortening of their lives'. By the beginning of July it had been rebuilt as an octagonal arena, and performances on Sundays had resumed.[2]

In the streets, fencers, acrobats, jugglers and others entertained the citizens, who might also have chanced upon someone performing some eccentric prank, probably being carried out for a challenge or bet. In February 1600 John Chamberlain described some recent larks: 'We have daily here many new experiments made, as the last weeke one came hopping from Charing Crosse into Powles bounde in a sacke, and this morning another caried up a horse and rode upon him on the top of Powles steeple, with divers other such wagers; and, among the rest, Green ... hath set up a printed paper, and doth challenge all commers at wrastling.'[3]

Those who wanted energetic exercise played ball games, including football. According to Stow, 'The ball is used by noblemen and gentlemen in tennis courts, and by people of meaner sort in the open fields and streets'; he further wrote that during the summer holidays 'the youths of this city have in the field exercised themselves in leaping, dancing, shooting, wrestling, casting of the stone or ball, etc'. But his was a nostalgic view, and although the young men used to exercise with practice swords and shields on holy days after evening prayer 'at their masters' doors', and the maidens, 'one of them playing on a timbrel, in sight of their masters and dames, to dance for garlands hung athwart the streets', these had been the activities of his lost youth, and he complained that they 'now being suppressed, worse practices within doors are to be feared'. He also noted that 'sliding upon the ice is now but children's play', and he deplored the decline of wrestling and archery, commenting gloomily that 'now of late years the wrestling is only practised on Bartholomew's day in the afternoon, and the shooting some three or four days after, in one afternoon, and no more'. The decline of archery he attributed to lack of space, as he put it 'want of room to shoot abroad', because of the 'closing in [of] the common grounds'. Stow grumbled that, instead of archery, the one-time bowmen would now 'creep into bowling alleys, and ordinary dicing houses, nearer home, where they have room enough to hazard their money at unlawful games'. This was also the conclusion of the Lord Mayor, who told the Privy Council in 1583 that archery had declined 'principally through the holding of such spectacles as bear-baiting, unchaste interludes and bargains of incontinence'. Yet twenty years after Stow was writing, Orazio Busino, a Venetian priest, could comment, 'Well nigh throughout the year they have archery meetings in the fields near London.'[4] Stephen Gosson had struck a nostalgic, and rather satirical, note some years earlier, in 1579, complaining that in the past both men and women had

> engaged in shootyng and darting, running and wrestling, and trying such maisteries, as eyther consisted in swiftnesse of feete, agilitie of body, strength of armes, or Martiall discipline. But the exercise that is nowe among us, is banqueting, playing, pipyng, and daucing, and all suche delightes as may win us to pleasure, or rocke us a sleepe.[5]

The inference that those who would have participated in regular archery and other active pursuits in the past had been followed by an indolent generation was not borne out by the amount of bell-ringing, also physically demanding and a popular pastime in Elizabethan London. Paul Hentzner, in 1598, wrote that 'in London it is common for a number of them ... to go up into some belfry, and ring the bells for hours together, for the sake of exercise'. Four years later Frederick Gershow, tutor to Philip Julius, Duke of Stettin-Pomerania, commented on the bell-ringing in London and was told that 'young people do that for the sake of exercise and amusement, and sometimes they lay considerable sums of money as a wager, who will pull a bell the longest or ring it in the most approved fashion'.[6] As well as being tolled for services and recreation, bells were rung in celebration annually on 17 November, the queen's accession day, and occasionally to mark events of national significance. The capture of the Earl of Northumberland in the aftermath of the rebellion in the north in 1569, the thwarting of the Parry Plot in 1585 and the Babington Plot in the following year, the execution of Mary, Queen of Scots in 1587, the defeat of the Spanish Armada in 1588 and 'the good success of our navy at Cadiz' in 1596 were all marked by the ringing of bells and lighting of bonfires in streets across the city.[7] These events were seen as deliverances from threats to the existing order by Catholics, but an exception was the response to news of the victory of the Christian fleet over the Ottoman navy at the Battle of Lepanto in 1571, which was a striking success for the Catholic powers. The chronicler Raphael Holinshed noted that 'there were bonfires made throughout the city, with banqueting and great rejoicing'. Clearly the outcome was seen as a victory for 'the Christian commonwealth', regardless of the divisions within it.[8]

Perhaps Stow was correct when he thought that gambling was the popular modern amusement. At the cockpit near Smithfield admission was a penny and the cocks fought on a round straw-covered area; someone placing bets would take a ringside seat. Gambling also took place in alehouses, which were lively meeting places for music and conviviality, with ballads pasted on the walls to encourage communal singing. Platter wrote that 'scattered about the city' were inns, taverns and beer gardens, 'where much amusement may be had with eating, drinking, fiddling, and the rest'. An aspect that he thought worth commenting on was that 'the women as well as the men, in fact more often than they, will frequent the taverns or ale-houses for enjoyment'.[9] The hostelry where Platter was lodging 'was visited by players almost daily'; in 1602 Gershow noted in his journal that 'in all England, it is the custom, that even in small villages the musicians wait on you for a small fee; in the morning about wakening time, they stand outside the chamber, playing religious songs'. The custom allowed musicians to make a living from such casual work, and more than one hundred men in Elizabethan London described themselves as 'minstrels'. Their interests were protected by 'the fellowship of minstrels freemen of the City of London', although its effectiveness as a guild was limited by the fact that musicians in the royal and aristocratic households were beyond its jurisdiction.[10]

Formal music could be enjoyed on Sundays and holidays at the Royal Exchange, where, according to Grenade, the six city waits 'produce wonderful sounds at 4 o'clock in the afternoon ... to the great pleasure of listeners, of whom there are very many'.[11] The concerts were begun in 1571 and the aldermen took an active interest in the waits, raising their annual salaries from £8 to £10 in that year and to £11 13*s* 4*d* in 1582. They also arranged for competitive examinations when there was a vacancy; places were so sought after that in 1582 the Earl of Leicester wrote to the aldermen requesting that one of his servants should be appointed. The composer Thomas Morley's *First Booke of Consort Lessons* (1599) was dedicated to the Lord Mayor and Aldermen, with the flattering comment: 'As the ancient custome is of this most honorable and renowned Cittie hath beene ever, to retaine and maintaine excellent and expert Musitians, to adorne your Honors favors, Feasts and solemne meetings; to those your Lordships Waits ... I recommend the same to your servants careful and skilfull handling.'[12]

The network of musicians in London included the Bassanos, successfully integrated into the local community around Bishopsgate after being forced out of the Charterhouse. Baptista's daughter Emilia secured a position in the Countess of Kent's household. Her musical skill, especially as a player of the virginals, and dusky good looks attracted attention, and when the countess introduced her at court she caught the eye of the queen. Emilia was also noticed by Elizabeth's Lord Chamberlain (and second cousin), Henry Carey, Lord Hunsdon, whose interest went well beyond admiration of her youth and musical abilities. She became his mistress; the physician and astrologer Simon Foreman noted in 1597 that 'the old Lord Chamberlain had kept her long', quite openly and indeed 'in great pomp'. In 1593 she gave birth to a son, Henry, and so she was married, to Alphonso Lanier.[13] The Laniers were another family of immigrant musicians, Huguenots who had arrived in England from Rouen in the early 1560s, a time of popular disturbances in the town as the growing Protestant community became increasingly assertive. Like the Bassanos, they had joined the royal musical establishment. Alphonso's father was a sackbut player and his mother was the daughter of the Mark Anthony Galliardello, who

John Gedney, twice Mayor of London in the mid-fifteenth century and Master of the Drapers' Company. (Author's collection)

The Fishmongers' Company's hall and adjacent streets in a plan-view of around 1513. (Author's collection)

An imagined view across a part of early Tudor London, showing Newgate in the foreground and the Franciscan Priory of the Greyfriars beyond; a reconstruction by H.W. Brewer. (Author's collection)

A London merchant with his writing materials and balance, from Caxton's *Game and Play of Chesse*, published around 1474. (Courtesy Jonathan Reeve JR1031b18p749 14001500)

A mason with his tools, depicted in Caxton's *Game and Play of Chesse*, published around 1474. (Author's collection)

In this fifteenth-century illustration 'Labour' is represented by those who dig and hew wood and stone. (Author's collection)

A tavern scene in the sixteenth century, with gaming at the tables. (Author's collection)

Men and women are enjoying the company in this tavern scene; there is plenty of food and drink and, despite the efforts of the justices, a card game is being played. (Author's collection)

A tailor and his customer. (Author's collection)

A printer's workshop shown in an illustration by Jost Amman of 1574. (Author's collection)

A scribe at his writing desk in the late fifteenth century. (Author's collection)

A communal meal at a well-provided board, from Chaucer's *Canterbury Tales* of 1485. (Author's collection)

Fish were a staple of the Londoners' diet and fishing on either side of the bridge was regulated, so this solitary fisherman is casting his line outside the city. From an edition published by Wynkyn de Worde. (Author's collection)

A monk who keeps the keys to the cellar is sampling the liquor while filling an ewer. (Author's collection)

Aldgate around 1500 redrawn 400 years later, with St Botolph's church outside the gate and Holy Trinity priory within it, on the right-hand side. (Author's collection)

A drawing of 'a most curious chimney-piece', apparently for the royal palace of Bridewell. (Author's collection)

An apothecary's shop, shown in a woodcut by Jost Amman, 1574. (Author's collection)

A dissection, shown in an edition published by Wynkyn de Worde in 1495. (Author's collection)

In the sick room a patient is being nursed by two women, one of whom stirs a potion in a pot on the hearth. (Author's collection)

Two apothecaries with their patients, one of whom is having blood taken and the other has brought a urine sample for inspection. (Author's collection)

Hans Holbein's drawing of a cup, of solid gold, for Jane Seymour, with her arms as queen on the cover. (Author's collection)

The southern section of London Bridge looking upstream, shown in an illustration by John Norden at the end of the sixteenth century. (Author's collection)

Left: A depiction of Thomas More's imaginary island of Utopia, from his account first published in 1516. (Author's collection)

Below: A feast in a fine room, with an elaborate ceiling and wall decorations, but it is attended only by men. (Author's collection)

Holy Trinity priory, with Aldgate beyond and then the suburb of Whitechapel, drawn by H.W. Brewer. (Author's collection)

Musicians in a gallery, perhaps at court, drawn by Hans Holbein. (Author's collection)

The mother has given birth to twins, one of whom is in a cradle while the other is held before the fire. (Author's collection)

The Holbein Gate of Whitehall Palace, built around 1532, shown in an engraving by George Vertue of 1725. (Author's collection)

The King Street Gate of Whitehall Palace, built as part of Henry VIII's improvements to the former palace of the archbishops of York in the early 1530s, from an engraving by George Vertue of 1725. (Author's collection)

Ludgate, with St Paul's cathedral beyond, before the destruction of its spire in 1561; drawn by H.W. Brewer. (Author's collection)

Portrait of John Fisher, Bishop of Rochester, by Hans Holbein, 1535. (Author's collection)

A self-portrait by Hans Holbein. (Author's collection)

John More, son of Thomas, in 1527, when he was nineteen, drawn by Hans Holbein. (Author's collection)

Above: Billingsgate and the legal quays between the bridge and the Tower, shown on the 'Agas' plan of the mid-sixteenth century. (Author's collection)

Below: The Brandon family, with the children dressed in the elaborate costume typical of an aristocratic family, drawn by Hans Holbein. (Author's collection)

Hans Holbein's design for a covered goblet for a goldsmith, from his 'English Sketch-book'. (Author's collection)

A study of a gentleman's costume in the 1530s; the elegantly dressed man nevertheless wears clogs, as a protection against cold and dirt. (Author's collection)

Portrait by Hans Holbein of an unknown man, perhaps a member of the French embassy to Henry VIII's court in 1533. (Author's collection)

A chalk drawing by Hans Holbein of Mary, Lady Heveningham, a cousin of Anne Boleyn. (Author's collection)

Portrait by Hans Holbein of an unknown lady. (Author's collection)

Portrait of an unknown lady, drawn by Hans Holbein, probably in 1527-8. (Author's collection)

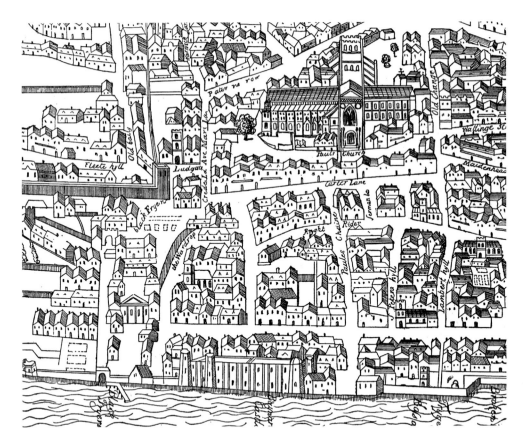

Above: St Paul's and the Blackfriars district in the mid-sixteenth century, after the cathedral's spire had been destroyed in 1561. Baynard's Castle stands on the riverfront; it was embellished by Henry VII *c.* 1501 and Anne of Cleves lived there for a time in 1540. (Author's collection)

Below: Bankside as depicted on the plan of London in Georg Braun and Franz Hogenberg's *Civitatis Orbis Terrarum* of 1572; it shows the two bear-baiting arenas that preceded the playhouses which were built in this district. (Courtesy Reeve JR1107b21p429 15501600)

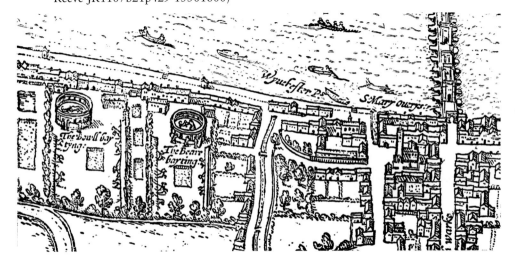

The interior of a wealthy family's house in the early Tudor period, imagined by Margery Whittington. (Author's collection)

Left: Cheapside looking west towards St Paul's, with the tower of St Mary-le-Bow church to the left; drawn by H. W. Brewer. (Author's collection)

Below: A crown minted in 1551, during Edward VI's reign, a period of high inflation. (Author's collection)

The imprisonment of four of the Protestant martyrs who were executed or died in prison during Mary's reign. (Author's collection)

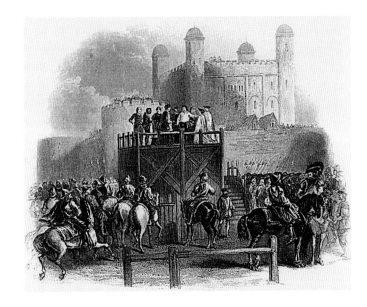

The execution of Lord Guildford Dudley, husband of Jane Grey, the nine-days queen, following Thomas Wyatt's rebellion against Mary in 1554. (Author's collection)

View of the city from the south c. 1550, by Anthony van Wyngaerde. (Courtesy Jonathan Reeve JR1875b46fp34 15001550)

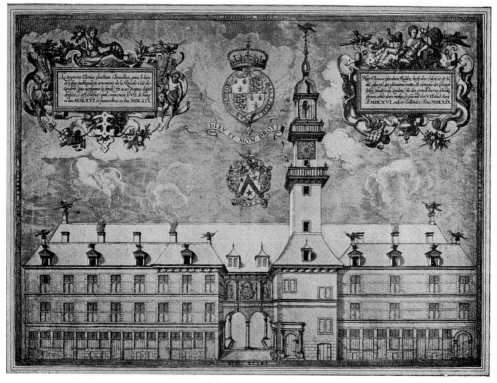

Above: The Royal Exchange, built on the initiative of Sir Thomas Gresham and completed in 1568. (Author's collection)

Below: The north section of London Bridge, looking upstream, drawn by John Norden in the late sixteenth century. (Author's collection)

Portrait of Sir Thomas Gresham, for many years the government's agent in Antwerp and the founder of almshouses in Broad Street and Gresham College. (Author's collection)

The Court of Wards and Liveries in session around 1585. (Courtesy Jonathan Reeve JR1068b5fp388 15501600)

The gateway to the church of St Bartholomew-the-Great, Smithfield, drawn in 1928. The stone doorway of the priory church was retained when the nave was demolished c. 1543; the two-storey structure above it was built in 1595. (Author's collection)

Schoolboys at their lessons, reading, writing, playing music and one of them is being birched by the master. (Author's collection)

Fish sellers gutting a fish for a customer. (Author's collection)

Water was distributed around the street from the conduits by water-carriers, who have poles on which to rest their load while the customers fill their vessels. (Author's collection)

Above: Billingsgate dock and market in 1598, a contemporary view drawn by Hugh Alley. (Courtesy Jonathan Reeve JR1061b4p788B 16001650)

Below: Eastcheap Market in 1598, drawn by Hugh Alley. (Courtesy Jonathan Reeve JR1060b4p788T 16001650)

Above: Nonesuch House on London Bridge was built in 1577–9 on the site of Drawbridge Gate; the drawbridge itself was replaced by a fixed roadway. This late-nineteenth-century drawing is by H. W. Brewer. (Author's collection)

Below: Plan-view of the district around the Temple and Fleet Street in the mid-sixteenth century, which was the legal quarter of the city. (Courtesy Jonathan Reeve JR1141b40p144 15501600)

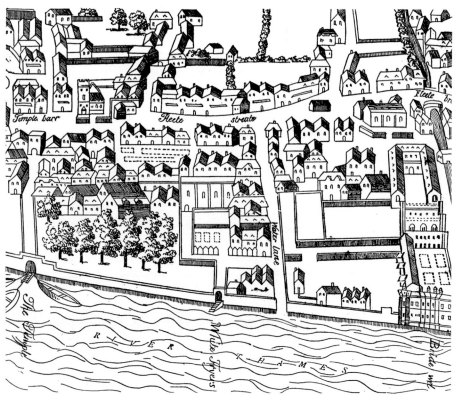

A glass made in London by the Venetian glassmaker Jacopo Verzelini and dated 1583. (Author's collection)

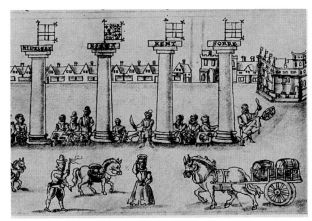

Gracechurch Market in 1598, drawn by Hugh Alley. (Author's collection)

A board game is being played at home by a husband and wife in this mid-sixteenth-century illustration. (Author's collection)

A sermon being delivered to a numerous congregation at Paul's Cross, the popular place for preaching, adjoining the cathedral. (Author's collection)

The nave of St Paul's cathedral, a thoroughfare, a place for the exchange of news and gossip and the transaction of business, drawn by Wenceslaus Hollar. (Author's collection)

A tall and decorated mid-sixteenth-century house at the corner of Chancery Lane and Fleet Street, drawn by J. T. Smith in 1789, ten years before it was demolished. (Author's collection)

Houses in Grub Street, believed to have been built in the fifteenth century; they were demolished in 1805. The etching is by J. T. Smith, dated 1791. (Author's collection)

In 1597 Sir Paul Pindar, diplomat, merchant and moneylender, acquired a site outside Bishopsgate, and the house that he built there had a finely carved façade. It was demolished in 1890 but the front was preserved in the Victoria and Albert Museum. Drawn by Roland W. Paul *c*. 1894. (Author's collection)

The buildings along the front of Staple Inn, Holborn, were erected in 1586 and survive as the finest group of half-timbered Elizabethan buildings in London; drawn by Gordon Home *c*. 1910. (Author's collection)

Left: A portrait of the printer and publisher John Day, drawn in 1562. (Author's collection)

Below: Plan of parts of Bishopsgate Street, Threadneedle Street and Cornhill, drawn in 1599; it includes the churches of St Martin Outwich and St Peter's, Cornhill and the Merchant Taylors' Company's hall. (Author's collection)

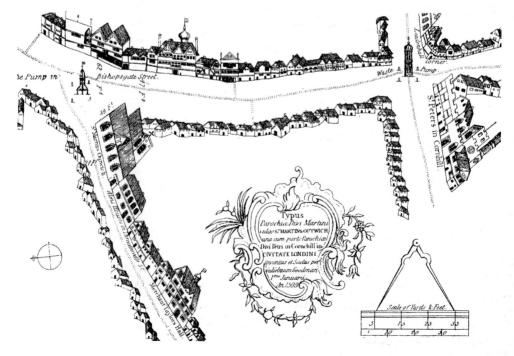

Above: A decorated car, or float, representing the Triumph of Neptune, for a late-sixteenth-century Lord Mayor's procession. (Author's collection)

Below: A theatrical performance in an inn yard during Elizabeth's reign, as imagined around 1870. (Author's collection)

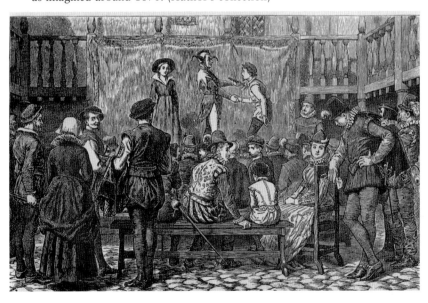

The Swan playhouse on Bankside, erected in 1595 and sketched by Johannes de Witt in the following year. His sketch was copied and that copy is the only surviving contemporary illustration of a theatre of Shakespeare's time. (Author's collection)

The engraved portrait of William Shakespeare by Martin Droeshout which was published on the title page of the First Folio edition of his works in 1623. (Author's collection)

Above: A card game in progress, possibly primero, which was introduced from Italy and became very popular during the second half of the sixteenth century. (Courtesy Jonathan Reeve JR1083b3fp472 15501600)

Below: Plan of the Tower of London drawn in 1597. (Courtesy Jonathan Reeve JR1133b41p91 15501600)

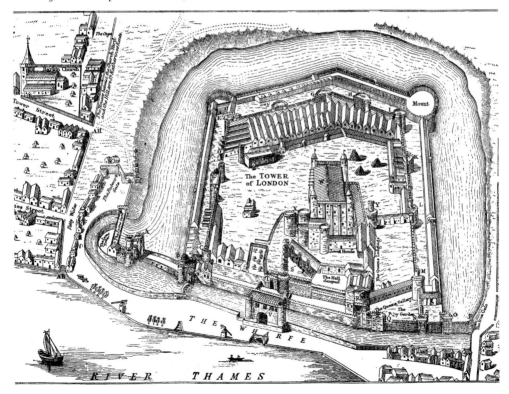

The grandiose tomb of Sir Christopher Hatton in St Paul's cathedral was drawn by William Dugdale before it was destroyed in the Great Fire. (Author's collection)

Engraving by the Swiss artist Joss Amman (1539–91) of a typical costume worn by 'A Lady from London'. (Author's collection)

A cabinet of curiosities; the accumulation of such collections became popular in the late sixteenth century, and this one was depicted by William Hogarth. (Author's collection)

had joined the king's consort of viols in 1545. He, too, had stayed in London and had settled in East Smithfield.[14]

Music formed a part of the annual Lord Mayor's Show as well as performances at the theatres, both of which developed considerably during the later sixteenth century. Each new Lord Mayor went through the 'Silent Ceremony' of swearing-in at the Guildhall on the feast of St Simon and St Jude (28 October) and on the next day went to Westminster to take his oath of office before the Barons of the Exchequer. Since the 1450s he had travelled to and from Westminster by barge within a flotilla of boats, returning to Baynard's Castle. He went from there in procession to Guildhall for his feast, which was followed by a service in St Paul's. The day was rounded off by a torchlight procession back to the Guildhall. The Lord Mayor's livery company bore most of the costs and was strongly represented in the processions; the Lord Mayor invariably was a member of one of the Great Twelve companies, which were large and wealthy enough to undertake the organisation and expense, ensuring a grand show to outdo the other companies' efforts. This was the chief day in the civic calendar and the citizens turned out in large numbers to participate or to watch. Grenade wrote in 1578 that 'from early morning you can see great preparations throughout the City. All the Halls, Companies and Estates assemble in a most magnificent array ... having a marvellous appearance.'[15]

In the morning the Lord Mayor and Aldermen were escorted to the mayoral barge, which was accompanied by a flotilla of the companies' barges 'deckyd with stremars' and many other craft. For the inauguration in 1566 of Christopher Draper, of the Ironmongers' Company, a contract to supply twenty boats and their crews was given to John Candish, a haberdasher. He was also to arrange for the music, specified as two trumpets, a drum and a flute, eight single and eight double basses, and to provide the uniforms, including those for the master and gunner of the foist, who were to wear sarcinet cassocks, silk night-caps and scarves.[16] The foist was a galley of eighteen or twenty tons, festooned with banners and streamers and carrying light cannon, which were discharged from time to time during the day. For instance, when the Lord Mayor boarded his barge 'some hundreds of guns fired a salute'. Grenade was so impressed by the spectacle on the river that he wrote that 'whoever sees the finery of the barges and boats in this convoy, their array, the number of people and the great triumph of the occasion would be astonished'. Lupold von Wedel, from Pomerania, witnessed the show in 1584 and the swearing-in of Wolston Dixie, a freeman of the Skinners' Company. He was fascinated by the scale of the armada: 'The river was covered with little boats, and the throng was so great that the number of vessels assembled was estimated at some hundreds.' Each livery company had its own barge and 'all the boats flaunted flags, whereby each guild could be recognised'. Trumpeters and musicians on the boats serenaded the company during the journeys to and from Westminster.[17] Henry Machyn's description of the scene in 1555 mentions two pinnaces, one painted white and blue, the other yellow and red, 'and the oars and gowne [guns] in lyke colour', and all the way the pinnaces fired their guns, perhaps drowning out the trumpets, drums and shawms (a woodwind instrument), and the waits. In 1571 Machyn commented that during the journey there was 'grett shutyng of gunes and trumpettes blohyng'.[18]

At Westminster the mayoral party disembarked and was followed by at least 200 people, with sixteen trumpeters and four men playing sackbuts or trombones, and seventy poor men, uniformly dressed in blue robes. As well as those members of the Lord Mayor's formal entourage, von Wedel saw 'many citizens wending their way to the Magistrates' Court', forming such a throng that 'although the courtyard is very large, there was no getting either in or out'. He noted, apparently with some surprise, that the crowd of onlookers contained women as well as men and that they mingled together. The Lord Mayor took the oath before the Lord Chancellor, Sir Thomas Bromley, and the flotilla then returned along the Thames.[19]

The main highlight of the day for the citizens was the procession from the wharf to St Paul's churchyard and then along Cheapside to the Guildhall. It was an impressive and colourful sight and consisted of a number of elements. First were the standards of the City and members of the Lord Mayor's livery company, accompanied by drummers and fifers, followed by up to 140 poor people in blue gowns, carrying javelins and shields with the coats-of-arms of the incoming and outgoing mayors. Behind them were

the standards of the monarch and the new Lord Mayor, with fifers
and ten trumpeters, then came eighty to a hundred 'bachelors',
who were to wait on the Lord Mayor during his term of office,
carrying out ritual duties, and they were followed by drummers,
fifers, twelve trumpeters and the City waits. There commonly seem
to have been twenty-four trumpeters in all, although Grenade saw
forty-eight in 1578, divided into three groups of sixteen. Between
the various sections in the parade were whifflers or gentlemen
ushers, whose role was to clear the way and keep back the crowds.
They were described in 1539 as being armed with a 'sworde or
a javelyn to kepe the people yn araye, wt chaynes abowte theyre
necks', although by Elizabeth's reign they carried white staves.
Then came the senior and junior members of the Lord Mayor's
company, with the City's officials behind them, and finally the
Lord Mayor and his predecessor, riding side-by-side and followed
by the aldermen, also on horseback. The whole procession could
consist of up to 350 people, and the members of the other livery
companies lined the route. In Cheapside the number of onlookers
was so great that space for the procession to pass was cleared
by men carrying squirts such as those used to quench fires, with
which 'they squirted water at the crowd, for the street was full
of people, so that they were forced to make way'. The role was
also performed by the 'wild men', who in 1556 cast 'squybe of
fyre afore the Bachelers'; in 1568 two men were assigned to 'serve
for woodhousis or Ivie man', and were to 'shote of Fyer with the
seid squybbes contynually'. The Merchant Taylors' Company's
account for 1575 noted that 'to make waye in the streetes, there
are certayne men apparelled lyke devells, and wylde men, with
skybbs [squibs, or firecrackers]'.[20] Pushing the onlookers back
increased the crush in the crowds and, according to Grenade, 'all
are so squashed that many people faint'. He estimated the crowd
to be 'more than 30 or 40,000 people forming a marvellous
throng'.[21]

Among the many sights, presentations, diversions and sounds,
probably the greatest attention was given to the pageant, described
by Grenade as 'a most magnificent portable theatre, completely
covered with gold and silver leaf in the shape of a mountain', and
by von Wedel as 'like a building pointed at the top, very quaintly

adorned with laurel-leaf, gilded and painted'.[22] In 1566 a Pageant-master was appointed for the first time, one Richard Baker, a painter-stainer, whose stated role was 'the making of the pageant'. In 1561, when the Lord Mayor reached St Paul's churchyard 'there met ym a pagantt gorgyously mad[e], with chylderyn, with dyvers instrumentes playng and syngyng'.[23] Seventeen years later Grenade wrote that on top of the pageant and across its front were 'several maidens most lavishly bedecked, representing several virtues such as Justice, Truth, Charity, Prudence and others similar. Also carried are figures of several wild and strange beasts, such as elephants, unicorns, leopards, griffons, camels, sirens and other such animals which are most wonderful to behold.' A train of gunpowder was laid around St Paul's churchyard with a small gun every few yards – he counted seventy-two – which were fired by the train when the Lord Mayor approached. Grenade found the effect to be 'strange and formidable to hear' and was such that 'it seems as if the great church of St. Paul's might fall to the ground, and there is not a house even in the outermost surroundings which does not shake vigorously'.[24] The gunfire and pyrotechnics during the show required considerable quantities of gunpowder; in 1567 the Ironmongers' Company paid one of its members £17 11s 5d for powder for the show.[25]

The feast in the Guildhall was a grand affair. Von Wedel counted 'sixty long tables, each some twenty paces in length, laid and well appointed', with more on the dais. The guests at the high table included senior figures from the court, members of the aristocracy and visiting diplomats. In a separate room were four long tables, 'at which sat maidens who had already begun to dine' before the Lord Mayor's arrival, and another room contained four more long tables 'occupied by women. Some of these women and girls were beautiful.' In one kitchen meat was being roasted at eight hearths, in another only boiled dishes were being prepared, and in a third 'pasties and suchlike' were baked. The feast was paid for by the Lord Mayor rather than his company, although with a subvention from the City chamber. Von Wedel was told that it would cost £500; Grenade's estimate was twice that sum, although William Smith put the number of diners at one thousand and the outlay at £400, with the sheriffs contributing £100 each. In 1557 the feast cost £331 12s 6d, when the main course was meat, and in the following year, when it was fish, the cost was £190 8s 5d, but those figures would not have included gifts of produce.[26] This was by no means the end of the Lord Mayor's expense in entertaining: 'For the whole of his office he must keep open table.' That comment by von Wedel was echoed by Baron Waldstein, who in 1600 noted that 'from the moment of his election he has to hold open house to everyone and continue to do so for the whole year'. He estimated that a Lord Mayor's outgoings were over £8,000, while his income from holding the post was only £2,000.[27]

In mid-afternoon the Lord Mayor attended a service at St Paul's. He left the building to a fanfare of trumpets and music and returned to the Guildhall by the light of more than 300 torches as the daylight began to fade. It surely was an exhausting day for all concerned, not least for the new incumbent, and an anxious one for those members of his company who had organised much of the event. But the outlay by the livery company, the Lord Mayor and sheriffs, on clothing, decorations, food, drink, accommodation for people and horses, and a host of other items, together with the expenditure by the citizens and visitors on their holiday day out, provided business for many and considerably benefited the city's economy. Grenade also perceptively noted the event's symbolic significance, with the observation that 'one should not be completely surprised at the use of such great magnificence for the entry of the Mayor of London, for it is one of the most excellent estates which exists in the whole of the kingdom of England ... after the royal dignity'.[28]

Lord Mayor's Day was punctuated by speeches, poetry and drama. In 1568 they were written by Richard Mulcaster, Master of the Merchant Taylors' School, and those written by George Peele for the inauguration of Wolston Dixie in 1585, the first to be published, were probably also the first by an established dramatist and poet. In 1591 Peele wrote the text for the inauguration of William Webbe. Peele's father James was a member of the Salters' Company and clerk of Christ's Hospital from 1569 until his death in 1585; he, too, had contributed to the pageants.

It became customary for talented writers to contribute the text. As the Lord Mayor's Show developed during the late sixteenth

century, so did the theatre. Players had traditionally acted for
the aristocracy and the court, but had such a low status that they
were equated with vagabonds. They drew a wider audience to
performances at inns, some of which were regular venues with a
permanent stage. This was the case at the Black Bull in Bishopsgate,
where plays were being staged by 1578 and which was licensed in
1583 for the Queen's Company of players. The Bell and the Cross
Keys, in Gracechurch Street, were also being used as inn theatres
during the second half of the 1570s, as was the Boar's Head in
Great Eastcheap and the Belle Sauvage on Ludgate Hill. These were
limited with regard to both the facilities for producing plays and
the size of the audiences that could be accommodated. There was
evidently a growing demand for such plays and entertainments,
and the solution was purpose-built playhouses, the first of which
was the Red Lion, erected in Whitechapel High Street in 1567; by
1600 the city had eleven active playhouses.

Bishopsgate developed a reputation as a haunt of the acting
profession, and to its north, beyond the gate, two playhouses were
erected. In his description of London, Stow mentioned that the
church of the former Holywell priory there had been pulled down
and 'many houses have been built for the lodgings of noblemen,
of strangers born, and other. And neare thereunto are builded two
publique houses for the acting and shewe of comedies, tragedies,
and histories, for recreation. Whereof one is called the Courtein,
the other the Theatre.' The Theatre was built in 1576 and the
Curtain in 1577. Grenade described them as 'two very fine theatres'
and noted that 'their agreeable appearance pleases men and any
onlookers', although he did comment that one, presumably the
Theatre, was 'magnificent in comparison with the other'.[29]

The first playhouse south of the river was also built in the late
1570s, in Newington Butts, beyond Southwark. This was a poor
site as it was difficult to reach, whereas Bankside was ideal, as the
patrons could arrive either across the bridge or by boat. The river
was full of small passenger boats, known as wherries, which were
regulated by the corporation from 1555; by the end of the century
there were said to be 3,000 of them. They were a comfortable
way to travel, taking two passengers and being 'charmingly
upholstered'. The only drawbacks to a journey by wherry were

the state of the river at the time, the discomfort if it was too choppy, and the danger when a journey involved passing beneath a bridge, which was a hazardous operation even for an experienced waterman. It was relatively safe at slack water, when the river levels upstream and downstream from the bridge were roughly equal, but at other times the flow was so rapid and turbulent that there was a risk of the boat being overturned or of the waterman losing control and his boat smashing against one of the starlings (the bases of the bridge's pillars). Prudent passengers would alight before the bridge and re-embark after it, but those who were bold and did not wish be seen to be faint-hearted stayed on. Accidents and fatalities did occur.

The bear gardens were already attracting patrons to Bankside before a playhouse was built on the site. The first was the Rose, erected in 1587, soon followed by the Swan, in 1595, and the Globe, in 1599. The Globe was substantially 'the Theatre' surreptitiously dismantled at the end of December 1598 and transported across the river to be reassembled on Bankside. The dramatic transformation was the outcome of a dispute between the landlord, Giles Allen, and the playhouse's managers, Cuthbert and Richard Burbage, the sons of James Burbage, who had invested quite heavily in the theatre. The rebuilt playhouse was a great success and the Rose's proprietors, Edward Alleyn and Philip Henslowe, responded by building a new theatre, the Fortune, at Golden Lane, Cripplegate.

The playhouses were unpopular with the City authorities and the Puritans virtually from the outset. Their arguments against the plays and players were partly moral, that they corrupted those who went to see them and were hang-outs for the criminal and the debauched, and partly economic, with the allegation that people, especially apprentices, neglected their work so that they could go to the entertainments. The patrons of playhouses were condemned in much the same terms as those who frequented bowling alleys and gaming houses. In 1580 Anthony Munday described them as 'light and lewd disposed persons, as harlots, cutpurses, cozeners, pilferers &c who under colour of hearing plays, devised divers and ungodly conspiracies'. Munday was a playwright himself and so not a detached critic. Stephen Gosson was also a poet and playwright, but one who wrote in a satirical tone, and he regarded the playhouses as being 'ful of adulterie' and described how the men there used 'such heaving, and shoving, such itching and shouldering to sit by women ... [with] such tickling, such toying, such smiling, such winking, and such manning them home, when the sports are ended, that it is a right comedy to mark their behaviour'.[30]

An unspecified occurrence at the Theatre in 1580 gave the Lord Mayor the opportunity to tell the Privy Council of the aldermen's objections to the playhouses. He wrote that the 'players of plays' at the Theatre 'and other such places', grouped with tumblers and other entertainers were

> a very superfluous sort of men, and of such faculty as the laws had disallowed; that the exercise of the plays was not only a great hindrance to the service of God, but also a great corruption of youth, with unchaste and wicked matters, the occasion of much incontinence, practices of many frays, quarrels, and other disorders.

He requested that plays should be prohibited in the City and the liberties.[31] The aldermen's opinions were influenced by incidents such as one at the Theatre in 1584, when 'a serving man in a blew coat' named Brown argued with 'certen poore boyes, handicraft prentises' and then drew his sword and wounded one of them. Even at the more refined indoor theatres, things could turn rough. Sir Richard Cholmley arrived too late to get a seat at a performance in the Blackfriars theatre in 1603 and so was obliged to take a stool, of which there was a fixed number. This was an uncomfortable way to watch, and so between every scene he stood up to stretch his legs 'as the custom was'. While he was on his feet another young gallant, who was a 'Lady's eldest son', provocatively took the stool, and would not return it. Cholmley politely led him outside and then challenged him to a duel, but his adversary did not have a sword; Cholmley rather cheekily offered to buy him one, but the watch arrived and so Cholmley had to satisfy his honour by inflicting 'two or three good blows' on the young man. Play-going could be hazardous, even for a cocky young aristocrat.[32]

The hostile attitudes persisted for the remainder of the century, and in 1592 the aldermen summarised them in a letter to the Archbishop of Canterbury. Their objections were that

> the youths of the City were greatly corrupted, and their manners infected with many evils and ungodly qualities, by reason of the wanton and profane devices represented on the stages. The apprentices and servants were withdrawn from their work, to the great hindrance of the trades and traders of the City, and the propagation of religion.

This was at a time when the playhouses were attracting large audiences drawn from across the social spectrum.[33] But there was a jurisdictional reason behind their approach to the archbishop, for the queen's Letters Patent to the Master of the Revels, Sir Edmund Tilney, had given him oversight of the players, plays and playhouses. Tilney had held the post, with the responsibility of arranging entertainments at court, since 1578 and he supported the players, not least because they could provide more accomplished performances at a cheaper rate than other productions, such as masques. In 1581 he obtained the authority to conscript workmen and buy materials, and he was given the right to order the players to perform their plays before him, together with the power to license, alter or suppress plays and to punish players and playwrights who did not comply. Tilney's role encroached upon the City's jurisdiction and the aldermen regarded him as an obstacle, shielding the players, as they tried to prevent plays being acted in the City, and so they wanted the archbishop's assistance in dealing with him.[34]

Support for the players in court circles was at odds with the corporation's steady hostility. In 1594 the Lord Mayor's reaction to the proposal to build the Swan playhouse was to write to Lord Burghley, the queen's leading minister, asking that all of London's playhouses should be pulled down. He wrote that they were 'the ordinary places of meeting for all vagrant persons and maisterles men that hang about the Citie, theeves, horsestealers, whoremongers, coozeners, connycatching persones, practizers of treason, and other such lyke'.[35] This was a wide-ranging condemnation, as was the reaction to the proposal to erect the Fortune playhouse, a few years later. The Privy Council received 'divers complaintes' because of the 'manyfolde abuses and disorders that have growen and do contynue by occasion of many houses erected and employed in and about the cittie of London for common stage-playes'. Their number and misgovernment 'hath bin and is dayly occasion of the ydle, ryoutous and dissolute living of great nombers of people, that leavinge all such honest and painefull course of life as they should followe, doe meete and assemble here, and of many particular abuses and disorders that doe thereupon ensue'. But the Council acknowledged that 'the use and exercise of such playes' was not 'evill in yt self' and should be tolerated in a well-governed state, and that the queen was 'pleased at some tymes to take delight and recreation in the sight and hearing of them'. Because of the queen's enjoyment, some public playhouses should be open for the players 'to keepe them in exercise' for when they performed before her majesty. It had not agreed to the earlier request for all playhouses to be demolished and now ruled that, as further regulation was needed, only two were to be permitted, one on Bankside and the other in Middlesex. As the Curtain was to be demolished or put to another appropriate use, the Council decided that the Fortune was to be the Middlesex playhouse, while the company playing on Bankside should choose its preferred theatre, which was the Globe. Performances at inn theatres were forbidden, and the two acting companies were to stage plays on only two days each week, to restrict the drawing of people 'from their trade and worke to misspend their tyme'. Playing on Sundays, during Lent and plague epidemics was forbidden. The owners and the players were liable to imprisonment if the Council's orders were not observed.[36]

The tension between the need for the players to remain proficient, so that they could put on good performances for the queen and the court during the long Christmas holiday, and the innate suspicion of the City authorities to the playhouses, had been present over the past twenty years or more. In 1581 the Privy Council had banned plays until Michaelmas, 29 September, because of the risk of plague, but in mid-November wrote to the Lord Mayor and Aldermen to tell them that as 'the sickness had almost ceased, and was not likely to increase at this time of the year', in order 'to relieve the poor players, and to encourage their being in readiness with convenient matters for Her Highness's solace this next Christmas', they should allow them to act again 'in the usual places'. Again, in 1583, the Council wrote to the Lord Mayor and Aldermen instructing them to permit the players to perform, so that they would be proficient when they acted before the queen and the court at Christmas.[37]

The Council also intervened in favour of the players at other times of the year. In April 1582 it wrote admitting that in the past it had given orders 'for the restraint of plays', but now 'for honest recreation sake, in respect that Her Majesty sometimes took delight in those pastimes', it thought it appropriate, because of the season of the year and the absence of plague, 'to allow of certain companies of players in London, partly that they might thereby attain more dexterity and perfection in that profession, the better to content Her Majesty'. Nevertheless, in order to maintain control over the plays that were performed, the City should appoint 'some proper person to consider and allow such plays only as were fitted to yield honest recreation and no example of evil'. The Lord Mayor's ban on plays at holidays should be withdrawn, and they should be prohibited only on the Sabbath. His response was to concur with the ban on Sunday playing, for although the players did not stage their performance until after evening service, all afternoon they 'took in hearers, and filled the places with such as were thereby absent from Church, and attended to serve God's enemies in an inn'. Moreover, the number of plague cases had increased, the weather was 'hot and perilous', and the law term and the meeting of Parliament were imminent, and so he asked the Council to 'continue their restraint of such plays', but did however support the proposal that 'the matter and manner of their plays' should be examined by 'some grave and discreet persons'.[38]

That role was fulfilled not by the City but by Tilney, who, while providing a buffer between the acting profession and its critics, was active as a censor. The play *Thomas More* of 1592–94, by Anthony Munday and Henry Chettle, dealt with More's response to Henry VIII's religious changes and the Evil May Day riots in 1517, taking a conciliatory line on the subject of foreigners in London. Tilney saw this section as a potential provocation to a London audience, and he wrote on the manuscript: 'Leave out

the insurrection wholly, and the cause thereof, and begin with
Sir Thomas More at the Mayor's sessions, with a report afterwards
of his good service ... a short report and not otherwise, at your
own perils.' The text was duly revised – the manuscript is in the
handwriting of five contributors, including that of Shakespeare –
although it may not have been performed during the Elizabethan
and Jacobean periods.[39] Despite such interventions, Elizabethan
dramatists were not shy of tackling contemporary issues, such as
the government's foreign policy. Platter commented that Londoners
'pass their time, learning at the play what is happening abroad ...
since the English for the most part do not travel much, but prefer to
learn foreign matters and take their pleasures at home'. Diplomatic
contacts and growing trade with the Muslim world attracted
enough public interest for some dramatists to use it as settings
for their plays, and more than sixty plays in London's playhouses
between 1576 and 1603 featured Turks, Moors and Persians.[40]

The playhouses resembled amphitheatres and were based upon
the design of the bear-baiting arenas at Bankside, with three tiers
of seating and the space in front of the stage occupied by those
standing; in the bear-baiting arenas the standing area was where the
baiting took place. The Rose had a capacity of roughly 1,950 until
it was enlarged in 1592, after which it could accommodate 2,400
patrons. A Dutch visitor, Johannes de Witt, who was in London in
1596, noted that the Swan had space for 3,000 spectators, and two
years later Paul Hentzner wrote that the plays were performed 'to
very numerous audiences'.[41] The modern Globe theatre, which is a
reproduction of the playhouse of 1599, has seating for 1,380 and
space for 700 standing. The indoor theatres were much smaller and
were used for boys' companies; the earliest was a room adapted for
the purpose at St Paul's, used from 1575 until 1591, and two were
at Blackfriars: the first was in use from 1576 until 1584 and the
second from 1600 by the Children of the Chapel.

Visitors to London who went to the playhouses probably were
unaware of the tensions between the acting companies, the City
and the court. Indeed, Grenade assumed that the location of the
Theatre and the Curtain was a decision of the aldermen, although
they were beyond the City's boundary. For those visitors who did
not understand English, the music and dancing rather than the

drama naturally featured in their descriptions. Thomas Platter was at the playhouses in 1599 and explained that daily, at two o'clock, there were two, or sometimes three, plays performed in London's playhouses. The raised stage meant that 'everyone has a good view', although the level of comfort varied according to admission price. Those who stood paid only a penny, while those who chose to sit entered by a separate door and paid another penny, and for a third penny a patron could enter by yet another door and sit in 'the most comfortable seats which are cushioned, where he not only sees everything well, but can also be seen'. Food and drink were taken round during the performance. The members of the cast were 'most expensively and elaborately costumed'. After a performance at the Globe of *Julius Caesar*, with a cast of fifteen, the actors 'danced very marvellously and gracefully together as is their wont, two dressed as men and two as women'. This was the usual practice and music played an integral part in the productions. Hentzner wrote that the performances 'were concluded with variety of dances, accompanied by excellent music and the excessive applause of those that are present'. According to Stephen Gosson, 'when any notable shew passeth over the stage, the people arise in their seates, & stand upright with delight and eagernesse to view it well'.[42] Samuel Kiechel, from Ulm, was at the playhouses in 1585 and he commented that when a new play was performed the members of the audience had to pay double the usual price – the receipts were from £10 to £12 for each performance. He also noted that the restrictions on the days when performances could take place were ignored, and in 1598 Hentzner wrote that plays were performed 'almost every day'.[43] The attempts to curtail the number of performances had clearly been ineffectual.

The indoor theatres were relatively expensive and so attracted a more genteel clientele. In his journal for 1602 Gerschow mentions three visits to the theatre by the Duke of Stettin-Pomerania and his entourage within a week. On 13 September they were at the Globe or the Rose, on the following day at the Fortune, and four days later they saw a play at the Blackfriars, which he described as 'the children's Theatre'. The boys were trained to sing and play musical instruments, and to perform a play once a week, for which 'the queen has provided them with an abundance of rich costumes'.

Despite the higher price, 'there is always a large audience, including many respectable women, because useful themes and much good doctrine, as we were informed by others, are presented there'. Gerschow was unable to follow the drama, but clearly enjoyed the music, for he wrote,

> For a whole hour beforehand a delightful performance of instrumental music is given on organs, lutes, pandoras, mandolins, viols and flutes; on this occasion a boy *cum voce tremula* sang sweetly to the accompaniment of a bass-viol, the like of which we have not heard on our whole journey, except possibly from the nuns in Milan.[44]

Gerschow's account touches on two aspects of the varied recreations in late-sixteenth-century London: music and theatre-going. His visit led to an example of London exerting cultural influence beyond England, for after returning to Pomerania the duke established a company of English players at his court in Wolgast.

12

London around 1600

London's topography changed a great deal during the sixteenth century. The monasteries came into lay ownership with new uses, some churches were demolished, others were rebuilt, St Paul's lost its spire and the City took control of the hospitals. The Royal Exchange was built, the Merchant Taylors' school and Gresham College were opened, and the first playhouses were erected. At Westminster, part of the palace was destroyed and Whitehall Palace became the principal royal residence, augmented by the new residences of St James's Palace, Bridewell and Somerset Place. Aristocrats and courtiers took houses close to the focus of royal power, in some cases supplanting senior clerics, and far more young gentlemen scholars attended the Inns of Court than hitherto. Most striking of all was the great increase in the city's size, as the suburbs began to spread ever outwards, unconstrained by the medieval city wall.

From the late 1530s the changes were noticed and chronicled by John Stow. He was born in 1525, the son and grandson of tallow chandlers in the parish of St Michael, Cornhill, but he became a tailor and was admitted to the Merchant Taylors' Company in 1547. The history and topography of London were his passions and he devoted his life to them until his death in 1605. His wife Elizabeth arranged for his monument in his parish church of St Andrew Undershaft, which shows him writing at a table in an alcove which has marble books on its inner walls. The inscription records: 'He exercised the most careful accuracy in searching ancient monuments, English annals, and records of the City of London. He wrote excellently and deserved well both of his own and subsequent ages.'

In his description of his own neighbourhood he noted: 'Now down St. Mary street, by the west end of the church towards the north, stand divers fair houses for merchants and other.' That brief summary of the housing and character of a street were typical of his survey, reflecting the city's social geography. In the wealthy central districts around Cheapside were streets such as Bread Street, 'now wholly inhabited by rich merchants; and divers fair inns be there, for good receipt of carriers and other travellers to the city'; Milk Street, with its 'many fair houses for wealthy merchants and other'; Foster Lane, where 'among many fair houses, there is one large inn for receipt of travellers called Blossoms inn'; but also the much less salubrious Honey Lane 'so called, not of the sweetness thereof, being very narrow, and somewhat dark'.[1] Cheapside itself gave visitors the same impression as it had done a hundred and more years earlier. Thomas Platter, in 1599, wrote: 'In one very long street called Cheapside dwell almost only goldsmiths and money changers on either hand, so that inexpressibly great treasures and vast amounts of money may be seen here.'[2]

Fine houses stood in the streets to the north of Cheapside, such as in Aldermanbury, where there were 'divers fair houses on both the sides, meet for merchants or men of worship', and Addle Street near Cripplegate was 'replenished with fair buildings on both sides'. Basinghall Street contained 'divers fair houses for merchants and others', as well as Blackwell Hall, focus of the cloth trade, which was rebuilt at a cost of £2,500 in 1588. The larger houses commonly stood close to more modest ones and tenements, as in Coleman Street, a little way to the east, described by Stow as 'a fair and large street, on both sides built with divers fair houses, besides alleys, with small tenements in great number'. He did not fail to note the incongruous setting of some houses of the wealthy citizens, such as in Lothbury, facetiously suggesting that in fact the name was a corruption of 'loathbury' because of the noise made by the brass and copper founders in their workshops there. Having cast their wares, such as candlesticks, dishes and spice mortars, they turned and finished them 'with the foot, turning and scrating (as some do term it), making a loathsome noise to the by-passers that have not been used to the like, and therefore by them disdainfully called Lothberie'. Nevertheless, he added that the south side of the street contained 'some fair houses and large for merchants'.[3]

Between Coleman Street and Poultry was Old Jewry, where the synagogue had been closed in 1272. Stow was intrigued by the succession of uses to which its site had been put. It had been granted to the Friars Penitent, and later was occupied first by a nobleman and then during the fifteenth century by two prominent mercers, who served as Mayor, Robert Large in 1439–40 and Hugh Clopton in 1492–3. By Stow's time the Windmill tavern stood there. Stow remembered the former Jewish enclave on the west side of the street north of St Olave's Church through to Ironmonger Lane being enclosed by a stone wall. Part of the site had been used for a royal wardrobe between the fourteenth and sixteenth centuries and it was still known as the Old Wardrobe in the mid-sixteenth century. By about 1600 sections of the outer wall had been removed and 'divers fair houses built thereupon'.[4]

Stow mentioned the locations of some of the Londoners' many trades as well as changes in the neighbourhoods occupied by particular tradesmen. Bread Street Hill contained 'divers fair houses, inhabited by fishmongers, cheesemongers, and merchants of divers trades', and Bucklesbury 'on both the sides throughout is possessed of grocers and apothecaries towards the west end thereof'. Fish Street Hill was home to 'fishmongers and fair taverns ... men of divers trades, grocers and haberdashers', and fishmongers lived in Friday Street, 'serving Friday's market' for fish. Watling Street's inhabitants were 'wealthy drapers, retailers of woollen cloth, both broad and narrow, of all sorts, more than in any one street of this city'. Stow mentioned that the drapers had formerly been in Lombard Street and Cornhill, but now were in Watling Street and Candlewick Street. Watling Street was one of the streets noted by Mancini more than a century earlier as being dominated by the cloth trade, and so the change which Stow described may have been under way before the sixteenth century. As well as Watling Street and Candlewick Street, Birchin Lane and an adjoining street 'hath been inhabited for the most part with wealthy drapers', and from

Birchin Lane 'down to the stocks, in the reign of Henry VI., had ye for the most part dwelling Fripperers or Upholders, that sold old apparel and household stuff'.[5]

In most cases Stow was not specific about when such changes had taken place, and of course the change itself had been a gradual process. The market in Poultry had given the street its name, but, he wrote, the poulterers were 'but lately departed from thence into other streets', namely Gracechurch Street and St Nicholas shambles. The pepperers and grocers of Soper Lane were now in Bucklesbury, the skinners from St Mary Axe had moved into Budge Row and Walbrook, the ironmongers had transferred their businesses from Old Jewry and Ironmonger Lane to Thames Street, while shoemakers and curriers of leather had moved to St Martin-le-Grand and London Wall near Moorgate. Some trades had dispersed to such an extent that he could not be specific, such as the vinters, formerly in the Vintry and now in 'divers places', and the cooks and pastelars, who were 'for the more part in Thames Street, the other dispersed into divers parts'. He mentioned trades that were apparently in terminal decline, such as 'the patten-makers, of St. Margaret, Pattens' lane, clean worn out' and the bowyers, from Bowyers Row near Ludgate, moved 'into divers places, and almost worn out with the fletchers'.[6]

The vicinity of Gutter Lane had been the base for a number of trades. Stow noted that the silversmiths there had been assigned by Edward I to mint coins, known as 'silver of Guthurun's lane'. By Stow's time the goldsmiths had mostly moved away from the lane into Cheapside. The miniaturist painter Nicholas Hilliard was apprenticed to a goldsmith and became a freeman of the company in 1569. For much of his career he was based at his workshop in a house called the Maidenhead in Gutter Lane as the company's tenant. The livery hall of the embroiderers, or broderers, was built in the lane in 1515, helped by a donation from John Throwstone, an embroiderer who was later a goldsmith. The area was also a focus for the saddlers, whose guild was in existence by at least the late twelfth century and received its charter in 1395. Its livery hall was close to St Vedast's church in Foster Lane.[7]

In the case of Grub Street a change of trades allowed Stow to indulge in one of his general complaints, for he believed that it had been inhabited by tradesmen connected with archery, but by the time that he was writing they had gone, to be replaced by 'bowling-alleys and dicing-houses, which in all places are increased, and too much frequented'. He claimed that the name Houndsditch was derived from the number of dogs thrown into the city ditch. By the end of the century the street was built up and already was known for its second-hand clothes business, which was to be one of the predominant trades there and in the nearby streets for the next four centuries.[8]

Stow was aware of the condition of the ditch around the city wall. He remembered that it had been cleaned in 1540 and 1549, and £814 had been spent on improving it in 1569. But cleaning and scouring had then been neglected and profits were made by letting out its banks. A rate was levied in 1595 to pay for cleaning the ditch once more, and a section had indeed been improved 'and made somewhat broader', but it was filling again very quickly because the ground around it had been raised. North of the Tower the ditch had formerly been kept open and clean, and it had been the practice to water horses there, but it was now enclosed and 'the banks thereof let out for garden-plots, carpenters' yards, bowling allies, and divers houses thereon built, whereby the city wall is hidden, the ditch filled up, a small channel left, and that very shallow'. Stow conveyed his despair at the long-term deterioration of the ditch with the comment 'and I will so leave it, for I cannot help it'.[9]

Some of the grand properties that were intermixed with the citizens' houses had been subdivided or put to another use. Stow recorded that Northumberland House in the parish of St Katherine Coleman had belonged to the earls of Northumberland and was occupied by them until at least the 1540s, but 'of late being left by the earls, the gardens thereof were made into bowling alleys, and other parts into dicing houses, common to all comers for their money, there to bowl and hazard'. More recently there had been further changes, because 'so many bowling alleys, and other houses for unlawful gaming, hath been raised in other parts of the city and suburbs, that this their ancient and only patron of misrule, is left and forsaken of her gamesters, and therefore turned into a number of great rents, small cottages, for strangers and others'.

In Old Fish Street Hill the former inn of the bishops of Hereford had become 'greatly ruinated, and is now divided into many small tenements; the hall and principal rooms, are a house to make sugar-loaves, etc.'. Part of the Crutched Friars had been taken by Jacob Verzelini, from Murano, sometime before 1568, who set up a glass works there, making Venetian glass. He received a royal patent in 1574, which stated that he had 'sette uppe within oure said cittie one furneys and sette on worke dyvers and sondrie parsonnes for the makynge of drynkynge glasses such as be accustomablie made in the towne of Morano'. But in August 1575 the works 'burst out into a terrible fire', which could not be checked because of the large stacks of wood stored there for fuel, so that the building was 'all consumed to the stone walls, which nevertheless greatly hindered the fire from spreading any further'. Verzelini then built another glass-house, in Broad Street, which was taken over by Sir Jerome Bowes in 1592, although he was a promoter and not a glassmaker by trade. There was a strong demand for high-quality glasses, for William Harrison wrote in the 1580s that the gentry now took both their wine and beer in Venetian glasses, in preference to gold and silver cups and goblets; the trade with Venice was so profitable that 'many become rich only with their new trade unto Murana ... from whence the very best are daily to be had'.[10]

Another monastic property had been transformed, for the buildings of the Poor Clares were replaced by 'divers fair and large storehouses for armour and habiliments of war, with divers workhouses, serving to the same purpose'.[11] The adjoining district of the Minories, close to the Tower, developed into London's gun quarter, a trade in which the city was dominant, as in many others.

At Cold Harborough in Thames Street, Poultney's Inn, built in the 1330s, was acquired in the late sixteenth century by the Earl of Shrewsbury, who demolished the surviving buildings and in their place erected 'a great number of small tenements, now letten out for great rents to people of all sorts'. Similarly, Oldbourne Hall in Shoe Lane 'is now letten out into divers tenements'. In 1574 the Privy Council had commented on the 'strangers, inmates and many lewd persons' on the site of St Martin-le-Grand – they were attracted by the right of sanctuary from justice that continued after the college's dissolution. Stow disapproved, as the privileges were not intended to benefit 'artificers, buyers and sellers'. Subdivision had occurred even in less grand properties, such as Pie Corner, on the edge of Smithfield, which had been the name of a hostelry 'sometimes a fair inn for receipt of travellers, but now divided into tenements'. But not all infilling in the aftermath of the dissolution of the monastic houses had been deleterious to a district. Stow wrote that in place of the White Friars, south of Fleet Street, there were 'many fair houses built, lodgings for noblemen and others'.[12]

The economy of Thames Street downstream from the bridge was inevitably based on seaborne trade, and it was a busy and somewhat insalubrious street due to the wharves and the cargoes that were unloaded or stored there. Yet both sides of the street contained 'many fair houses large for stowage, built for merchants', who wished to be close to the places where their goods were landed and from where they could distribute them. The streets running north from Thames Street were steep. St Mary-at-Hill is the name of both a church and a street; Stow explained that the church was 'called on the hill, because of the ascent from Billingsgate' and he remarked that the street 'on both sides is furnished with many fair houses for merchants'. Dowgate Hill took its name from a water gate where the Walbrook entered the Thames and was noted for its steepness. Stow described a fatal accident during a downpour during an afternoon in September 1574, when water cascaded down the channels and an eighteen-year-old youth, attempting to jump across one of them, lost his footing and was swept away. Attempts to check his catastrophic progress down the street were unsuccessful and, according to Stow, he had drowned before he hit a cart wheel at the water gate.[13]

Across the river, Southwark consisted of 'divers streets, ways, and winding lanes, all full of buildings, inhabited'. St Olave's Church was described as 'a fair and meet large church, but a far larger parish especially of aliens or strangers, and poor people'. Eastwards from St Olave's, Stow mentioned 'continual building on both the sides, with lanes and alleys', and beyond them were many other 'small tenements builded, replenished with strangers and other, for the most part poor people'.[14] Southwark was still home to the watermen and to incomers, especially from the Low Countries.

The river-based trades and foreigners which characterised Southwark were features that it shared throughout the century with St Katherine's on the north side of the river, east of the Tower. The hospital there had been 'of late years inclosed about, or pestered with small tenements and homely cottages, having inhabitants, English and strangers, more in number than in some city in England'. The district was described as 'Petty Flanders' and had a Flemish burial ground. The enumeration of immigrants in 1573 recorded 425 foreigners there, 328 of them Dutch. The precinct attracted those who were not freemen of the City, because it was just outside its jurisdiction. Close by, on Tower Hill, Stow complained that its area was by the end of the century 'greatly diminished by building of tenements and garden-plots, etc.'. Sir John Peyton, newly appointed Lieutenant of the Tower, commissioned a survey in 1597, which reported that eighty houses had been built in the previous forty years on Tower Hill within the Tower's jurisdiction, and that these were 'of late inhabited by Strangers manie of them being very poore & disordred persons, by meanes wherof contentions & quarrells are daily moved'. Because of the increase in population there was not enough room for burials, which in 'tymes of infection wilbe moste dangerous & in other respects very inconvenient'.[15]

In other districts around the edge of the city the housing was poor, and Stow commented that in Golden Lane (then Golding Lane) the street 'on both the sides is replenished with many tenements of poor people'. The suburbs were growing rapidly and outside Aldgate the street was 'not only fully replenished with buildings outward, and also pestered with divers alleys, on either side to the bars, but to White Chappell and beyond'. Stow complained about the 'filthy cottages' and rubbish dumps in Whitechapel that stretched for half a mile beyond St Mary's church, which, he complained, presented 'no small blemish to so famous a city to have so unsavoury and unseemly an entrance or passage thereunto'. Another main road into the city passed through the extra-mural suburb beyond Bishopsgate. In response to the plague epidemic of 1563 the City set out a new burial ground there in 1569, on a part of Bethlehem Hospital's lands, in anticipation of future need, although it was used as a general burial ground and not only for epidemic burials. The cemetery was in an area recognised to be at risk from the disease, and Stow wrote that north of the hospital 'many houses have been built with alleys backward, of late time too much pestered with people (a great cause of infection)'. The street up to Shoreditch had 'a continual building of small and base tenements, for the most part lately erected'.[16]

The riverside was being developed at the same time. At Wapping, along the river east of the Tower, a gallows had stood for executing pirates, and there was 'never a house standing within these forty years; but since the gallows being after removed farther off, a continual street, or filthy strait passage, with alleys of small tenements, or cottages, [is] built, inhabited by sailors' victuallers, along by the river of Thames, almost to Radcliff, a good mile from the Tower'. As well as the new small houses along the river, Stow also mentioned that 'of late years shipwrights and (for the most part) other marine men, have built many large and strong houses for themselves, and smaller for sailors ... almost to Poplar, and so to Blake wall'.[17]

Not all routes out of the city had been developed in the same way, however. Someone travelling beyond Newgate from St Andrew's church up Holborn Hill would pass 'divers fair built houses', and beyond them, in the High Street of St Giles-in-the-Fields, there were 'divers fair buildings, hostelries, and houses for gentlemen and men of honour'. Fetter Lane, between Holborn and Fleet Street, was 'of late years on both sides built through with many fair houses'. Stow called it Fewter Lane and, in one of his speculations on the origins of names, he took that to mean 'the lane of idle people'. The word 'faitour' was used to describe impostors or cheats, such as those who feigned illness, although in Old French it meant 'lawyer'. Going northwards along Gray's Inn Lane would take a traveller through a district containing the inn, the hall of which was built in 1556–8 and the gatehouse in 1593, and along the street itself, which Stow described as 'furnished with fair buildings and many tenements on both the sides, leading to the fields toward Highgate and Hamsted'.[18] But fine houses along a street frontage could conceal shoddy houses to their rear. Off Holborn were Gold Lane, 'now on both sides built with small tenements', and Leather Lane, which was 'lately replenished with houses built'. Stow's description conveys the population growth and overcrowding that were features of the city during the late sixteenth century, with rebuilding, subdivision of existing buildings and infilling of open spaces. Even in the centre, at St Leonard's, Foster Lane the parish's population had recently 'mightily increased'. St Michael Cornhill was separated from Cornhill by its churchyard, and Stow admired it as 'a fair and beautiful church', yet he complained that since the 1540s houses had been built in the churchyard between the church and the street, 'whereby the church is darkened and other ways annoyed'. Stow was especially sensitive to the changes at St Michael's, because both his parents and grandparents were buried there.[19]

On the north side of Holborn was Ely House, the London residence of the bishops of Ely. The accommodation was larger than the bishops generally required and in the sixteenth century members of the aristocracy became their tenants. They included Thomas Wriothesly, Earl of Southampton (1505–50), and, later in the century, Sir Christopher Hatton, one of Elizabeth's favourites. Hatton coveted the palace and with the queen's support pressed the bishop, Richard Cox, to release it to him. In 1576 Cox granted Hatton a twenty-one-year lease of the gatehouse and other parts of the buildings, in addition to fourteen acres of land. Hatton built a house to the west of the bishops' residence, which with repairs cost almost £1,900. He then demanded the freehold, which Cox refused, but the queen obtained a mortgage of the property, which she passed on to Hatton. The episcopal residence was thereby divided, rather awkwardly, between the Hatton family and the bishopric. Bishop Cox died in 1581 and Hatton, created Lord Chancellor in April 1587, died at his house there in 1591.

Another senior officer of state lived in the City. Sir Francis Walsingham was one of the two Secretaries of State from 1573 to 1578 and again from 1581 until his death in 1590. He used his house in Seething Lane as the centre of his operations, including intelligence gathering. Stow wrote that the street contained 'divers fair and large houses' and noted that Walsingham's house had been built by Sir John Allen, a mercer, who was Lord Mayor in 1525–6 and again in 1535–6; he was also a member of the Privy Council. Hatton and Walsingham were both buried in St Paul's, rather than Westminster Abbey. Hatton's tomb was a grandiose one, described by Stow as 'a most sumptuous monument' and he included in his *Survey* two lines by 'a merry poet': 'Philip and Francis have no tombe, For great Christopher takes all the roome.'[20] (Philip and Francis were Sir Francis Walsingham and his son-in-law Sir Philip Sidney, and a few years after Stow's own death the suggestion was made that he was the 'merry poet'.)

Sir Francis Drake took a lease of a property known as the Herbar in Dowgate in 1588. Stow described it as a 'great old house'; it was rebuilt in 1584 by Sir Thomas Pullison, Lord Mayor, and 'was afterward inhabited by Sir Francis Drake, that famous mariner', as his London house, until he sold the lease in 1593 to Alderman Paul Banning.[21] Drake's contemporary Sir John Hawkins, naval commander and merchant, lived for thirty years in the parish of St Dunstan-in-the-East. For a time during the 1590s the Charterhouse was occupied by the Earl of Cumberland. Londoners would regularly see these and other great men and members of their households as they went along the streets. The City was not isolated from the royal and government enclave at Westminster.

The citizens could also ogle visiting diplomats and their entourages as they arrived at Tower Wharf and when they went in procession to Whitehall Palace. Some visiting diplomats lived in the City: the Imperial ambassador François van der Delft was lodged at Bridewell Palace from 1545 to 1550, and in 1553 Antoine de Noailles, the French ambassador, stayed there. The Portuguese ambassador lived in the Charterhouse for a time during the 1570s, and when André Hurault, Sieur de Maisse, arrived in London in 1597 as the French ambassador he was 'lodged in a house that the Queen had commanded for me wherein Drake had formerly lodged', which must refer to the Herbar.[22] In August 1600 the Moroccan ambassador arrived in London and was lodged at Alderman Ratcliffe's house, near the Royal Exchange, with his delegation of fifteen men, who as diplomats from a Muslim state were a novelty in England and attracted much attention. In the following month the czar's ambassador disembarked and he and his party of twenty other persons were 'kindly used and dietted for 8 moneths space, at the sole charges of the companie of the Muscovie Marchants'. The Moroccans had been maintained at the queen's expense.[23]

As the largest city and busiest port, London was the focus for recruiting soldiers for the wars against Spain, in the Low Countries and in Ireland. Continental officers also recruited in England. Recruiting officers would collect their men in the city before they took ship. During the Armada campaign in 1588 the city was patrolled, with chains rigged across the streets as barriers. The trained bands were put in readiness and 6,000 men were enrolled in four regiments, divided into forty companies. These were assembled and drilled twice a week. An enumeration showed that there were 17,083 men in London aged between seventeen and seventy who were judged to be fit to serve. The City was required to send a detachment of 1,000 to the army that was assembled at Tilbury during the summer, which was 14,000 strong. The defeat of the Spanish fleet removed the possibility of invasion and brought a sense of relief; flags from the defeated fleet were hung on the battlements of St Pauls's, then carried to Cheapside Cross before being displayed on London Bridge. At St Martin-in-the-Fields the churchwardens paid two shillings 'for ringinge at her maties goinge & comynge to & from ye Campe at Tilbury in Essex'.[24]

Londoners faced another alarming threat in 1601 when the Earl of Essex led a band of armed supporters in an insurrection. Not since Wyatt's rebellion in 1554 had the citizens experienced such an insurgency in their streets. A courtier, soldier and one of the queen's closest favourites, as well as being a rival of Robert Cecil, her chief minister, Essex had enjoyed influence and popularity during the previous decade. The relation had soured, chiefly because of his conduct during a futile campaign to suppress the rebellion in Ireland, which had begun with high expectations and a rousing send-off from London. He exceeded his orders in agreeing a truce with the rebel leader, the Earl of Tyrone, and then returned post-haste to London, without permission, to explain his conduct. His folly was compounded when he burst in on the queen in her private apartments before she was ready to receive visitors. The earl was prohibited from attending court and, as his influence ebbed away, he simmered at Essex House in the Strand with a group of supporters that included Shakespeare's patron, the Earl of Southampton. Eventually, on Sunday 8 February, the dam of rising frustration burst and, after taking hostage four privy councillors sent to negotiate, up to 300 armed men under Essex's command surged out of the building and headed for the City, not for Whitehall.

They made their way along Fleet Street and up Ludgate Hill, but found the gates at Ludgate closed against them. When they claimed that they came in the queen's name the gates were opened to let them through. Essex hoped to pick up recruits in the City, perhaps from the congregation at the Sunday sermon at Paul's Cross, where he might also find many of the aldermen and persuade them to support his cause. But his wild tales of plots, Spanish and otherwise, against the queen and himself did not carry conviction, and few wanted to attach themselves to his rash enterprise. He went as far as the house in Fenchurch Street belonging to one of the sheriffs, Sir Thomas Smythe, the commander of the trained bands, where he spent time taking refreshment, before Smythe excused himself on the pretext of needing to consult the Lord Mayor. Essex's hope of gaining the support of some of the trained bands had been a forlorn one, and he and his followers then attempted to return the way they had come; but Essex had been declared a traitor, and a force was hastily assembled by the Earl of Cumberland and the Bishop of London. Shots were fired in Gracechurch Street, and when the insurgents reached the west end of Cheapside they were 'chardged about Saint Paules churchyard' by the government's men. Essex's page was killed, and retreating into Cheapside they were again attacked by Cumberland's force. They then went down to the river at Queenhithe and 'there taking as manie boates as they could get, cut the ropes and rowed themselves to Essex house'. When they arrived they discovered that the hostages had been released by one of Essex's cronies who, aware of the impending failure of the scheme, wished to recover some credit at Whitehall, and a siege began, with the defenders stacking books in the windows to block musket fire. Eventually the earls yielded to the inevitable and gave themselves up.[25] They were tried and convicted: Essex was executed, within the Tower, while Southampton was reprieved and received a pardon from King James soon after his accession two years later. The citizenry had supported Essex during his years of royal favour but must have been dismayed by this venture, which threatened the stability of the nation's and the City's governments.

Despite the many changes chronicled by Stow and others, some aspects of the London scene had changed little during the sixteenth century. Timber and tile were still the common building materials, and it remained the practice not to have ostentatious fronts to buildings. William Harrison, writing in the 1580s, commented that it was common in England, 'for example, in most streets of London', that the greatest houses 'have outwardly been very simple and plain to sight, which inwardly have been able to receive a duke with his whole train, and lodge them at their ease'.[26]

As the population increased, so did the level of everyday activity in the streets, markets, shops and workshops. Consequently, the streets were more crowded than before, and congestion, both of pedestrians and vehicles, remained a characteristic and frustrating feature of the city. Jacob Rathgeb, Secretary to the Duke of Württemberg, was in London in 1592 and found that the crowds were such that 'one can scarcely pass along the streets, on account of the throng', and Platter's reaction a few years later was very similar, that 'one simply cannot walk along the streets for the crowd'. This was not a great exaggeration, for Grenade had discovered, fourteen years earlier, that Thames Street was 'extremely narrow, even too narrow. For, owing to the vast quantity of goods which land there, it is necessary to use many large and heavy carts to carry them. As a result, the street is often so blocked that sometimes passers-by are brought to a standstill for a long time.'[27] Thames Street posed a particular problem for the reasons which Grenade mentioned. The number of vessels on the river had increased, as had the volume of the cargoes landed, while the street had remained the same. Indeed, visitors were impressed by the sheer amount of shipping in the Thames, such as de Maisse, who found it 'a magnificent sight to see the number of ships and boats which lie at anchor, insomuch that for two leagues [roughly six miles] you see nothing but ships that serve as well for war as for traffic'.[28]

Something needed to be done, and a set of regulations was introduced by the Common Council in 1586 aimed at reducing stoppages in 'Thames Strete and other Narrowe lanes and places within this Cittie'. The blockages were attributed to the number of vehicles and the stubbornness of their drivers, who would not give way. In Ben Jonson's *Every Man in his humour* (1598), the character Brainworm says to his fellows 'would we were e'en pressed [conscripted], to make porters of; and serve out the remnant of our days, in Thames Street, or at Custom House quay, in a civil war, against the carmen'.[29] Under the regulations of 1586, the carmen if they were intransigent faced imprisonment and the confiscation of their vehicle for a month. Other streets were obstructed by parked vehicles, such as Cheapside and 'many other places of the Cittie to which Carrmen do usuallie resorte'. A set of rules governing parking was issued in 1586, specifying the places where carters could wait for business and the numbers of carts. In streets where markets were held, the orders distinguished between market hours and other times – for example six carts could wait at Leadenhall during market hours and twice that number 'when market is done'. The same arrangement applied at the Royal Exchange, where seven carts could wait 'when the Exchange is done', but none during trading hours. In all, when no market was being held a maximum of sixty-seven carts was allowed to wait for business in the City centre.[30]

As well as the movement of goods, the numbers of people and the range of shops, there was a strong undercurrent of intellectual activity in Elizabethan London, not readily apparent to observers, but an important element nonetheless. Informal networks of enthusiasts were formed to share experiences and information on aspects of mathematics, botany and medicinal recipes, and to compare the contents of their cabinets of curiosities, which were becoming increasingly popular. One of the finest such cabinets in late Elizabethan London was that of Walter Cope, described by Stow as his 'worshipfull frend', which was also witnessed by Platter, who described it as 'stuffed with queer foreign objects in every corner'. They included items from Africa, India and China, charms, weapons and musical instruments, and 'remnants of nature' such as a 'twisted horn of a bull seal', a hairy caterpillar, fish, birds and a pelican's beak.[31] The most prominent group of naturalists at the time lived in the Lime Street area.

Like the polymath John Dee, an influential figure in a range of fields including astrology and alchemy, they were in touch with their Continental counterparts, either directly or through members of the Dutch and French churches in London, such as Emanuel van Meteren, a merchant from Antwerp who lived in London for almost the whole of Elizabeth's reign. Their members rarely ventured into print with their discoveries, perhaps because of the structure of the medical profession and for fear of provoking the wrath of the College of Physicians or the Barber-Surgeons' Company. But they did engage in controversies with more publicity-minded experts. James Garret was a Flemish apothecary in London and in 1597 his stinging criticism of the accuracy of the draft of John Gerard's forthcoming *The Herball or Generall historie of plantes* was enough to cause its publishers, Bonham and John Norton, to delay publication until it was revised. Gerard had also plagiarised others' work without acknowledgment. The book was revised and did eventually appear; it proved to be enduringly popular. Although the Lime Street group shunned Gerard, he was remembered through his book, whereas they were not – they had not published their findings.[32]

Perhaps awareness that authors did not fare so well financially from publication deterred the enthusiasts and collectors. John Stow received twenty shillings and fifty copies 'for his pains in the *Brief Chronicle*', published in 1588, and £3 and forty copies for *A Survey of London*, which appeared ten years later. He told the lawyer John Manningham that he 'made no gains by his travails'.[33] Those who kept journals while travelling abroad, such as merchants, artisans and diplomats, also generally failed to publish their accounts. Some did reach a wider public nevertheless, through the efforts of Richard Hakluyt (1552?–1616), the son of a member of the Skinners' Company. Hakluyt was ordained in 1580 and was appointed a prebendary of Westminster Abbey in 1602, but his chief role was as a collector and assimilator of information on voyages, and as a vigorous advocate of exploration and colonisation. His influential *The Principall Navigations, Voiages and Discoveries of the English Nation* was published in 1589 as a single volume, with a much enlarged three-volume edition in a folio format appearing in 1598–1600. Hakluyt travelled no further afield than Paris, but was the intellectual force behind the expanding horizons of Elizabethan Londoners.

There certainly was enough capacity in London's printing trade for the output of the various groups if they had wished to venture into print. The metropolis dominated the trade. Printers such as Henry Bynneman, whose patron was Sir Christopher Hatton, and John Day kept three or four presses working in their shops. Some indication of the scale of Bynneman's business and the size of the market for books in London is indicated by the fact that when he died in 1584 he had 19,000 books in stock. The market for printed works was large and literate; de Maisse observed that 'there is no youth in the world, poor or rich, that has greater chance of learning than in England'.[34] There was also a market for printed music; in 1575 the queen granted to the composer Thomas Tallis and his younger colleague William Byrd the monopoly of publishing any songs 'that may serve for musicke either in Churche or chamber, or otherwise to be either plaid or soonge'.[35] The queen's printers were kept busy with statutes, proclamations, and even self-justificatory accounts of current news, such as one distributed nationally in 1563 that attributed the failure of the expedition sent to assist the Huguenots in Le Havre to an outbreak of plague there. Sir William Cecil was probably anxious to shift the blame for a foreign policy mishap away from himself.[36]

Such hectic activity, when considered with the congestion in the streets and on the river, reflected the city's industrious and prospering society. By the time that the Tudor dynasty came to an end with Elizabeth's death in 1603, London's population had increased fourfold since Henry VII had taken the throne. This was just one reflection of how dominant the city was within England, in terms of its economic, social, political, legal and cultural influence. And the capital had gained a far wider international reach, too, through its merchants trading with an expanding range of ports across much of the world, and the greater volume and ever-widening range of fine goods that were imported; many such goods reached London's myriad shops and households. Problems remained, for growth brought with it overcrowding and bad living conditions for the poor, and plague outbreaks could not be prevented – the deadliest epidemic yet to hit the city began a few weeks after the queen's death and continued through the summer and autumn of 1603.

The rapid recovery from that and subsequent outbreaks, down to 1665, demonstrated London's social and economic resilience. But the fabric of the city that Stow had known was steadily eroded, by the gradual replacement of buildings, new tastes in materials and styles, Londoners' changing needs and the losses inflicted by fires. A blaze at the north end of the bridge in 1633 wrecked about a third of the houses on the structure itself and nearly eighty more in the parish of St Magnus the Martyr; the Great Fire in 1666 swept away 13,200 houses in the heart of the city, as well as St Paul's, eighty-seven churches, six consecrated chapels and fifty-two halls of the livery companies; and a fire in Southwark ten years later destroyed 620 houses. The properties were rebuilt, but the destruction of Tudor London continued, so that few major clusters remain. The Tower, the Charterhouse, the Guildhall, Westminster Abbey, Westminster Hall and Staple Inn in Holborn, Barnard's Inn nearby, the Merchant Taylors' Company's hall, the halls at the Middle Temple and Gray's Inn, the gatehouses of St John's priory, St James's Palace, Lambeth Palace, Lincoln's Inn and St Bartholomew-the-Great, as well as a number of churches, were all standing when Elizabeth died, and remain – albeit restored, rebuilt or altered. The royal Palace of Whitehall, the focus of the Tudor court and government, was destroyed by a blaze in 1698, and that part of Westminster Palace which had escaped the flames in 1512 was gutted in 1834, with the exception of the hall. The sites of those two royal palaces are now occupied by government offices and the Houses of Parliament. And yet beneath the Ministry of Defence building in Whitehall can be found Henry VIII's wine cellar, which was the undercroft of Cardinal Wolsey's York Place, the predecessor of Whitehall Palace. Parts of Tudor London do indeed remain, but they have to be sought out.

Notes

Abbreviations

APC   *Acts of the Privy Council*
CSPVen   *Calendar of State Papers Relating to English Affairs in the Archives of Venice*
HMC   Historical Manuscripts Commission
L&P   *Letters and Papers, Foreign and Domestic, Henry VIII*
LMA   London Metropolitan Archives
ODNB   Oxford Dictionary of National Biography
TED   R. H. Tawney and Eileen Power, *Tudor Economic Documents*, 3 vols, London, Longmans, 1925
TNA   The National Archives

1 – A Large and Magnificent City

1. Malcolm Letts, *The Travels of Leo of Rozmital through Germany, Flanders, England, France, Spain, Portugal and Italy 1465-1467*, Hakluyt Society, 2nd series, CVIII, 1955, pp. 45, 51, 54.
2. Letts, *Travels of Leo of Rozmital*, pp. 26, 30, 32, 40, 41, 45, 51. For the population of the Flemish cities, Jonathan Israel, *The Dutch Republic: Its Rise, Greatness, and Fall 1477–1806*, Oxford, Clarendon Press, 1995, p. 114.
3. Dominic Mancini, *The Usurpation of Richard the Third*, ed. C. A. J. Armstrong, Oxford, OUP, 1936, pp. 71, 125. C. H. Williams, *English Historical Documents 1485–1558*, London, Eyre & Spottiswood, 1967, pp. 188–9. Charlotte Augusta Sneyd, ed., *A Relation, or rather a true account, of the Island of England*, London, Camden Soc., 1847, pp. 42, 45.
4. Mark Ford, ed., *London: A History in Verse*, Cambridge, Mass, & London, Harvard University Press, 2012, pp. 1, 56–8. Williams, *English Historical Documents*, p. 205.
5. W. G. Hoskins, English provincial towns in the early sixteenth century, in *The Early Modern Town: A Reader*, ed. Peter Clark, London, Longman, 1976, pp. 92–3.

6. Cited in Barney Sloane, *The Black Death in London*, Stroud, History Press, 2011, p. 148.
7. C. L. Kingsford, ed., *Chronicles of London*, Oxford, Clarendon Press, 1905, p. 85. Philippe de Commynes, *Memoirs: The Reign of Louis XI 1461–83*, ed. Michael Jones, London, Penguin, 1972, pp. 194, 397.
8. Chris Skidmore, *Bosworth: The Birth of the Tudors*, London, Weidenfeld & Nicolson, 2013, p. 334.
9. Francis Bacon, *The History of the Reign of King Henry VII*, London, Hesperus, 2007, p. 9.
10. Polydore Vergil, *Anglica Historia*, 1555, ch. xxvi.
11. Kingsford, ed., *Chronicles of London*, p. 193.
12. J. D. Mackie, *The Earlier Tudors, 1485–1558*, Oxford, OUP, 1952, p. 55.
13. Allen B. Hinds, ed., *Calendar of State Papers, Milan*, London, HMSO, 1912, no. 553.
14. Mancini, *Usurpation of Richard the Third*, p. 125.
15. Mancini, *Usurpation of Richard the Third*, pp. 125, 127. Letts, *Travels of Leo of Rozmital*, p. 51.
16. Williams, *English Historical Documents*, p. 189.
17. Mancini, *Usurpation of Richard the Third*, p. 127.
18. Letts, *Travels of Leo of Rozmital*, p. 54. Williams, *English Historical Documents*, p. 189.
19. W. D. Robson-Scott, *German Travellers in England 1400–1800*, Oxford, Blackwell, 1953, p. 16. Sneyd, *A Relation*, pp. 42–3.
20. John Stow, *The Survey of London*, ed. H. B. Wheatley, Dent, London, 1987, p. 308.
21. Letts, *Travels of Leo of Rozmital*, p. 51. Mancini, *Usurpation of Richard the Third*, p. 125. Williams, *English Historical Documents*, p. 189.
22. Williams, *English Historical Documents*, p. 189.
23. R. A. B. Mynors, A. Dalzell and J. M. Estes, eds, *The Correspondence of Erasmus: Letters 1356 to 1534, 1523 to 1524*, vol. 10, Toronto, University of Toronto Press, 1992, p. 471.
24. Dan Lochman, 'Between Country and City: John Colet, Thomas More, and Early Modern Perceptions of London', *Literary London: Interdisciplinary Studies in the Representation of London*, vol. 4, March 2006.
25. Susan Bruce, ed., *Three Early Modern Utopias*, Oxford, OUP, 1999, p. 54.
26. Letts, *Travels of Leo of Rozmital*, p. 53. Bruce, *Three Early Modern Utopias*, p. 54.
27. Derek Keene, *Cheapside before the Great Fire*, London, ESRC, 1985, p. 19.
28. Sneyd, *A Relation, or rather a true account*, p. 42. *CSPVen*, vol. 4, 1527–1533, no. 682. Williams, *English Historical Documents*, p. 189.
29. Margaret Wood, *The English Mediaeval House*, London, Dent, 1965, p. 292.
30. J. G. Nichols, ed., *Chronicle of the Grey Friars of London*, Camden Soc., vol. 53, 1852, p.28. W. D. Hamilton, ed., *A Chronicle of England during the reigns of the Tudors, from A.D. 1485 to 1559, by Charles Wriothesley*, Camden Soc., 2nd series, vol. 11, 1875, I, pp. 5–6.
31. H. S. Cobb, ed., *The Overseas Trade of London: Exchequer Customs Accounts 1480–1*, London Record Soc., 1990, items 11, 204.

32. L. F. Salzman, *Building in England Down to 1540. A Documentary History*, Oxford, Clarendon Press, 1952, p. 185.
33. TED, III, p. 83.
34. Salzman, *Building in England*, p. 560.
35. Henry Littlehales, ed., *The Medieval Records of A London City Church: St Mary At Hill, 1420–1559*, London, Trübner, 1905, pp. 22–5.
36. Mancini, *Usurpation of Richard III*, p. 127.
37. Williams, *English Historical Documents*, p. 189.
38. Stow, *Survey of London*, p. 155.
39. John Guy, *A Daughter's Love: Thomas & Margaret More*, London, Fourth Estate, 2008, pp. 10–13.
40. Stow, *Survey of London*, pp. 66, 121, 232–3.
41. Stow, *Survey of London*, p. 161. Tracy Borman, *Thomas Cromwell*, London, Hodder & Stoughton, 2014, pp. 47–8, 135–9.
42. Letts, *Travels of Leo of Rozmital*, p. 52. Mancini, *Usurpation of Richard III*, p. 127. Robson-Scott, *German Travellers*, p. 15.
43. Rawdon Brown, *Four Years at the Court of Henry VIII*, London, Smith, Elder, 1854, II, p. 69.
44. Brown, *Court of Henry VIII*, I, p. 87.
45. CSPVen, vol. 4, no. 682.

2 – An Organised Society

1. C. H. Williams, *English Historical Documents 1485-1558*, London, Eyre & Spottiswood, 1967, p. 190.
2. Charlotte Augusta Sneyd, ed., *A Relation, or rather a true account, of the Island of England*, London, Camden Soc., 1847, p. 201.
3. Rawdon Brown, *Four Years at the Court of Henry VIII*, London, Smith, Elder, 1854, I, p. 67.
4. Williams, *English Historical Documents*, p. 190.
5. Peter Gwyn, *The King's Cardinal: The Rise and Fall of Thomas Wolsey*, London, Barrie & Jenkins, 1990, p. 438.
6. Malcolm Letts, *The Travels of Leo of Rozmital through Germany, Flanders, England, France, Spain, Portugal and Italy 1465–1467*, Hakluyt Society, 2nd series, CVIII, 1955, pp. 52, 54. Mark Ford, ed., *London: A History in Verse*, Cambridge, Mass, & London, Harvard University Press, 2012, p. 57. *CSPVen*, vol. 4, 1527–1533, no. 682. W. D. Robson-Scott, *German Travellers in England 1400–1800*, Oxford, Blackwell, 1953, pp. 8–9, 17. J. A. Cramer, ed., *The Second Book of the Travels of Nicander Nucius, of Corcyra*, Camden Soc., 1841, p. 10.
7. *CSPVen*, vol. 4, 1527–1533, no. 682.
8. Sneyd, *A Relation, or rather a true account*, pp. 24, 43.
9. Barbara Hanawalt, *Growing up in Medieval London*, Oxford, OUP, 1993, p. 139.
10. Sylvia M. Thrupp, *The Merchant Class of Medieval London*, Ann Arbor, University of Michigan Press, 1989 edn, pp. 104, 111, 158.
11. Steve Rappaport, *Worlds within worlds: structures of life in sixteenth-century London*, Cambridge, CUP, 1989, pp. 36–7, 40. Cramer, ed., *Travels of Nicander Nucius*, p. 10.

12. Caroline M. Barron, *London in the Later Middle Ages: Government and People 1200–1500*, Oxford, OUP, 2004, pp. 218–23.

13. Tom Girtin, *The Mark of the Sword: A narrative history of the Cutlers' Company 1189–1975*, London, Hutchinson Benham, 1975, pp. 65, 86.

14. Thomas Allen, *History and Antiquities of London, Westminster, Southwark, and Parts Adjacent*, London, George Virtue, 1839, III, p. 93.

15. Rappaport, *Worlds within worlds*, p. 48.

16. This and the following paragraphs are based upon: Reginald R. Sharpe, ed., *Calendar of Letter-Books of the City of London: L, Edward IV-Henry VII*, London, 1912, from 1485.

17. Danny Danziger and John Gillingham, *1215: The Year of Magna Carta*, London, Hodder & Stoughton, 2003, p. 292.

18. Charles Welch, *History of The Tower Bridge*, London, Smith, Elder, 1894, pp. 96–7. John Stow, *The Survey of London*, ed. H. B. Wheatley, Dent, London, 1987, p. 370. L&P, III, items 1528–9.

19. Williams, *English Historical Documents*, p. 190.

20. Sneyd, *A Relation, or rather a true account*, pp. 21, 25, 28.

21. Dan Lochman, 'Between Country and City: John Colet, Thomas More, and Early Modern Perceptions of London', *Literary London: Interdisciplinary Studies in the Representation of London*, vol. 4, March 2006.

22. Johan Huizinga, *Erasmus of Rotterdam*, London, Phaidon, 1952, p. 233.

23. John Caius, *A boke or counseill against the disease commonly called the sweate or sweatyng sicknesse*, 1552, p. 22.

24. L&P, II, i, no. 115.

25. John Cherry, *Medieval Goldsmiths*, London, British Museum Press, 2011, p. 76. Allen B. Hinds, ed., *Calendar of State Papers, Milan*, London, HMSO, 1912, no. 552.

26. *Chronicle of London, from 1089 to 1483*, London, 1827, reprinted, Felinfach, Llanerch, 1995, p. 146.

27. TNA, LR2/61, ff. 103v–4v.

28. Thrupp, *Merchant Class of Medieval London*, p. 179. Caroline M. Barron, 'Forster, Agnes (d. 1484)', ODNB.

29. W. D. Hamilton, ed., *A Chronicle of England during the reigns of the Tudors, from A.D. 1485 to 1559, by Charles Wriothesley*, Camden Soc., 2nd series, vol. 11, 1875, I, p. 137.

30. Barron, *London in the Later Middle Ages*, pp. 104–5.

31. H. S.Cobb, ed., *The Overseas Trade of London: Exchequer Customs Accounts 1480–1*, London Record Soc., 1990, passim.

32. Cobb, ed., *Overseas Trade of London* items 40.55. Williams, *English Historical Documents*, p. 90.

33. Rappaport, *Worlds within worlds*, pp. 130–2.

34. J. G. Nichols, ed., *Chronicle of the Grey Friars of London*, Camden Soc., vol. 53, 1852, p. 27.

35. Nichols, ed., *Chronicle of the Grey Friars*, pp. 26–7.

36. Eric Bennett, *The Worshipful Company of Carmen of London*, London, Simpkin Marshall, 1952, pp. 10–17.

3 – Continental Connections

1. C. H. Williams, *English Historical Documents 1485-1558*, London, Eyre & Spottiswood, 1967, p. 189.
2. L&P, XVII, 1542, item 881, no. 17.
3. John Oldland, 'London's Trade in the Time of Richard III', *The Ricardian*, XXIV, 2014, pp. 6–7.
4. Dominic Mancini, *The Usurpation of Richard the Third*, ed. C. A. J. Armstrong, Oxford, OUP, 1936, p. 164.
5. J. G. Nichols, ed., *Chronicle of the Grey Friars of London*, Camden Soc., vol. 53, 1852, p. 25. Edward Hall, *Hall's Chronicle; Containing the History of England, During the Reign of Henry the Fourth ... to the End of the Reign of Henry the Eighth*, London, 1809, pp. 467–8.
6. TED, II, pp. 16–17.
7. E. M. Carus-Wilson, *Medieval Merchant Venturers*, London, Methuen, 1967 edn, pp. xxx, 151–2, 156, 159–60, 182.
8. Allen B Hinds, ed., *Calendar of State Papers, Milan*, London, HMSO, 1912, no. 552.
9. Vincent Gillespie and Susan Powell, eds, *A Companion to the Early Printed Book in Britain, 1476–1558*, Cambridge, Brewer, 2014, pp. 54–5.
10. N. F. Blake, 'Caxton, William, 1415x24–1492'; 'Worde, Wynkyn de (*d.*1534/5)', ODNB.
11. Oldland, 'London's Trade', *The Ricardian*, pp. 1–3, 8–9.
12. TED, I, p. 295.
13. Charles Welch, *History of The Tower Bridge*, London, Smith, Elder, 1894, pp. 94, 97.
14. Rawdon Brown, *Four Years at the Court of Henry VIII*, London, Smith, Elder, 1854, II, pp. 69–75. TED, III, pp. 82–90.
15. Theodor Dumitrescu, *The Early Tudor Court and International Musical Relations*, Aldershot, Ashgate, 2007, pp. 87–93.
16. Brown, *Court of Henry VIII*, I, p. 301.
17. Dumitrescu, *Early Tudor Court*, pp. 70–1, 99–100.
18. Roger Lockyer, ed., *Thomas Wolsey late Cardinal ... by George Cavendish his gentleman-usher*, London, Folio Soc., 1962, p. 53.
19. David Lasocki, 'Bassano, Alvise (*d.* 1554)', ODNB.
20. Peter Holman, *Four and Twenty Fiddlers: The Violin at the English Court 1540–1690*, Oxford, OUP, 1993, pp. 78–9.
21. TNA, C4/8/1.
22. Mary Rose archive, ID No.81A1191. Lasocki, 'Bassano, Alvise (*d.* 1554)', ODNB.
23. Kim W. Woods, Carol M. Richardson and Angeliki Lymberopoulou, *Viewing Renaissance Art*, London, Yale University Press, 2007, p. 270. David Starkey, ed., *Henry VIII: A European Court in England*, London, Collins & Brown, 1991, pp. 32–3.
24. Benvenuto Cellini, *The Life of Benvenuto Cellini*, ed. John Addington Symonds, London, Heron Books, undated, pp. 19–20.
25. Desiderius Erasmus, *Praise of Folly*, London, Penguin, 1993, p. 84.

26. Hans Devisscher, ed., *Antwerp, story of a metropolis*, Ghent, Martial & Snoeck, 1993, pp. 206–7.
27. John Guy, *A Daughter's Love: Thomas & Margaret More*, London, Fourth Estate, 2008, pp. 118, 170.
28. Günther Oestmann, 'Kratzer, Nicolaus, (*b.* 1486/7, *d.* after 1550)', ODNB. Willem Hackmann, 'Nicolaus Kratzer: the King's Astronomer and Renaissance Instrument-Maker', in Starkey, ed., *Henry VIII: A European Court*, pp. 70–3.
29. Susan Foister, 'Holbein, Hans, the younger (1497/8–1543)'; 'Hornebout [Hornebolt], Lucas (*d*, 1544)', ODNB.
30. L&P, X, no. 351.
31. Joan Simon, *Education and Society in Tudor England*, Cambridge, CUP, 1967, pp. 73, 95.
32. John Stow, *The Survey of London*, ed. H. B. Wheatley, Dent, London, 1987, pp. 68–9, 166.
33. Sir George Clark, *A History of the Royal College of Physicians*, I, Oxford, Clarendon Press, 1964, pp. 40–66, 79.

4 – In Sickness and in Poverty

1. Victor Cornelius Medvei and John L. Thornton, *The Royal Hospital of Saint Bartholomew 1123–1973*, London, St Bartholomew's Hospital, 1974, p. 23.
2. W. D. Hamilton, ed., *A Chronicle of England during the reigns of the Tudors, from A.D. 1485 to 1559*, by Charles Wriothesley, Camden Soc., 2nd series, vol. 11, 1875, I, pp. 77–8.
3. John Stow, *Annales, or a general Chronicle of England*, 1631, p. 470. Hamilton, ed., *Chronicle*, I, p. 81.
4. J. G. Nichols, ed., *Chronicle of the Grey Friars of London*, Camden Soc., vol. 53, 1852, p. 28. Hamilton, ed., *Chronicle*, I, pp. 6, 10–11.
5. Caroline M. Barron and Matthew Davies, eds, *The Religious Houses of London and Middlesex*, London, University of London, 2007, pp. 155–9.
6. Christine Merie Fox, 'Henry VII's Almshouse at Westminster', *London Topographical Record*, XXXI, 2015, pp. 29–33.
7. Caroline M. Barron, *London in the Later Middle Ages: Government and People 1200–1500*, Oxford, OUP, 2004, pp. 298–9. Ian Archer, *The History of the Haberdashers' Company*, Chichester, Phillimore, 1991, p. 13. *The endowed charities of ... London*, 1829, pp. 222, 290.
8. Ida Darlington, ed., *London Consistory Court Wills 1492–1547*, London Record Soc., vol. 3, 1967, no. 219.
9. Stow, *Annales*, p. 481.
10. CSPVen, vol. 2, 1509–1519, no. 945.
11. L&P, II, no. 3558, app. no. 38.
12. R. A. B. Mynors and D. F. S. Thomson, *The Correspondence of Erasmus*, vol. II, Toronto & Buffalo, University of Toronto Press, 1975, p. 290.
13. Peter Gwyn, *The King's Cardinal: The Rise and Fall of Thomas Wolsey*, London, Barrie & Jenkins, 1990, pp. 440–1. L&P, IV, no. 4510.
14. Cited in *The Westminster Review*, 1871, p. 45.
15. Mynors and Thomson, *Correspondence of Erasmus*, p. 259.
16. CSPVen, vol. 2, 1509–19, p. 142.

17. Gwyn, *King's Cardinal*, p. 441. F. P. Wilson, *The Plague in Tudor and Stuart London*, Oxford, OUP, 1927, pp. 34–5,56–7.
18. Eric Bennett, *The Worshipful Company of Carmen of London*, London, Simpkin Marshall, 1952, p. 14.
19. LMA, Corporation of London, Common Council Journal, XXV, f. 55.
20. L&P, XIII pt 1, p. 520.
21. CSPVen, vol. 5, 1534–1554, no. 934.
22. Nichols, ed., *Chronicle of the Grey Friars*, p. 70.
23. Paul L. Hughes and James F. Larkin, *Tudor Royal Proclamations Volume I The Early Tudors (1485–1553)*, London, Yale University Press, 1964, pp. 204, 234–5, 259–60, 323. Thomas Paynell, *Moche profitable treatise against the pestilence*, 1534.
24. LMA, Corporation of London, Common Council Journal, XXV, ff. 48–9.
25. Susan Bruce, ed., *Three Early Modern Utopias*, Oxford, OUP, 1999, pp. 64–5.
26. Gwyn, *King's Cardinal*, p.436. Maria Hayward, *Rich Apparel: Clothing and the Law in Henry VIII's England*, Farnham, Ashgate, 2009, p. 20.
27. Charlotte Augusta Sneyd, ed., *A Relation, or rather a true account, of the Island of England*, London, Camden Soc., 1847, pp. 34, 36. Rawdon Brown, *Four Years at the Court of Henry VIII*, London, Smith, Elder, 1854, I, p. 67.
28. C. H. Williams, *English Historical Documents 1485–1558*, London, Eyre & Spottiswood, 1967, p. 208.
29. Nichols, ed., *Chronicle of the Grey Friars*, pp. 30, 35, 37, 39. Hamilton, ed., *Chronicle*, I, pp. 134–5.
30. Bruce, ed., *Three Early Modern Utopias*, p. 24.
31. Linda Clark, ed., *Of Mice and Men: Image, Belief and Regulation in Late Medieval England*, Woodbridge, Boydell, 2005, pp. 153–4.
32. Gwyn, *King's Cardinal*, p. 439. Marjorie Keniston Mackintosh, *Controlling Misbehaviour in England, 1370–1600*, Cambridge, CUP, 1998, pp. 99–101.
33. Neville Williams, *Henry VIII and his court*, London, Weidenfeld and Nicolson, 1971, p. 46.
34. L&P, XVII, item 443.
35. Stow, *Annales*, p. 480.
36. Maarten Hell, Emma Los and Norbert Middelkoop, *Portrait Gallery of the Golden Age*, Amsterdam, Amsterdam Museum, 2014, p. 21.
37. L&P, XIV pt 1, January–July 1539, nos. 940, 941. Hamilton, ed., *Chronicle*, I, pp. 95–7, 99–100.
38. Nichols, ed., *Chronicle of the Grey Friars*, p. 35.
39. Nichols, ed., *Chronicle of the Grey Friars*, p. 42. Hamilton, ed., *Chronicle*, I, p. 85.
40. Charles Welch, *History of the Tower Bridge*, London, Smith, Elder, 1894, pp. 105, 107.
41. *State Papers, Volume I, King Henry the Eighth: Correspondence between the King and his Ministers, 1530–1547*, London, John Murray, 1831, p. 443.
42. TED, I, pp. 115–17.
43. Bruce, ed., *Three Early Modern Utopias*, pp. 57–8.
44. Tom Girtin, *The Mark of the Sword: A narrative history of the Cutlers' Company 1189–1975*, London, Hutchinson Benham, 1975, p. 95.

5 – *Churches, Cloisters and Heretics*

1. John Stow, *The Survey of London*, ed. H. B. Wheatley, Dent, London, 1987, pp. 159, 303, 363.
2. William St.John Hope, *The History of the London Charterhouse*, London, SPCK, 1925, pp. 100–4. Reginald R. Sharpe, ed., *Calendar of Wills Proved and Enrolled in the Court of Husting, London, A.D.1258-A.D.1688*, II, London, John E. Francis, 1890, pp. 233, 309, 572–3, 578–9, 621.
3. TNA, SC6/H.VIII/2396. L&P, XVIII pt 1, p. 132; XXI pt 1, p. 767. Stow, *Survey of London*, p. 372.
4. Stow, *Survey of London*, p. 128.
5. L&P, II, i, no. 115. Caroline M. Barron and Matthew Davies, eds, *The Religious Houses of London and Middlesex*, London, University of London, 2007, p. 86.
6. *Cal. Patent Rolls, 1441–6*, p. 104. *Cal. Close Rolls, 1441–7*, p. 415. *Cal. Papal Registers, 1471–1484*, p. 260.
7. TNA, SC12/25/55, mm.4–19. E. Margaret Thompson, *The Carthusian Order in England*, London, SPCK, 1930, pp. 193–6.
8. TNA, E33/13/1; E23/3.
9. G. W. S. Curtis, ed., *The Passion and Martyrdom of the Holy English Carthusian Fathers: The Short Narration by Dom Maurice Chauncy*, London, SPCK, 1935, pp. 17–18.
10. Stow, *Survey of London*, p. 115. Barron and Davies, eds, *Religious Houses*, pp. 93, 147, 157–8.
11. Barron and Davies, eds, *Religious Houses*, p. 126.
12. Stow, *Survey of London*, p. 128.
13. L&P, IV, 1524–30, no. 952.
14. Sharpe, ed., *Calendar of Wills*, p. 621.
15. L&P, VIII, Jan–July 1535, nos 160, 161. L&P, IX, Aug–Dec 1535, no. 1168.
16. Susan Brigden, *London and the Reformation*, London, Faber, 1989, pp. 46, 64. J. G. Nichols, ed., *Chronicle of the Grey Friars of London*, Camden Soc., vol. 53, 1852, p. 32.
17. C. H. Williams, *English Historical Documents 1485-1558*, London, Eyre & Spottiswood, 1967, p. 656.
18. Stow, *Survey of London*, pp. 131–2. Simon Bradley and Nikolaus Pevsner, *The Buildings of England: London 1: The City of London*, London, Penguin, 1997, pp. 192–3.
19. Stow, *Survey of London*, pp. 181, 281.
20. Stow, *Survey of London*, pp. 226–7.
21. C. J. Kitching, ed., *London and Middlesex Chantry Certificate 1548*, London Record Soc., 16, London, 1980, items 63, 69.
22. Brigden, *London and the Reformation*, pp. 47, 49–61.
23. Brigden, *London and the Reformation*, pp. 36–7.
24. Brigden, *London and the Reformation*, pp. 49–51.
25. Ida Darlington, ed., *London Consistory Court Wills 1492–1547*, London Record Soc., 3, 1967, item 96. L&P, III, 1519–23, no. 3175; IV, 1524–30, no. 952.
26. G. A. Williamson, ed., *Foxe's Book of Martyrs*, London, Secker & Warburg, 1965, p. 70.
27. BL, Cotton MSS, Cleop. E.iv, f. 42. Barron & Davies, eds, *Religious Houses*, pp. 17–18.

28. W. D. Hamilton, ed., *A Chronicle of England during the reigns of the Tudors, from A.D. 1485 to 1559, by Charles Wriothesley*, Camden Soc., 2nd series, vol. 11, 1875, I, p. 7.

29. Cited in S. Thompson, 'Fitzjames, Richard (*d.* 1522)', ODNB.

30. Peter Gwyn, *The King's Cardinal: The Rise and Fall of Thomas Wolsey*, London, Barrie & Jenkins, 1990, p. 40.

31. L&P, II, no. 215. Hamilton, ed., *Chronicle*, p. 9 note g.

32. Williamson, ed., *Foxe's Book of Martyrs*, p. 90.

33. James McDermott, 'Lok, Sir William (1480–1550), mercer and merchant adventurer', ODNB.

34. Paul Arblaster, Gergely Juhász and Guido Latré, eds, *Tyndale's Testament*, Turnhout, Brefols, 2002, pp. 35–7, 118–19, 153. David Daniell, 'Preface' to W. R. Cooper, ed., *The New Testament Translated by William Tyndale*, London, British Library, 2000, pp. xv–xvi.

35. John D. Fudge, *Commerce and Print in the Early Reformation*, Leiden, Brill, 2007, p. 190.

36. L&P, IV(2), no. 4218.

37. Cited in, Arblaster et al, *Tyndale's Testament*, p. 35.

38. Peter Marshall, 'Pakington, Robert (*b.* in or before 1489, *d.* 1536), member of parliament and murder victim', ODNB.

39. *Letters of Henry VIII, 1526–29*, London, Stationery Office, 2001, p. 53.

6 – Dissolutions and New Foundations

1. Caroline M. Barron and Matthew Davies, eds, *The Religious Houses of London and Middlesex*, London, University of London, 2007, pp. 255–7.

2. Barron and Davies, eds, *Religious Houses*, pp. 24, 87.

3. L&P, XIV pt I, Jan–July 1539, item 1354 no. 52; pt II, Aug–Dec 1539, item 133.

4. W. D. Hamilton, ed., *A Chronicle of England during the reigns of the Tudors, from A.D. 1485 to 1559, by Charles Wriothesley*, Camden Soc., 2nd series, vol. 11, 1875, I, p. 87.

5. Susan Brigden, *London and the Reformation*, London, Faber, 1989, p. 395.

6. G. A. Williamson, ed., *Foxe's Book of Martyrs*, London, Secker & Warburg, 1965, pp. 153–4.

7. Hamilton, ed., *Chronicle*, I, p. 86.

8. J. V. Kitto, ed., *St Martin-in-the-Fields: the Accounts of the Churchwardens, 1525–1603*, London, 1901, accounts June 1525–March 1530, pp. 1–20.

9. Hamilton, ed., *Chronicle*, I, pp. 81, 84.

10. John Stow, *The Survey of London*, ed. H. B. Wheatley, Dent, London, 1987, pp. 175, 186.

11. Stow, *Survey of London*, pp. 183, 205, 288.

12. Stow, *Survey of London*, pp. 189, 275.

13. L&P, vol. IX Aug–Dec 1535, items 812, 1059.

14. L&P, XIV part 1 Jan–July 1539, item 967. APC, I, pp. 108, 112, 120.

15. J. G. Nichols, ed., *Chronicle of the Grey Friars of London*, Camden Soc., vol. 53, 1852, p. 52.

16. William St.John Hope, *The History of the London Charterhouse*, London, SPCK, 1925, pp. 178–83. David Knowles and W. F. Grimes, *Charterhouse*, London, Longmans, 1954, p. 86.

17. Stow, *Survey of London*, p. 372.
18. Hamilton, ed., *Chronicle*, I, p. 113.
19. Stow, *Survey of London*, pp. 276, 305.
20. Stow, *Survey of London*, pp. 145, 210.
21. CSPVen, vol. 5, 1534–1554, item 934.
22. Charles Welch, *History of the Tower Bridge*, London, Smith, Elder, 1894, p. 77.
23. Stow, *Survey of London*, pp. 128–9.
24. Nichols, ed., *Chronicle of the Grey Friars*, p. 58.
25. Hamilton, ed., *Chronicle*, I, p. 161. Stow, *Survey of London*, pp. 268, 275.
26. Stow, *Survey of London*, p. 264.
27. Stow, *Survey of London*, p. 166.
28. Hugh Dunthorne, *Britain and the Dutch Revolt 1560–1700*, Cambridge, CUP, 2013, pp. 135–6. Dirk W. Rodgers, 'À Lasco [Laski], John (1499–1560)', ODNB.
29. Victor Cornelius Medvei and John L. Thornton, *The Royal Hospital of Saint Bartholomew 1123–1973*, London, St Bartholomew's Hospital, 1974, pp. 22–5.
30. William C. Carroll, *Fat King, Lean Beggar: Representation of Poverty in the Age of Shakespeare*, Ithaca and London, Cornell University Press, 1996, p. 100. Stow, *Survey of London*, p. 150.
31. TED, II, p. 312.
32. Eric Ives, *The Reformation Experience*, Oxford, Lion Hudson, 2012, p. 182.
33. Paul Slack, *From Reformation to Improvement: Public Welfare in Early Modern England*, Oxford, Clarendon Press, 1998, pp. 20–1.
34. Carroll, *Fat King, Lean Beggar*, pp. 98, 112.
35. Raphael Holinshed, *Holinshed's Chronicles of England, Scotland, and Ireland*, III, London, 1808, p. 1062.
36. Stow, *Survey of London*, p. 113.
37. Slack, *Reformation to Improvement*, pp. 21–2.
38. Hamilton, ed., *Chronicle*, II, pp. 36, 40.

7 – Troubled Times

1. Ida Darlington, ed., *London Consistory Court Wills 1492–1547*, London Record Soc., vol. 3, 1967, nos 183, 207.
2. C. M. Clode, ed., *Memorials of the Guild of Merchant Taylors of the Fraternity of St. John the Baptist in the City of London*, London, 1875, pp. 13, 109.
3. APC, II, pp. 275–7.
4. W. D. Hamilton, ed., *A Chronicle of England during the reigns of the Tudors, from A.D. 1485 to 1559, by Charles Wriothesley*, Camden Soc., 2nd series, vol. 11, 1875, II, pp. 1, 41.
5. Hamilton, ed., *Chronicle*, II, pp. 1, 9. Eric Ives, *The Reformation Experience*, Oxford, Lion Hudson, 2012, pp. 194–5.
6. Henry Littlehales, ed., *The Medieval Records of a London City Church: St Mary At Hill, 1420–1559*, London, Trübner, 1905, pp. 385–91.
7. John Stow, *The Survey of London*, ed. H. B. Wheatley, Dent, London, 1987, pp. 130–1. John Cherry, *Medieval Goldsmiths*, London, British Museum Press, 2011, pp. 76–7. Tom Girtin, *The Mark of the Sword: A narrative history of the Cutlers' Company 1189–1975*, London, Hutchinson Benham, 1975, p. 102.

8. Susan Wabuda, 'Ridley, Nicholas, *c.*1502–1555', ODNB. Hamilton, ed., *Chronicle*, II, p. 38.

9. Clode, ed., *Memorials of the Guild of Merchant Taylors*, p. 103. HMC, *Calendar of the Cecil Papers in Hatfield House, Volume 1, 1306–1571*, London, 1883, p. 103.

10. APC, II, pp. 521–2.

11. J. G. Nichols, ed., *Chronicle of the Grey Friars of London*, Camden Soc., vol. 53, 1852, p. 67.

12. J. G. Nichols, ed., *The Diary of Henry Machyn Citizen and Merchant-Taylor of London (1550–1563)*, Camden Soc., 1848, p. 20.

13. Girtin, *Mark of the Sword*, p. 100. Nichols, ed., *Chronicle of the Grey Friars*, pp. 60–2, 65.

14. Susan Brigden, *London and the Reformation*, London, Faber, 1989, pp. 520–6.

15. Harry Kelsey, *Philip of Spain King of England*, London, I. B. Tauris, 2012, pp. 90, 91, 108. Brigden, *London and the Reformation*, p. 556. *Calendar of State Papers, Spain, vol. 13, 1554–1558*, pp. 49–50.

16. Brigden, *London and the Reformation*, pp. 530–1.

17. Littlehales, ed., *St Mary at Hill*, pp. 397, 403–4, 407.

18. Nichols, ed., *Diary of Henry Machyn*, p. 165.

19. Hamilton, *Chronicle*, II, pp. 99–100.

20. APC, IV, p. 349. Hamilton, ed., *Chronicle*, II, pp. 114, 117, 127.

21. *Calendar of State Papers, Spain, Volume 12, 1554*, pp. 64–5.

22. Brigden, *London and the Reformation*, p. 546.

23. Brigden, *London and the Reformation*, pp. 606–20.

24. Brigden, *London and the Reformation*, pp. 600–4.

25. Williamson, ed., *Foxe's Book of Martyrs*, p. 456.

26. Nichols, ed., *Diary of Henry Machyn*, p. 178.

27. Wallace MacCaffrey, *Elizabeth I*, London, Edward Arnold, 1993, p. 51.

28. Barrett L. Beer, *Tudor England Observed: The World of John Stow*, Stroud, Sutton, 1998, p. 96.

29. Littlehales, ed., *St Mary at Hill*, pp. 411–13.

30. J. V. Kitto, ed., *St Martin-in-The-Fields: the Accounts of the Churchwardens, 1525–1603*, London, 1901, pp. 167–78.

31. Nichols, ed., *Diary of Henry Machyn*, pp. 208, 209, 241.

32. Hamilton, ed., *Chronicle*, II, pp. 143, 146.

33. Peter Sherlock, *Monuments and Memory in Early Modern England*, Aldershot, Ashgate, 2008, pp. 166–7.

34. MacCaffrey, *Elizabeth I*, pp. 114–24.

8 – Prices and Trade

1. J. G. Nichols, ed., *The Diary of Henry Machyn Citizen and Merchant-Taylor of London (1550–1563)*, Camden Soc., 1848, p. 163.

2. David Loades, *Henry VIII*, Stroud, Amberley, 2011, p. 308. G. D. Ramsay, *The City of London in international politics at the accession of Elizabeth Tudor*, Manchester, Manchester University Press, 1975, pp. 50–1.

3. APC, I, p. 284. W. D. Hamilton, ed., *A Chronicle of England during the reigns of the Tudors, from A.D. 1485 to 1559, by Charles Wriothesley*, Camden Soc., 2nd series, vol. 11, 1875, I, pp. 151–2.

4. Hamilton, ed., *Chronicle*, I, p. 148.

5. Hamilton, ed., *Chronicle*, I, p. 158.

6. APC, II, p. 275.

7. Tom Girtin, *The Mark of the Sword: A narrative history of the Cutlers' Company 1189–1975*, London, Hutchinson Benham, 1975, p. 97.

8. Thomas Smith, *A Discourse of the Common Weal of this Realm of England*, ed. Elizabeth Lamond, Cambridge, CUP, 1954, p. 83.

9. J. D. Gould, *The Great Debasement: Currency and the Economy in Mid-Tudor England*, Oxford, Clarendon Press, 1970, p. 83.

10. Gould, *Great Debasement*, pp. 56–7.

11. Steve Rappaport, *Worlds within worlds: structures of life in sixteenth-century London*, Cambridge, CUP, 1989, pp. 128–45.

12. Smith, *Discourse of the Common Weal*, p. 163.

13. Hamilton, ed., *Chronicle*, I, pp. 145, 147, 156, 163, 175; II, pp. 15, 37, 45, 47, 66.

14. Hamilton, ed., *Chronicle*, I, p. 141; II, pp. 15, 29, 30, 46–7, 66.

15. Hamilton, ed., *Chronicle*, II, pp. 70–1, 80–1, 105, 113.

16. Hamilton, ed., *Chronicle*, I, pp. 153–4. John Cordy Jeaffreson, ed., *Middlesex County Records: Volume 1, 1550–1603*, London, 1886, p. 22.

17. Rappaport, *Worlds within worlds*, pp. 146–7, 150–3, 168–70.

18. Gould, *Great Debasement*, pp. 136–7.

19. TED, III, pp. 130–5.

20. TED, I, p. 114. Rappaport, *Worlds within worlds*, pp. 47–8.

21. Clare Williams, *Thomas Platter's Travels in England*, London, Jonathan Cape, 1937, pp. 156–7. William Brenchley Rye, *England as seen by foreigners in the days of Elizabeth and James the First*, London, John Russell Smith, London, 1865, reprinted 2005, p. 7.

22. CSPVen, vol. 6, 1555–1558, no. 884.

23. Ramsay, *City of London*, pp. 49, 74 n. 79.

24. Ramsay, *City of London*, pp. 46–50. APC, vol. 4, pp. 279–81.

25. T. S. Willan, *Studies in Elizabethan Foreign Trade*, Manchester, Manchester University Press, 1959, p. 51.

26. G. B. Harrison and R. A. Jones, eds, *A Journal of all that was accomplished by Monsieur De Maisse, Ambassador in England from King Henri IV to Queen Elizabeth Anno Domini 1597*, London, Nonesuch Press, 1931, pp. 46–7.

27. K. R. Andrews, *Elizabethan Privateering*, Cambridge, CUP, 1964, pp. 16–18, 32–4.

28. Harrison and Jones, eds, *Journal of ... Monsieur De Maisse*, p. 67.

29. Willan, *Elizabethan Foreign Trade*, pp. 313–23. Charles Welch, 'Myddelton, Sir Thomas (1549x56–1631)', revised by Trevor Dickie, ODNB. Rye, *England as seen by foreigners*, p. 104.

30. Harrison and Jones, eds, *Journal of ... Monsieur De Maisse*, pp. 2–3.

31. T. S. Willan, *The Inland Trade*, Manchester, Manchester University Press, 1976, pp. 10, 26–31.

32. Willan, *Inland Trade*, pp. 7, 18–24.
33. Alan D. Dyer, *The City of Worcester in the sixteenth century*, Leicester, Leicester University Press, 1973, p. 105.
34. D. M. Palliser, York under the Tudors: The Trading Life of the Northern Capital, in Alan Everitt, ed., *Perspectives in English Urban History*, London, Macmillan, 1973, pp. 51–2.
35. Willan, *Inland Trade*, pp. 6, 11–13. John Stow, *The Survey of London*, ed. H. B. Wheatley, Dent, London, 1987, pp. 242–3.
36. Rye, *England as seen by foreigners*, p. 52.
37. LMA, Corporation of London, Common Council Journal, XIX, f. 186v.
38. L. Grenade, *The Singularities of London, 1578*, ed. Derek Keene and Ian W. Archer, London Topographical Soc., 175, 2014, p. 105. Malcolm Thick, 'Intensive rabbit production in London and nearby counties in the sixteenth, seventeenth, and eighteenth centuries: an alternative to alternative agriculture', *Agricultural History Review*, vol. 64, 2016, pp. 1–16.
39. Malcolm Thick, 'Market Gardening in England and Wales', in *The Agrarian History of England and Wales, V 1640–1750, pt ii, Agrarian Change*, ed. Joan Thirsk, Cambridge, CUP, 1985, p. 505.
40. John Cordy Jeaffreson, ed., *Middlesex County Records: Volume 1, 1550–1603*, Middlesex County Records Soc., 1886, p. 233.
41. Willan, *Inland Trade*, p. 13. Andrew B. Appleby, *Famine in Tudor and Stuart England*, Stanford, Stanford University Press, 1978, pp. 86, 91.

9 – Cheerful Givers

1. W. R. Cooper, ed., *The New Testament: Translated by William Tyndale*, London, British Library, 2000, p. 390.
2. John Stow, *The Survey of London*, ed. H. B. Wheatley, Dent, London, 1987, p. 117.
3. Shakespeare, *Henry V*, act 1 sc.1.
4. Stow, *Survey of London*, pp. 104, 106, 114, 157, 268.
5. Ian W. Archer, *The Pursuit of Stability: Social Relations in Elizabethan London*, Cambridge, CUP, 1991, p. 177; 'The Charity of Early Modern Londoners', *Trans Royal Hist. Soc.*, 6th series, XII, 2002, p. 237.
6. Thomas Girtin, *The Golden Ram: A Narrative History of the Clothworkers' Company, 1528–1958*, London, Worshipful Company of Clothworkers, 1958, pp. 304–5.
7. Robert Tittler, *Townspeople and Nation: English Urban Experiences, 1540–1640*, Stanford, Stanford University Press, 2001, pp. 103–10.
8. Joan Simon, *Education and Society in Tudor England*, Cambridge, CUP, 1967, p. 306.
9. T. S. Willan, *Studies in Elizabethan Foreign Trade*, Manchester, Manchester University Press, 1959, pp. 191–4.
10. Willan, *Elizabethan Foreign Trade*, p. 194. Ian W. Archer, 'Ramsey {née Dale; other married name Avery}, Mary, Lady Ramsey (d.1601)', ODNB.
11. Stow, *Survey of London*, p. 156.
12. Stow, *Survey of London*, p. 173.

13. L. Grenade, *The Singularities of London, 1578*, ed. Derek Keene and Ian W. Archer, London Topographical Soc., 175, 2014, p. 118.

14. Stow, *Survey of London*, pp. 154–5.

15. Ian W. Archer, 'Spencer, Sir John (*d*.1610)', ODNB.

16. John Nichols, *The Progresses, Processions, and Magnificent Festivities, of King James the First*, I, 1828, p. 160.

17. Ian W. Archer, 'Isham, John (1525–1596)', ODNB.

18. W. K. Jordan, *The Charities of London 1480–1660*, London, Routledge, 2006, pp. 31, 36, 37, 50.

19. Tittler, *Townspeople and Nation*, pp. 101, 121 n. 7.

20. Archer, *Pursuit of Stability*, p. 169.

21. Sarah Williams, ed., *Letters written by John Chamberlain during the Reign of Queen Elizabeth*, Camden Soc., 1861, p. 122.

22. Archer, *Pursuit of Stability*, p. 178.

23. Archer, *Pursuit of Stability*, p. 180.

24. J. G. Nichols, ed., *The Diary of Henry Machyn Citizen and Merchant-Taylor of London (1550–1563)*, Camden Soc., 1848, p. 262.

25. Simon Adams, ed., *Household Accounts and Disbursement Books of Robert Dudley, Earl of Leicester, 1558–1561, 1584–1586*, Camden Soc., 5th series, vol. 6, 1995, pp. 200–1, 203–4.

26. Archer, *Pursuit of Stability*, p. 180.

27. W. K. Jordan, *Philanthropy in England 1480–1660*, London, Routledge, 1959, p. 362.

28. John Stow, *Annales*, ed. Edmond Howes, 1631, pp. 586, 607.

29. Nichols, ed., *Diary of Henry Machyn*, pp.239-40. Stow, *Survey of London*, pp. 199–200. LMA, Common Council Journal, XXI, f. 34r.

30. Edward Griffith, *Cases of supposed exemption from poor rates … with a preliminary sketch of the ancient history of the parish of St. Andrew Holborn*, London, 1831, pp. xxxviii–ix, which gives the month of the explosion as July. Stow, *Annales*, ed. Howes, p. 696.

31. W. H. and H. C. Overall, eds, *Analytical Index To the Series of Records Known As the Remembrancia 1579–1664*, London, 1878, pp. 60–1.

32. J. G. Nichols, ed., *Chronicle of the Grey Friars of London*, Camden Soc., vol. 53, 1852, p. 49. W. D. Hamilton, ed., *A Chronicle of England during the reigns of the Tudors, from A.D. 1485 to 1559, by Charles Wriothesley*, Camden Soc., 2nd series, vol. 11, 1875, I, p. 161; II, p. 6.

33. Stow, *Survey of London*, p. 303.

34. Stow, *Survey of London*, pp. 292, 296. Patrick Collinson, *Archbishop Grindal, 1519–1583: The Struggle for a Reformed Church*, Berkeley, University of California Press, 1979, pp. 153–4.

35. Ian W. Archer, *Religion, Politics, and Society in Sixteenth Century England*, Camden Soc., 5th series, 22, 2003, p. 80 n. 129.

36. Derek Keene, Arthur Burns and Andrew Saint, eds, *St Paul's: The Cathedral Church of London 604–2004*, New Haven & London, Yale University Press, 2004, p. 173.

37. William Dugdale, *The History of St Paul's Cathedral in London, from its Foundation until these Times*, London, 1658, p. 134.

38. Dugdale, *St Paul's*, p. 134. Collinson, *Archbishop Grindal*, p.160. Overall and Overall, eds., *Analytical Index*, I, 336.

39. Overall and Overall, eds., *Analytical Index*, I, 278, 326.

40. Williams, ed., *Letters written by John Chamberlain*, p. 90.

41. Keene et al, eds, *St Paul's*, p. 51.

42. Collinson, *Archbishop Grindal*, pp. 155–6. Thomas Girtin, *The Golden Ram: A Narrative History of the Clothworkers' Company 1528–1958*, London, The Worshipful Company of Clothworkers, 1958, pp. 308–9.

43. Deborah E. Harkness, *The Jewel House: Elizabethan London and the Scientific Revolution*, New Haven & London, Yale University Press, 2007, pp. 2–3.

44. J. M. S. Brooke and A. W. C. Hallen, *The Transcript of the Registers of the United Parishes of S. Mary Woolnoth and S. Mary Woolchurch Haw ... 1538 to 1760*, London, 1886, p. li.

45. Keene et al, eds, *St Paul's*, p. 173.

46. Stow, *Survey of London*, p. 297.

47. Overall and Overall, eds., *Analytical Index*, I, 278. Keene et al, eds, *St Paul's*, p. 173.

10 – Growing Pains

1. W. D. Hamilton, ed., *A Chronicle of England during the reigns of the Tudors, from A.D. 1485 to 1559, by Charles Wriothesley*, Camden Soc., 2nd series, vol. 11, 1875, I, pp. 128–9,134. Betty R. Masters, ed., *Chamber Accounts of the Sixteenth Century*, London Record Soc., 20, 1984, pp. 1–30.

2. G. D. Ramsay, *The City of London in international politics at the accession of Elizabeth Tudor*, Manchester, Manchester University Press, 1975, pp. 35–6.

3. APC, I, pp. 172–3.

4. John Cordy Jeaffreson, ed., *Middlesex County Records: Volume 1, 1550–1603*, London, 1886, p. 19.

5. John Stow and Edmund Howes, *Annales, or A General Chronicle of England*, 1631, p. 689.

6. Frank Aydelotte, *Elizabethan Rogues and Vagabonds*, London, Cass, 1967, pp. 81, 152–4.

7. Hamilton, ed., *Chronicle*, II, pp. 42, 105.

8. W. H. and H. C. Overall, *Analytical Index To the Series of Records Known As the Remembrancia 1579–1664*, London, 1878, pp. 164–5.

9. Aydelotte, *Elizabethan Rogues and Vagabonds*, pp. 79–82, 95.

10. Henry Ellis, *Original Letters Illustrative of English History*, II, London, 1824, pp. 283–6.

11. Joel F. Harrington, *The Faithful Executioner: Life and Death in the Sixteenth Century*, London, Bodley Head, 2013, p. 97.

12. Hamilton, ed., *Chronicle*, I, pp. 145–6; II, p. 71.

13. Sarah Williams, ed., *Letters written by John Chamberlain during the Reign of Queen Elizabeth*, Camden Soc., 1861, p. 135. Barrett L. Beer, *Tudor England Observed: The World of John Stow*, Stroud, Sutton, 1998, p. 45.

14. John Howes, 'A Famyliar and Frendly Discourse', in TED, III, p. 442. Andrew Gurr, *Playgoing in Shakespeare's London*, 2nd edn, Cambridge, CUP, 1996, p. 222.

15. *Calendar of the Cecil Papers in Hatfield House, Volume 2, 1572–1582*, London, HMSO, 1888, pp. 164, 222.

16. L. Grenade, *The Singularities of London, 1578*, ed. Derek Keene and Ian W. Archer, London Topographical Soc., 175, 2014, p. 141. William Brenchley Rye, *England as seen by foreigners in the days of Elizabeth and James the First*, London, John Russell Smith, 1865, reprinted 2005, p. 192 n. 22.

17. Grenade, *Singularities*, p. 145.

18. Grenade, *Singularities*, pp. 50–1.

19. Tom Girtin, *The Mark of the Sword: A narrative history of the Cutlers' Company 1189–1975*, London, Hutchinson Benham, 1975, pp. 143, 149. Ian W. Archer, *The History of the Haberdashers' Company*, Chichester, Phillimore, 1991, pp. 61, 63.

20. Sir George Clarke, *A History of the Royal College of Physicians of London*, Oxford, Clarendon Press, 1964, pp. 114–15. Margaret Pelling and Frances White, 'Cornet, Charles', 'Gossen, Gerard or Garrett', in *Physicians and Irregular Medical Practitioners in London 1550–1640*, London, Centre for Metropolitan History, 2004.

21. E. S. Roberts, ed., *The Works of John Caius, TM.D.*, 'A boke or counseil against the ... sweate or sweatyng sicknesse (1552)', p. 11, Cambridge, CUP, 1912.

22. APC, 1577–1578, pp. 387–8.

23. LMA, Corporation of London, Common Council Journal, XX pt 2, f. 453v.

24. Paul L. Hughes and James F. Larkin, *Tudor Royal Proclamations, Volume II The Later Tudors (1553–1587)*, London & New Haven, Yale University Press, 1969, pp. 420, 432. APC, 1577–1578, pp. 22, 40.

25. HMC, *Calendar of the Manuscripts of the Marquess of Salisbury*, vol.II, 1888, p. 224.

26. LMA, Common Council Journal, XIX, f. 217r; XX pt I, ff. 62r,126v,163v.

27. HMC, *Manuscripts of the Marquess of Salisbury*, vol. II, p. 222.

28. LMA, Corporation of London, Common Council Journal, XXI, ff. 285r-6v.

29. LMA, Corporation of London, Common Council Journal, XIX, ff. 186,187.

30. LMA, Corporation of London, Common Council Journal, XVIII, f. 136r–v; XXI, f. 351v.

31. LMA, Corporation of London, Common Council Journal, XX, part i, f. 113r.

32. Lawrence Manley, ed., *London in the Age of Shakespeare: An Anthology*, London & Sydney, Croom Helm, 1986, pp. 184–5. C. C. Knowles and P. H. Pitt, *The History of Building Regulation in London 1189–1972*, London, Architectural Press, 1972, pp. 12–13.

33. Ian W. Archer, *The Pursuit of Stability: Social Relations in Elizabethan London*, Cambridge, CUP, 1991, p. 184.

34. Williams, ed., *Letters written by John Chamberlain*, p. 142.

35. John Howes, 'Famyliar and Frendly Discourse', in TED, III, pp. 427, 428, 429, 438.

36. Howes, 'Famyliar and Frendly Discourse', in TED, III, pp. 429, 437–8.

37. Howes, 'Famyliar and Frendly Discourse', in TED, III, p. 437.

38. APC, 1592, pp. 182–3, 203–4, 221, 232; 1592–3, pp. 22–3, 342–3.

39. Edwin Freshfield, *The Vestry Minute Book of The Parish of St. Margaret Lothbury in the City of London 1571–1677*, London, 1887, pp. 25–30.

40. Stephen Porter, *Lord Have Mercy Upon Us: London's Plague Years*, Stroud, Tempus, 2005, pp. 75–7.

11 – Recreation and Show

1. Anna Keay, *The Elizabethan Tower of London: The Haiward and Gascoyne plan of 1597*, London Topographical Soc., 158, 2001, p. 28.

2. John Stow, *The Survey of London*, ed. H. B. Wheatley, Dent, London, 1987, p. 360. Clare Williams, *Thomas Platter's Travels in England*, London, Cape, 1937, pp. 168–70.

3. Sarah Williams, ed., *Letters written by John Chamberlain during the Reign of Queen Elizabeth*, Camden Soc., 1861, p. 102.

4. Stow, *Survey of London*, p. 86–7, 95–6. *CSPVen*, vol. 15, 1617–1619, p. 257. W. H. and H. C. Overall, *Analytical Index To the Series of Records Known As the Remembrancia 1579–1664*, London, 1878, p. 17.

5. Stephen Gosson, *The Schoole of Abuse*, 1579, trans. R. S. Bear, The University of Oregon, 2000.

6. William Brenchley Rye, *England as seen by foreigners in the days of Elizabeth and James the First*, London, John Russell Smith, 1865, new edn 2005, p. 111. Lawrence Manley, *Literature and culture in early modern London*, Cambridge, CUP, 1995, p. 41.

7. David Cressy, *Bonfires and Bells: National Memory and the Protestant Calendar in Elizabethan and Stuart England*, London, Weidenfeld & Nicolson, 1989, pp. 75–6, 90–1.

8. Jerry Brotton, *This Orient Isle: Elizabethan England and the Islamic World*, London, Allen Lane, 2016, p. 70.

9. Lawrence Manley, ed., *London in the Age of Shakespeare*, Beckenham, Croom Helm, 1986, pp. 39–40.

10. Iain Fenlon, ed., *The Renaissance: From the 1470s to the end of the 16th century*, London, Macmillan, 1989, pp. 328–9.

11. L. Grenade, *The Singularities of London, 1578*, ed. Derek Keene and Ian W. Archer, London Topographical Soc., 175, 2014, p. 117.

12. Overall and Overall, *Analytical Index*, p.275. Fenlon, ed., *The Renaissance*, p. 328.

13. Lorna Hutson, 'Lanier [née Bassano], Emilia (*bap.* 1569, *d.* 1645)', ODNB.

14. Michael I. Wilson, 'Lanier, Nicholas, (*bap.*1588, *d.*1666), musician and art dealer', ODNB.

15. Grenade, *Singularities*, p. 129.

16. William Carew Hazlitt, *The Livery Companies of the City of London*, London, 1892, pp. 310–11.

17. Grenade, *Singularities*, p. 129. Victor von Klarwill, *Queen Elizabeth and some Foreigners*, London, John Lane The Bodley Head, 1928, pp. 325–6.

18. J. G. Nichols, ed., *The Diary of Henry Machyn Citizen and Merchant-Taylor of London (1550–1563)*, Camden Soc., 1848, pp. 96, 270–1, 294.

19. Von Klarwill, *Queen Elizabeth and some Foreigners*, p. 326.
20. Philip Butterworth, *Theatre Of Fire: Special Effects in Early English and Scottish Theatre*, London, Soc. for Theatre Research, 1998, pp. 24–5.
21. Von Klarwill, *Queen Elizabeth and some Foreigners*, p.327. Grenade, *Singularities*, pp. 131, 133.
22. Grenade, *Singularities*, p. 129. Von Klarwill, *Queen Elizabeth and some Foreigners*, p. 327.
23. Nichols, ed., *Diary of Henry Machyn*, p. 271.
24. Grenade, *Singularities*, pp. 130–1.
25. Butterworth, *Theatre Of Fire*, p. 14.
26. Von Klarwill, *Queen Elizabeth and some Foreigners*, pp. 326–7. Grenade, *Singularities*, pp. 133, 183.
27. G. W. Groos, ed., *The Diary of Baron Waldstein. A Traveller in Elizabethan England*, London, Thames & Hudson, 1981, p. 172.
28. Grenade, *Singularities*, p. 135.
29. Stow, *Survey of London*, p. 377. Grenade, *Singularities*, pp. 78, 82.
30. Julian Bowsher, *Shakespeare's London Theatreland: Archaeology, History and Drama*, London, Museum of London Archaeology, 2012, p. 30. John Dover Wilson, *Life in Shakespeare's England*, Cambridge, CUP, 1913, p. 166.
31. Overall and Overall, *Analytical Index*, I, 9.
32. Andrew Gurr, *Playgoing in Shakespeare's London*, Cambridge, CUP, 2nd edn, 1996, pp. 70–1, 215, 265.
33. Overall and Overall, eds, *Alphabetical Index*, I, 635, 646.
34. Richard Dutton, 'Tilney, Edmund (1535/6–1610)', ODNB.
35. Gurr, *Playgoing*, p. 139.
36. APC, 30, 1599–1600, pp. 395–8, 411.
37. Overall and Overall, eds, *Alphabetical Index*, I, 295, 553–4.
38. Overall and Overall, eds, *Alphabetical Index*, I, 317, 319.
39. Anthony Munday and others, *Thomas More*, London, Nick Hern Books, 2005, pp. xvi,xxi.
40. Williams, *Thomas Platter's Travels*, p. 170. Brotton, *This Orient Isle*, p. 176.
41. Rye, *England as seen by foreigners*, p. 215.
42. Gurr, *Playgoing*, pp. 219, 222. Rye, *England as seen by foreigners*, p. 215.
43. Rye, *England as seen by foreigners*, pp. 88, 215.
44. W. D. Robson-Scott, *German Travellers in England 1400–1800*, Oxford, Blackwell, 1953, pp. 62–3.

12 – London around 1600

1. John Stow, *The Survey of London*, ed. H. B. Wheatley, Dent, London, 1987, pp. 132, 242–33, 264, 309.
2. Clare Williams, *Thomas Platter's Travels in England*, London, Cape, 1937, p. 157.
3. Stow, *Survey of London*, pp. 248, 254, 259, 262, 266.
4. Stow, *Survey of London*, p. 253.
5. Stow, *Survey of London*, pp. 74, 178, 190, 317, 233, 309, 313.
6. Stow, *Survey of London*, pp. 74–5, 167.
7. Stow, *Survey of London*, p. 281.

8. Stow, *Survey of London*, pp. 116–17, 382–3.

9. Stow, *Survey of London*, pp. 20–1, 115.

10. Stow, *Survey of London*, pp. 134, 135, 318. Harry J. Powell, *Glass Making in England*, Cambridge, CUP, 1923, pp. 29–30. Lothrop Withington, ed., *Elizabethan England*, London, Walter Scott, 1876, p. 90.

11. Stow, *Survey of London*, p. 115.

12. Stow, *Survey of London*, pp. 276, 333, 347, 354.

13. Stow, *Survey of London*, pp. 123–4, 187–8, 206.

14. Stow, *Survey of London*, pp. 359, 371.

15. Stow, *Survey of London*, pp. 113–14. Anna Keay, *The Elizabethan Tower of London: The Haiward and Gascoyne plan of 1597*, London Topographical Soc., 158, 2001, pp. 60, 62.

16. Stow, *Survey of London*, pp. 116, 149, 376, 378, 383.

17. Stow, *Survey of London*, pp. 375, 376.

18. Stow, *Survey of London*, p. 347, 349, 389.

19. Stow, *Survey of London*, pp. 175–6, 274, 332.

20. Stow, *Survey of London*, p. 302.

21. Stow, *Survey of London*, p. 207.

22. G. B. Harrison and R. A. Jones, eds, *A Journal of all that was accomplished by Monsieur De Maisse, Ambassador in England from King Henri IV to Queen Elizabeth Anno Domini 1597*, London, Nonesuch Press, 1931, p. 3.

23. John Stow and Edmund Howes, *Annales, or A General Chronicle of England*, 1631, pp. 791–2.

24. J. V. Kitto, ed., *St Martin-in-the-Fields: the Accounts of the Churchwardens, 1525–1603*, 1901, p. 406.

25. HMC, *Calendar of the Manuscripts of the Most Honourable the Marquess of Bath*, V, London, HMSO, 1980, pp. 278–9.

26. Withington, ed., *Elizabethan England*, p. 115.

27. William Brenchley Rye, *England as seen by foreigners in the days of Elizabeth and James the First*, London, John Russell Smith, 1865, reprinted 2005, p. 7. Williams, *Thomas Platter's Travels*, p. 174. L. Grenade, *The Singularities of London, 1578*, ed. Derek Keene and Ian W. Archer, London Topographical Soc., 175, 2014, p. 92.

28. Harrison and Jones, eds, *Journal of … Monsieur De Maisse*, pp. 2–3.

29. Ben Jonson, *Every Man in his Humour*, ed. Simon Trussler, London, Methuen, 1986, p. 43, Act 3: Sc 1.

30. Eric Bennett, *The Worshipful Company of Carmen of London*, London, Simpkin Marshall, 1952, pp. 26–7.

31. Peter C. Mancall, *Hakluyt's Promise: An Elizabethan Obsession for an English America*, New Haven & London, Yale University Press, 2007, pp. 156–7.

32. Deborah E. Harkness, *The Jewel House: Elizabethan London and the Scientific Revolution*, New Haven & London, Yale University Press, 2007, pp. 15–19.

33. Frank Arthur Mumby, *Publishing and Bookselling*, London, Jonathan Cape, 1934 edn, p. 89.

34. Harrison and Jones, eds, *Journal of … Monsieur De Maisse*, p. 13.

35. Craig Monson, 'Byrd, William (1539x43–1623)', ODNB.

36. Andrew Pettegree, *The Invention of News: How the world came to know about itself*, New Haven & London, Yale University Press, 2014, p. 87.

Bibliography

Anon, *The endowed charities of ... London*, 1829

Anon, *Chronicle of London, from 1089 to 1483*, London, 1827, reprinted, Felinfach, Llanerch, 1995

Anon, *Letters of Henry VIII, 1526–29*, London, Stationery Office, 2001

Adams, Simon, ed., *Household Accounts and Disbursement Books of Robert Dudley, Earl of Leicester, 1558–1561, 1584–1586*, Camden Soc., 5th series, vol. 6, 1995

Allen, Thomas, *History and Antiquities of London, Westminster, Southwark, and Parts Adjacent*, London, George Virtue, 1839

Andrews, K. R., *Elizabethan Privateering*, Cambridge, CUP, 1964

Appleby, Andrew B., *Famine in Tudor and Stuart England*, Stanford, Stanford University Press, 1978

Arblaster, Paul, Gergely Juhász and Guido Latré, eds, *Tyndale's Testament*, Turnhout, Brefols, 2002

Archer, Ian W., *The Pursuit of Stability: Social Relations in Elizabethan London*, Cambridge, CUP, 1991

Archer, Ian, *The History of the Haberdashers' Company*, Chichester, Phillimore, 1991

Archer, Ian W., *Religion, Politics, and Society in Sixteenth Century England*, Camden Soc., 5th series, 22, 2003

Archer, Ian W., 'The Charity of Early Modern Londoners', *Trans Royal Hist. Soc.*, 6th series, XII, 2002

Aydelotte, Frank, *Elizabethan Rogues and Vagabonds*, London, Cass, 1967

Bacon, Francis, *The History of the Reign of King Henry VII*, London, Hesperus, 2007

Barron, Caroline M., *London in the Later Middle Ages: Government and People 1200–1500*, Oxford, OUP, 2004

Barron, Caroline M., and Matthew Davies, eds, *The Religious Houses of London and Middlesex*, London, University of London, 2007

Beer, Barrett L., *Tudor England Observed: The World of John Stow*, Stroud, Sutton, 1998

Bennett, Eric, *The Worshipful Company of Carmen of London*, London, Simpkin Marshall, 1952

Bowsher, Julian, *Shakespeare's London Theatreland: Archaeology, History and Drama*, London, Museum of London Archaeology, 2012

Bradley, Simon, and Nikolaus Pevsner, *The Buildings of England: London 1: The City of London*, London, Penguin, 1997

Brigden, Susan, *London and the Reformation*, London, Faber, 1989

Brooke, J. M. S., and A. W. C. Hallen, *The Transcript of the Registers of the United Parishes of S. Mary Woolnoth and S. Mary Woolchurch Haw ... 1538 to 1760*, London, 1886

Brotton, Jerry, *This Orient Isle: Elizabethan England and the Islamic World*, London, Allen Lane, 2016

Brown, Rawdon, *Four Years at the Court of Henry VIII*, London, Smith, Elder, 1854

Bruce, Susan, ed., *Three Early Modern Utopias*, Oxford, OUP, 1999

Butterworth, Philip, *Theatre Of Fire: Special Effects in Early English and Scottish Theatre*, London, Soc. for Theatre Research, 1998

Caius, John, *A boke or counseill against the disease commonly called the sweate or sweatyng sicknesse*, 1552

Carroll, William C., *Fat King, Lean Beggar: Representation of Poverty in the Age of Shakespeare*, Ithaca and London, Cornell University Press, 1996

Carus-Wilson, E. M., *Medieval Merchant Venturers*, London, Methuen, 1967

Cellini, Benvenuto, *The Life of Benvenuto Cellini*, ed. John Addington Symonds, London, Heron Books, undated

Cherry, John, *Medieval Goldsmiths*, London, British Museum Press, 2011

Clark, Sir George, *A History of the Royal College of Physicians*, I, Oxford, Clarendon Press, 1964

Clark, Linda, ed., *Of Mice and Men: Image, Belief and Regulation in Late Medieval England*, Woodbridge, Boydell, 2005

Clark, Peter, ed., *The Early Modern Town: A Reader*, London, Longman, 1976

Clode, C. M., ed., *Memorials of the Guild of Merchant Taylors of the Fraternity of St. John the Baptist in the City of London*, London, 1875

Cobb, H. S., ed., *The Overseas Trade of London: Exchequer Customs Accounts 1480–1*, London Record Soc., 1990

Collinson, Patrick, *Archbishop Grindal, 1519–1583: The Struggle for a Reformed Church*, Berkeley, University of California Press, 1979

Commynes, Philippe de, *Memoirs: The Reign of Louis XI 1461–83*, ed. Michael Jones, London, Penguin, 1972

Cooper, W. R., ed., *The New Testament Translated by William Tyndale*, London, British Library, 2000

Cramer, J. A., ed., *The Second Book of the Travels of Nicander Nucius, of Corcyra*, Camden Soc., 1841

Cressy, David, *Bonfires and Bells: National Memory and the Protestant Calendar in Elizabethan and Stuart England*, London, Weidenfeld & Nicolson, 1989

Curtis, G. W. S., ed., *The Passion and Martyrdom of the Holy English Carthusian Fathers: The Short Narration by Dom Maurice Chauncy*, London, SPCK, 1935

Danziger, Danny, and John Gillingham, *1215: The Year of Magna Carta*, London, Hodder & Stoughton, 2003

Darlington, Ida, ed., *London Consistory Court Wills 1492–1547*, London Record Soc., vol. 3, 1967

Devisscher, Hans, ed., *Antwerp, story of a metropolis*, Ghent, Martial & Snoeck, 1993

Dugdale, William, *The History of St Paul's Cathedral in London, from its Foundation until these Times*, London, 1658

Dumitrescu, Theodor, *The Early Tudor Court and International Musical Relations*, Aldershot, Ashgate, 2007

Dunthorne, Hugh, *Britain and the Dutch Revolt 1560–1700*, Cambridge, CUP, 2013

Dyer, Alan D., *The City of Worcester in the sixteenth century*, Leicester, Leicester University Press, 1973

Ellis, Henry, *Original Letters Illustrative of English History*, London, 1824

Erasmus, Desiderius, *Praise of Folly*, London, Penguin, 1993

Everitt, Alan, ed., *Perspectives in English Urban History*, London, Macmillan, 1973

Fenlon, Iain, ed., *The Renaissance: From the 1470s to the end of the 16th century*, London, Macmillan, 1989

Ford, Mark, ed., *London: A History in Verse*, Cambridge, Mass, & London, Harvard University Press, 2012

Fox, Christine Merie, 'Henry VII's Almshouse at Westminster', *London Topographical Record*, XXXI, 2015

Freshfield, Edwin, *The Vestry Minute Book of The Parish of St. Margaret Lothbury in the City of London 1571–1677*, London, 1887

Fudge, John D., *Commerce and Print in the Early Reformation*, Leiden, Brill, 2007

Gillespie, Vincent, and Susan Powell, eds, *A Companion to the Early Printed Book in Britain, 1476–1558*, Cambridge, Brewer, 2014

Girtin, Thomas, *The Golden Ram: A Narrative History of the Clothworkers' Company, 1528–1958*, London, Worshipful Company of Clothworkers, 1958

Girtin, Tom, *The Mark of the Sword: A narrative history of the Cutlers' Company 1189–1975*, London, Hutchinson Benham, 1975

Gosson, Stephen, *The Schoole of Abuse*, 1579, trans. R. S. Bear, The University of Oregon, 2000

Gould, J. D., *The Great Debasement: Currency and the Economy in Mid-Tudor England*, Oxford, Clarendon Press, 1970

Grenade, L., *The Singularities of London, 1578*, ed. Derek Keene and Ian W. Archer, London Topographical Soc., 175, 2014

Griffith, Edward, *Cases of supposed exemption from poor rates ... with a preliminary sketch of the ancient history of the parish of St. Andrew Holborn*, London, 1831

Groos, G. W., ed., *The Diary of Baron Waldstein. A Traveller in Elizabethan England*, London, Thames & Hudson, 1981

Gurr, Andrew, *Playgoing in Shakespeare's London*, 2nd edn, Cambridge, CUP, 1996

Guy, John, *A Daughter's Love: Thomas & Margaret More*, London, Fourth Estate, 2008

Gwyn, Peter, *The King's Cardinal: The Rise and Fall of Thomas Wolsey*, London, Barrie & Jenkins, 1990

Hall, Edward, *Hall's Chronicle; Containing the History of England, During the Reign of Henry the Fourth ... to the End of the Reign of Henry the Eighth*, London, 1809

Hamilton, W. D., ed., *A Chronicle of England during the reigns of the Tudors, from A.D. 1485 to 1559, by Charles Wriothesley*, Camden Soc., 2nd series, vol. 11, 1875

Hanawalt, Barbara, *Growing up in Medieval London*, Oxford, OUP, 1993

Harkness, Deborah E., *The Jewel House: Elizabethan London and the Scientific Revolution*, New Haven & London, Yale University Press, 2007

Harrington, Joel F., *The Faithful Executioner: Life and Death in the Sixteenth Century*, London, Bodley Head, 2013

Harrison, G. B., and R. A. Jones, eds, *A Journal of all that was accomplished by Monsieur De Maisse, Ambassador in England from King Henri IV to Queen Elizabeth Anno Domini 1597*, London, Nonesuch Press, 1931

Hayward, Maria, *Rich Apparel: Clothing and the Law in Henry VIII's England*, Farnham, Ashgate, 2009

Hazlitt, William Carew, *The Livery Companies of the City of London*, London, 1892

Hell, Maarten, Emma Los and Norbert Middelkoop, *Portrait Gallery of the Golden Age*, Amsterdam, Amsterdam Museum, 2014

Holinshed, Raphael, *Holinshed's Chronicles of England, Scotland, and Ireland*, London, 1808

Holman, Peter, *Four and Twenty Fiddlers: The Violin at the English Court 1540–1690*, Oxford, OUP, 1993

Hope, William St.John, *The History of the London Charterhouse*, London, SPCK, 1925

Hughes, Paul L., and James F. Larkin, *Tudor Royal Proclamations Volume I The Early Tudors (1485–1553)*, London, Yale University Press, 1964; *Volume II The Later Tudors (1553–1587)*, London & New Haven, Yale University Press, 1969

Huizinga, Johan, *Erasmus of Rotterdam*, London, Phaidon, 1952

Israel, Jonathan, *The Dutch Republic: Its Rise, Greatness, and Fall 1477–1806*, Oxford, Clarendon Press, 1995

Ives, Eric, *The Reformation Experience*, Oxford, Lion Hudson, 2012

Jeaffreson, John Cordy, ed., *Middlesex County Records: Volume 1, 1550–1603*, Middlesex County Records Soc., 1886

Jordan, W. K., *Philanthropy in England 1480–1660*, London, Routledge, 1959

Jordan, W. K., *The Charities of London 1480–1660*, London, Routledge, 2006

Keay, Anna, *The Elizabethan Tower of London: The Haiward and Gascoyne plan of 1597*, London Topographical Soc., 158, 2001

Keene, Derek, *Cheapside before the Great Fire*, London, ESRC, 1985

Keene, Derek, Arthur Burns and Andrew Saint, eds, *St Paul's: The Cathedral Church of London 604–2004*, New Haven & London, Yale University Press, 2004

Kelsey, Harry, *Philip of Spain King of England*, London, I. B. Tauris, 2012

Kingsford, C. L., ed., *Chronicles of London*, Oxford, Clarendon Press, 1905

Kitching, C. J., ed., *London and Middlesex Chantry Certificate 1548*, London Record Soc., 16, London, 1980

Kitto, J. V., ed., *St Martin-in-the-Fields: the Accounts of the Churchwardens, 1525–1603*, London, 1901

Klarwill, Victor von, *Queen Elizabeth and some Foreigners*, London, John Lane The Bodley Head, 1928

Knowles, C. C., and P. H. Pitt, *The History of Building Regulation in London 1189–1972*, London, Architectural Press, 1972

Knowles, David, and W. F. Grimes, *Charterhouse*, London, Longmans, 1954

Letts, Malcolm, *The Travels of Leo of Rozmital through Germany, Flanders, England, France, Spain, Portugal and Italy 1465–1467*, Hakluyt Society, 2nd series, CVIII, 1955

Littlehales, Henry, ed., *The Medieval Records of A London City Church: St Mary At Hill, 1420–1559*, London, Trübner, 1905

Loades, David, *Henry VIII*, Stroud, Amberley, 2011

Lochman, Dan, 'Between Country and City: John Colet, Thomas More, and Early Modern Perceptions of London', *Literary London: Interdisciplinary Studies in the Representation of London*, vol. 4, March 2006

Lockyer, Roger, ed., *Thomas Wolsey late Cardinal ... by George Cavendish his gentleman-usher*, London, Folio Soc., 1962

MacCaffrey, Wallace, *Elizabeth I*, London, Edward Arnold, 1993

Mackie, J. D., *The Earlier Tudors, 1485–1558*, Oxford, OUP, 1952

Mackintosh, Marjorie Keniston, *Controlling Misbehaviour in England, 1370–1600*, Cambridge, CUP, 1998

Mancall, Peter C., *Hakluyt's Promise: An Elizabethan Obsession for an English America*, New Haven & London, Yale University Press, 2007

Mancini, Dominic, *The Usurpation of Richard the Third*, ed. C. A. J. Armstrong, Oxford, OUP, 1936

Manley, Lawrence, ed., *London in the Age of Shakespeare*, Beckenham, Croom Helm, 1986

Masters, Betty R., ed., *Chamber Accounts of the Sixteenth Century*, London Record Soc., 20, 1984, pp. 1–30.

Medvei, Victor Cornelius, and John L. Thornton, *The Royal Hospital of Saint Bartholomew 1123–1973*, London, St Bartholomew's Hospital, 1974

Mumby, Frank Arthur, *Publishing and Bookselling*, London, Jonathan Cape, 1934

Mynors, R. A. B., A. Dalzell and J. M. Estes, eds, *The Correspondence of Erasmus: Letters 1356 to 1534, 1523 to 1524*, vol. 10, Toronto, University of Toronto Press, 1992

Mynors, R. A. B., and D. F. S. Thomson, *The Correspondence of Erasmus*, vol. II, Toronto & Buffalo, University of Toronto Press, 1975

Nichols, J. G., ed., *The Diary of Henry Machyn Citizen and Merchant-Taylor of London (1550–1563)*, Camden Soc., 1848

Nichols, J. G., ed., *Chronicle of the Grey Friars of London*, Camden Soc., vol. 53, 1852

Nichols, John, *The Progresses, Processions, and Magnificent Festivities, of King James the First*, I, 1828

Oldland, John, 'London's Trade in the Time of Richard III', *The Ricardian*, XXIV, 2014

Overall, W. H. and H. C., eds, *Analytical Index To the Series of Records Known As the Remembrancia 1579–1664*, London, 1878

Paynell, Thomas, *Moche profitable treatise against the pestilence*, 1534.

Pettegree, Andrew, *The Invention of News: How the world came to know about itself*, New Haven & London, Yale University Press, 2014

Porter, Stephen, *Lord Have Mercy Upon Us: London's Plague Years*, Stroud, Tempus, 2005

Porter, Stephen, *Shakespeare's London: Everyday Life in London 1580–1616*, Stroud, Amberley, 2009

Powell, Harry J., *Glass Making in England*, Cambridge, CUP, 1923

Ramsay, G. D., *The City of London in international politics at the accession of Elizabeth Tudor*, Manchester, Manchester University Press, 1975

Rappaport, Steve, *Worlds within worlds: structures of life in sixteenth-century London*, Cambridge, CUP, 1989

Roberts, E. S., ed., *The Works of John Caius, TM.D.* Cambridge, CUP, 1912

Robson-Scott, W. D., *German Travellers in England 1400–1800*, Oxford, Blackwell, 1953

Rye, William Brenchley, *England as seen by foreigners in the days of Elizabeth and James the First*, London, John Russell Smith, London, 1865, reprinted 2005

Salzman, L. F., *Building in England Down to 1540. A Documentary History*, Oxford, Clarendon Press, 1952

Sharpe, Reginald R., ed., *Calendar of Letter-Books of the City of London: L, Edward IV–Henry VII*, London, 1912

Sharpe, Reginald R., ed., *Calendar of Wills Proved and Enrolled in the Court of Husting, London, A.D.1258–A.D.1688*, II, London, John E. Francis, 1890

Sherlock, Peter, *Monuments and Memory in Early Modern England*, Aldershot, Ashgate, 2008

Simon, Joan, *Education and Society in Tudor England*, Cambridge, CUP, 1967

Skidmore, Chris, *Bosworth: The Birth of the Tudors*, London, Weidenfeld & Nicolson, 2013

Slack, Paul, *From Reformation to Improvement: Public Welfare in Early Modern England*, Oxford, Clarendon Press, 1998

Sloane, Barney, *The Black Death in London*, Stroud, History Press, 2011

Smith, Thomas, *A Discourse of the Common Weal of this Realm of England*, ed. Elizabeth Lamond, Cambridge, CUP, 1954

Sneyd, Charlotte Augusta, ed., *A Relation, or rather a true account, of the Island of England*, London, Camden Soc., 1847

Starkey, David, ed., *Henry VIII: A European Court in England*, London, Collins & Brown, 1991

Stow, John, *Annales, or a general Chronicle of England*, ed. Edmond Howes, 1631

Stow, John, *The Survey of London*, ed. H. B. Wheatley, Dent, London, 1987

Tawney, R. H., and Eileen Power, *Tudor Economic Documents*, 3 vols, London, Longmans, 1925

Thick, Malcolm, 'Intensive rabbit production in London and nearby counties in the sixteenth, seventeenth, and eighteenth centuries: an alternative to alternative agriculture', *Agricultural History Review*, vol. 64, 2016, pp. 1–16

Thirsk, Joan, ed., *The Agrarian History of England and Wales, V 1640–1750, pt ii, Agrarian Change*, Cambridge, CUP, 1985

Thompson, E. Margaret, *The Carthusian Order in England*, London, SPCK, 1930

Thrupp, Sylvia M., *The Merchant Class of Medieval London*, Ann Arbor, University of Michigan Press, 1989

Tittler, Robert, *Townspeople and Nation: English Urban Experiences, 1540–1640*, Stanford, Stanford University Press, 2001

Vergil, Polydore, *Anglica Historia*, 1555

Welch, Charles, *History of The Tower Bridge*, London, Smith, Elder, 1894

Willan, T. S., *Studies in Elizabethan Foreign Trade*, Manchester, Manchester University Press, 1959

Willan, T. S., *The Inland Trade*, Manchester, Manchester University Press, 1976

Williams, C. H., *English Historical Documents 1485-1558*, London, Eyre & Spottiswood, 1967

Williams, Clare, *Thomas Platter's Travels in England*, London, Jonathan Cape, 1937

Williams, Neville, *Henry VIII and his court*, London, Weidenfeld & Nicolson, 1971

Williams, Sarah, ed., *Letters written by John Chamberlain during the Reign of Queen Elizabeth*, Camden Soc., 1861

Williamson, G. A., ed., *Foxe's Book of Martyrs*, London, Secker & Warburg, 1965

Wilson, F. P., *The Plague in Tudor and Stuart London*, Oxford, OUP, 1927

Wilson, John Dover, *Life in Shakespeare's England*, Cambridge, CUP, 1913

Withington, Lothrop, ed., *Elizabethan England*, London, Walter Scott, 1876

Wood, Margaret, *The English Mediaeval House*, London, Dent, 1965

Woods, Kim W., Carol M. Richardson and Angeliki Lymberopoulou, *Viewing Renaissance Art*, London, Yale University Press, 2007

Index

Addle St 208
Aldermanbury 208
Aldersgate 127
Aldgate 12, 15, 171, 214
Alehouses 16, 76, 191
All Hallows Stane 103
All Hallows the Great 107, 154
All Hallows the Less 77
All Hallows, Bread St 90
All Hallows, Gracechurch 90
All Hallows, Honey Lane 97
Allen, Giles 199
Allen, Sir John 216
Alleyn, Edward 199
Almshouses 64, 67-8, 153-4, 158
Ammonio, Andreas 69
Amsterdam 142, 155
Antwerp 9-10, 48, 49, 50, 51, 52, 55, 58, 97, 127, 133, 139, 140, 141-2, 146, 156, 157, 160
Apprentices 29-30, 140-1
Archery 77-8
Armourers' Company 31, 176
Arnold, Richard 96
Arthur, Prince 62, 85
Artillery Garden, Society of the 78
Ascham, Roger 128
Audley, Sir Thomas 106, 107
Augmentations, Court of 105, 106, 120
Augsburg 52, 151, 184
Augustinian Friary 84, 106, 110
Austin Friars 20, 22, 60, 90, 97, 106
Aylmer, John 165, 167

Bacon, Francis 178
Badoer, Andrew 27, 75
Baker, Richard 196
Baltic Sea 52, 136, 142, 144, 145, 150, 155
Bankside 188, 198, 199, 202, 204
Banning, Paul 217
Barbary Company 144
Barber Surgeons' Company 63, 117, 178, 222
Barnard's Castle 43
Barnard's Inn 224
Barne, Sir George 138
Barnes, Robert 97, 128
Bartholomew Fair 79, 80, 121
Basel 58, 60
Basinghall St 208
Bassano family 56-7, 60, 192
Batmanson, John 99
Baynard's Castle 24, 133, 147, 193
Beamond, Thomas 67
Bear Garden 189, 199, 204
Becket, Thomas à 17, 107, 130
Bedlam, see Bethlehem Hospital
Beggars 65, 73, 74, 94, 161, 171, 184
Bell-ringing 11, 90, 190-1
Bergen-op-Zoom 51
Bermondsey Abbey 86, 106
Berwick 148
Bethlehem Hospital 65, 104, 111, 214
Bibles 96-8, 102
Billingsgate 15, 20, 42, 66, 137, 138, 213

Billingsley, Richard 101
Birchin Lane 209
Birckmann, Franz 52, 96
Bishopsgate 12, 42, 169, 198, 214
Black Death 11-12, 20, 84
Black Friars 83, 84, 88, 107
Blackfriars 106
Blackfriars playhouse 200, 204, 205-6
Blacksmiths' Company 31
Blackwell Hall 47, 114, 208
Blanch Appleton 32
Blossoms Inn 149, 208
Blue Coat School see Christ's Hospital
Boar's Head, playhouse 198
Boleyn, Anne 99
Bolton 149
Bonfoire, Robert 177
Bonner, Edmund 102, 119, 123, 126, 128, 166
Bonvix, alisas Bonvise, Anthony 47
Book trade 52, 105, 167, 222-3
Borough, The 43
Botolph Wharf 20
Boulogne 132
Bowes, Sir Jerome 212
Bowes, Martin 100, 104
Bowling alleys 76, 171-2, 211
Bowyers Row 210
Bread St 42, 66, 113, 208
Bread Street Hill 209
Brescia 57
Breten, Thomas 13
Brewers' Company 68
Bridewell Hospital 111-13, 155, 168, 172, 174

Bridewell Palace 43-4, 85, 207, 217
Bridge House 35, 54
Bridge Ward Without 115
Bristol 11, 156
Brittany 52, 137
Broad St 157, 158, 212
Broken Wharf 185
Bromley, Sir Thomas 194
Brown, William 117
Bruges 9, 10, 26, 49, 51, 52, 53, 142
Brune, Walter and Rose 65
Brussels 9, 10
Bucklesbury 19, 22, 209, 210
Budge Row 16, 210
Bulmar, Bevis 185
Burbage family 199
Burcot 148
Busino, Orazio 190
Bynneman, Henry 223
Byrd, William 223

Cabot, John 50
Caen 147
Caius, John 37, 178
Calais 49, 132
Campeggio, Cardinal Lorenzo 85
Candish, John 193
Candlewick St 16, 43, 209
Canonbury 159
Canterbury 115
Capel, Sir William 24
Carlisle 11
Carmelite Friars see White Friars
Carthusians 37, 84, 99, 100
Carwarden, Sir Thomas 107, 127
Cavendish, George 56
Caxton, William 52
Cecil, William, Lord Burghley 112, 201, 223
Cellini, Benvenuto 58
Cephalonia 52
Chamberlain, John 183, 189
Champneys, Sir John 22
Chancery, Inns of 15, 109
Chantries 91, 102, 116-17
Chapel Royal 128-9, 204
Chapman, Thomas 101
Chapuys, Eustace 60
Charles V 122, 123
Charterhouse, The 39, 57, 84-5, 86, 87-8, 89, 94, 99-100, 101, 105-6, 108, 128, 217
Cheapside 16, 17, 20, 24, 31, 38, 41-2, 79, 98, 124, 130, 138, 166, 194, 195, 208, 210, 218, 219, 221, 224

Chelsea 151
Chester 11, 149
Chester Inn 108
Chettle, Henry 203
Chircheman, John 67
Cholmeley, William 140
Cholmley, Sir Richard 55, 208
Christ's Hospital 113, 114, 155, 156, 168
Churches, parish 83, 90-1, 102-5, 109, 117-19
Churchyard, Thomas 160
Clemens, Peter 163
Clerkenwell 79
Clink Liberty 16
Cloak Lane 31
Clopton, Hugh 209
Cloth trade 16, 46-7, 53, 139-41, 148
Clothworkers' Company 32, 68, 154, 155, 166
Coldharbour 20, 212
Coleman St 31, 208, 209
Colet, John 19, 60-2, 90, 94
Cologne 10, 51, 52, 96
Commynes, Philippe de 12
Companies, livery 29, 31-6, 117, 133, 140-1, 176-7, 193
Compton, William, Lord 159
Constantinople 10
Coopers' Company 154
Cope, Walter 221
Corinth 40
Cornet, Charles 177
Cornhill 15, 38, 42, 157, 173, 185, 209, 216
Coventry 11, 115
Coverdale, Miles 102
Cox, Richard 216
Cranmer, Thomas 62, 110, 118, 126
Cremona 57
Crete 52
Crime 75-7, 170-5
Cripplegate 199
Cromwell, Thomas 22-3, 60, 72, 80, 99, 107, 157
Crooked Lane 162
Crosby Hall 22, 47, 159
Cross Keys 198
Crossed Friars 89-90, 101
Crutched Friars 212
Cumberland, George, Earl of 146, 217, 219
Curtain, The 198, 202, 204
Custom House 20, 66, 157, 221
Cutlers' Company 31, 68, 119, 176

Damme 51

Day, John 127, 223
Dee, John 221
Delft, Francois van der 217
Denmark 48, 110, 136, 143
Diet 36-8
Dimmock, John 144
Dixie, Wolstan 194, 197
Dobbs, Sir Richard 113
Dogs 74, 181-2, 211
Dowgate 217
Dowgate Hill 213
Drake, Sir Francis 217
Draper, Christopher 193
Drapers' Company 68, 134
Dudley, Edmund 24
Dudley, John, Duke of Northumberland 121
Dudley, Lord Guildford 121, 125
Dugdale, Sir William 165
Durham 11
Durham House 109, 121
Dutch Church 106, 110, 175, 221
Dyers' Company 33

East India Company 144, 155, 156, 158
East Smithfield 162, 193
Eastcheap 16, 22, 41, 43, 150, 198
Eastland Company 144
Edward III 22
Edward IV 12, 48, 79
Edward VI 109, 110, 112, 116, 121
Elizabeth, Queen 109, 110, 113, 116, 128, 130, 145, 147, 157, 172, 223
Elizabeth of York 25, 57
Elsing Spital 65, 109, 115
Ely House 216
Emden 142
Empson, Richard 24
Erasmus, Desiderius 18, 28, 37, 55, 58-9, 61-2, 69, 71, 98, 119
Essex 35, 121, 147
Essex House 218
Essex, Robert, Earl of 218-20
Evil May Day 54-5, 119, 203
Executions 126-7
Exeter 11, 49

Fairs 79-80, 114
Faversham 147
Fenchurch St 16, 120, 218
Fetter Lane 162, 215
Fires 20, 64, 66, 109, 163, 212, 224

Fish   37, 40, 42-3, 51, 143, 150
Fish St   170
Fish Street Hill   42, 209
Fishmongers' Company   40, 117
Fitzjames, Richard   94-5
Fitzwilliams, William   90
Flanders   46, 47, 49, 51, 52, 56
Fleet St   52, 125, 215, 218
Fleet, River   16, 42-3
Fleetwood, William   172-3, 174, 180
Flemish   16, 46, 54, 214
Florence   10, 17, 27, 46
Florida   145
Forman, Robert   97
Fortune, The   199, 202, 205
Foster Lane   124, 208, 210
Foster, Stephen and Agnes   39
Foxe, John   127
France   143, 176
Franciscius, Andreas   10, 16, 17, 18, 20, 22, 26, 27, 36, 40, 46
Frankfurt   52, 145
Frankland, William   154
Franklin, John   167
Fraternities   92-3
French Church   110, 175, 221
Friars   34, 86
Friday St   42
Frith, John   128
Fugger family   133, 184
Fulham   151
Fullers' Company   32, 33, 48

Galliardello, Mark Anthony   192
Gallors, Nicholas Des   110
Gaming   76-7
Garland, John   90
Garret, James   222
Gascony   52
Genoa   27, 46, 155
Gerard, John   222
Germany   46, 51, 127, 136, 143, 145, 148, 155, 176
Gershow, Frederick   190, 191, 205-6
Ghent   9, 10
Gibson, Avise   153
Gillis, Pieter   58, 59
Girdlers' Company   68
Giustinian, Sebastian   24, 54, 56, 69
Globe, The, playhouse   199, 202, 204, 205
Gloucester   115
Gold Lane   215

Golden Lane   199, 214
Goldsmiths   17
Goldsmiths' Company   29, 38
Goldsmiths' Row   17
Gosson, Stephen   190, 199, 205
Gossenius, Gerard   177
Gracechurch St   38, 42, 43, 198, 210, 219
Gray's Inn   215, 224
Gray's Inn Lane   215
Great Fire   19, 224
Great Yarmouth   148, 151
Grenade, L.   150, 157, 174-5, 193, 194-7, 198, 204, 220
Gresham College   158, 207
Gresham, John   156
Gresham, Sir Richard   66
Gresham, Sir Thomas   141, 144, 156-8
Grey Friars   38, 83, 88
Grey, Lady Jane   121, 125
Griffiths, William   77
Grindal, Edmund, Archbishop of Canterbury   128, 165, 167
Grocers' Company   30, 31, 63, 67, 154, 156
Grocyn, William   61
Grove, Nicholas   116
Grub St   210
Guildhall   16, 193, 194, 196, 224
Gunpowder   162-3, 196
Gutter Lane   210
Gybbes, John   101

Haberdashers' Company   68, 162, 173, 176
Hackney   151
Hakluyt, Richard   222
Hall, Edward   27, 55
Halstead   156
Hamburg   142, 143
Hanseatic League   40, 47, 48, 142
Harrison, William   212, 220
Harvel, Edmund   56
Hat-makers   33
Hatton, Sir Christopher   168, 216
Hawkins, Sir John   217
Helston   148
Heneage, Sir Thomas   170
Henley-on-Thames   149
Henry VII   12, 24, 25, 48, 50, 57, 67, 68, 87, 88, 157
Henry VII's almshouse   67
Henry VIII   55-7, 58, 77, 85, 88, 98, 105, 108, 111, 114, 122, 132
Henslowe, Philip   199

Hentzner, Paul   147, 175, 190, 204, 205
Hickman, Rose   97, 127
Hide, George   116
Hill, Thomas   13, 38
Hilliard, Nicholas   210
Hills, Richard   153
Hinde, Thomas   91
Holbein, Hans   58-60
Holborn   15, 138, 151, 215, 216
Holborn Bridge   43
Holgill, William   68
Holinshed, Raphael   113, 191
Holland   20, 137, 151
Holland, Roger   126
Holmden, Edward   156
Holy Trinity the Less   126
Holy Trinity, Aldgate   37, 84, 86-7, 88, 89, 100, 106, 152
Holy Trinity, Minories   161
Honey Lane   42, 208
Horenbout, Lucas   60
Hospitals   64-5, 67, 68, 109-14, 115
Houghton, John   99, 100
Houndsditch   152, 211
Howes, John   111, 112, 174, 184-5
Huguenots   223
Hull   147
94-6
Hunsdon, Henry, Lord   192
Hunter, William   126

Iceland   48, 51
Immigration   53-5, 175-6
Influenza   12
Inns of Court   15, 170, 207
Ipswich   115, 149
Ironmonger Lane   209, 210
Ironmongers' Company   29
Isham, John   160
Islington   172

Jennings, Sir Stephen   90
Joan of Kent   119
Jonson, Ben   220
Judd, Andrew   153
Jurden, Henry   117

Katherine of Aragon   99
Keble, Henry   91
Kensington   151
Kerbie, John   90
Keswick   148, 149, 151
Kiechel, Samuel   205
King's Lynn   47, 147
Kingston-upon-Thames   21, 125
Knightrider St   63

Knolles, Thomas 39
Kratzer, Nicolaus 59-60

Lambe, William 154
Lambeth Palace 224
Lamport 160
Lanier, Alphonso 192
Large, Robert 209
Lasko, John à 110
Latimer, Hugh 112, 126
Latimer, John, Lord 86
Laxton, Sir William 91, 133
Layton, Richard 113
Lea, River 148-9
Leadenhall 33, 35, 48, 157, 161, 221
Leadenhall St 119
Leather Lane 215
Le Havre 223
Leicester, Robert, Earl of 161, 192
Leland, John 86
Levant Company 144, 155
Levison, Nicholas 90
Lily, William 61
Lime St 221, 222
Linacre, Thomas 61-3
Lincoln's Inn 162, 224
Livorno 155
Lock, William 97
Lodge, Sir Thomas 91
Lollardy 94, 102
Lombard St 46, 100, 157, 209
London Bridge 11, 12, 17-18, 20, 42, 66, 74, 107, 125, 170, 175, 224
London Wall 210
Long, John 91
Lord Mayor's show 193-7
Lothbury 208
Lowe, Thomas 145
Lucca 27, 46
Ludgate 15, 39, 125, 219
Ludgate Hill 15, 166, 198, 219
Lyme Regis 148

Machyn, Henry 132, 194
Maisse, André Hurault, Sieur de 145, 146, 147, 217, 220, 223
Major, or Mair, John 11
Mancini, Domenico 10, 14, 15, 16, 18, 21, 23, 48, 209
Manningham, John 222
Manutius, Aldus 62
Mark Lane 32
Market gardening 150-1
Markets 35, 41-3, 136, 150
Marshalsea prison 123
Martens, Dirk 59

Mary, Queen 110, 116, 121, 122, 125, 128, 132
Maypoles 119, 120
Mazzoni, Guido 57
Mechelen 9
Memo, Dionysius 55-6
Mercers' Company 29, 30, 31, 49, 50, 52, 61-2, 67, 98, 109, 115, 117, 130, 154, 156, 160
Merchant Adventurers' Company 49-50, 53, 55, 142, 143-4, 145, 160
Merchant Taylors' Company 31, 67, 117, 120, 153, 195, 207, 224
Merchant Taylors' School 154, 207
Merchants 11, 143-7, 160-1
Messina 40
Meteren, Emanuel van 222
Metsys, Quentin 58, 59
Michiel, Giovanni 143
Middelburg 20, 142, 147
Middlemore, Hugh 99
Milan 10, 17, 57
Milborne, Sir John 89
Militia 77-8, 134, 218
Milk St 42, 208
Milton 147, 148
Mincing Lane 32, 147
Minories 212
Monasteries 83-90; 100-2, 105-8
Monkwell St 153
More, Sir Thomas 18-19, 22, 37, 39, 58, 59, 69, 74, 76, 81, 96, 99, 111, 203-4
Morley, Thomas 192
Morocco 144, 146, 155, 156, 217
Morris, Peter 185
Mortality, Bills of 72, 180
Morwen, John 166
Mulcaster, Richard 197
Munday, Anthony 199, 203
Munich 52
Muscovy Company 144
Music 55-7, 191-3, 206
Myddelton, Sir Thomas 146

Nantwich 162
Naples 10
Netherlands 141-3, 175
New Fish Street 42
Newcastle 11, 148
Newgate 15, 39, 100, 215
Newgate St 16, 106
Newington Butts playhouse 198
Nicholas, Sir Ambrose 153
Noialles, Antoine de 124, 217

Norfolk, Thomas, Duke of 130
Norland, Thomas 13
Normandy 20
North, Sir Edward 106, 108
Northumberland House 211
Norton Folgate 60
Norwich 11, 150
Nucius, Nicander 28, 30
Nuremburg 52, 145, 173

Old Bailey 171
Old Fish Street Hill 212
Old Jewry 209, 210
Oldbourne Hall 212
Opiciis, Benedictus de 55
Oudenarde 51
Oxford 115, 125, 148, 155

Pace, Richard 61
Packington, Augustine 96
Packington, Robert 98
Padua 178
Paesschen, Hendryck van 157
Pardon Churchyard 109
Paris 10, 112, 222
Paris Garden, Bankside 189
Parish Clerks' Company 68
Parish registers 72
Parvish, Henry 145
Pasqualigo, Piero 24
Paternoster Row 164
Paul's Cross 24, 54, 66, 105, 119, 123, 124, 218
Paul's Wharf 171
Paulet, William 106
Paynell, Thomas 73
Peele, George 197
Peyton, Sir John 214
Philip II 122, 125
Physicians, College of 62-3, 177-8, 222
Pie Corner 213
Pie-bakers' Company 34
Pilkington, James 166
Pisa 46
Pistoia 71
Plague 11-12, 41, 68-9, 70-4, 80, 141, 178-82, 184-7, 202, 214, 223
Platter, Thomas 143, 174, 189, 191, 204, 205, 208, 220, 221
Playhouses 198-206
Plymouth 147
Pole, Edmund 122
Pope, Sir Thomas 106
Popham, Sir John 84
Poplar 215
Popplau, Nikolaus von 27
Population 10, 25, 182, 223
Porter, John 102

Portsoken Ward 88, 100, 136
Poultney's Inn 212
Poultry 16, 31, 42, 209, 210
Poverty 64, 65-6, 93-4, 139, 161-2
Poyntz, Ferdinando 147
Prices 41, 74, 135-8, 150
Printing 52
Privateering 145-6
Pullison, Sir Thomas 217
Purveyance 43-4

Queenhithe 15, 138

Ramsey, Lady Mary 156, 161
Ramsey, Sir Thomas 156
Ratcliff 153, 162, 215
Rathgeb, Jacob 143, 220
Rawson, Richard 13
Red Lion playhouse 198
Rede, Sir Robert 84
Reid, Richard 133
Renard, Simon 123
Revell, John 165, 167
Rich, Sir Richard 133
Richard III 12, 48
Richmond, John 169
Ridley, Nicholas 110, 112, 113, 119, 123, 126
Ridolfi, Roberto 130
Roach, Sir William 133
Rochester 147
Rogers, John 102, 126
Rome 10, 17
Rose, The, playhouse 199, 204, 205
Rouen 145, 192
Rovezzano, Benedetto da 58
Royal Exchange 157-8, 207, 217, 221
Rozmital, Leo of 9
Rue, Andrew and John 52
Ruremund, Christofell van 97
Ruremund, Hans van 96
Ryc 147

Sagudino, Nicolo 54
St Alphage 109
St Andrew, Holborn 61, 162, 215
St Andrew Undershaft 60, 90, 119, 207
St Andrew's Hill 43
St Anne, Aldersgate 109, 127
St Anne-in-the-Willows 163
St Anthony's School 61, 110
St Augustine, London Wall 107
St Bartholomew's fair 79, 80
St Bartholomew's Hospital 88, 106

St Bartholomew's priory 39, 64, 111
St Botolph, Aldgate 87, 117, 187
St Botolph, Billingsgate 103
St Botolph, Bishopsgate 60, 103, 161, 187
St Dunstan-in-the-East 217
St Edmund the King 91
St Ethelberga, Bishopsgate St 124
St Ewin, Newgate Market 106
St George, Botolph Lane 104
St Giles, Cripplegate 109, 128, 163
St Giles-in-the-Fields 124, 215
St Helen, Bishopsgate 153, 156, 158
St Helen, Bishopsgate nunnery 47, 86, 89, 101
St James Clerkenwell 186
St James the Less hospital 79
St James's fair 79
St James's Palace 207, 224
St John Zachary 92
St John's priory 39, 90, 94, 224
St Katherine Coleman 211
St Katherine Cree 107, 119
St Katherine, Fraternity of 44, 72
St Katherine's Hospital 25, 67, 88, 114, 115
St Katherine-by-the-Tower 16, 114, 187, 214
St Leonard, Foster Lane 104, 216
St Magnus the Martyr 20, 79, 224
St Margaret Lothbury 186
St Margaret Moses 126
St Margaret Pattens 66, 103, 210
St Margaret, Westminster 25, 124
St Martin-in-the-Fields 103, 129, 186, 218
St Martin, Ironmonger Lane 118
St Martin-le-Grand 66, 89, 107, 172, 177, 210, 212
St Martin Ludgate 163
St Martin-in-the-Vintry 93
St Mary Aldermary 91
St Mary Axe 210
St Mary Bethlehem, see Bethlehem Hospital
St Mary without Bishopsgate 65, 111
St Mary Bothaw 103
St Mary de Graces 101

St Mary-at-Hill 118-19, 123, 129, 213
St Mary Magdalene, Bermondsey 86
St Mary Matfellon 94
St Mary Outwich 155
St Mary Overy 64, 84, 89, 106, 125
St Mary-le-Querne 42
St Mary-le-Strand 109
St Mary Woolchurch Haw 42, 167
St Mary Woolnoth 89
St Mary's nunnery 39, 88, 101
St Matthew, Friday St 118
St Michael, Cornhill 93, 207, 216
St Michael Paternoster Royal 67
St Mildred, Bread St 66
St Nicholas, Cole Abbey 117, 123
St Nicholas Shambles 106, 171, 210
St Olave, Southwark 125, 183, 213
St Omer 52
St Paul's cathedral 16, 24, 67, 96, 102, 103, 109, 118, 163-8, 189, 193, 197, 216-17, 218, 224
St Paul's churchyard 16, 52, 129, 196, 219
St Paul's School 61-2, 115
St Peter the Apostle 90
St Peter, Cornhill 61, 103, 117
St Saviour (St Mary Overy), Southwark 183
St Saviour, Bermondsey 86
St Sepulchre 101
St Thomas of Acon 61, 110
St Thomas's Hospital 64, 113-14, 155
St Vedast, Foster Lane 124, 210
Salisbury 11
Sandwich 147
Savorgnano, Mario 20, 27, 28
Savoy Hospital 68, 113, 123, 172
Schaseck 9, 17, 19, 23, 25, 28
Schaumburg, Wilmolt von 17
Schools 61-2, 110, 114, 115, 153, 154-5, 156
Seething Lane 216
Serne's Tower 22
Seville 40
Seymour, Edward, Duke of Somerset 108-9, 116
Shaa, Sir John 90

Shakespeare, William 77, 151, 153, 204
Shene 43
Shoe Lane 212
Shoreditch 13, 101, 121, 151, 215
Sidney, Sir Philip 217
Skevington, Sir John 89, 93
Skinners' Company 68
Skipton 154
Sluis 51
Smith, Sir Thomas 134
Smith, William 173, 196
Smithfield 64, 76, 79, 119, 126, 191, 213
Smythe, Sir Thomas 219
Somerset Place 109, 207
Soncino, Raimondo de 38, 51
Soper Lane 210
Soranzo, Giacomo 73, 107
Southampton 53
Southampton, Thomas, Earl of 218-19
Southwark 15-16, 33, 54, 64, 79, 89, 115, 125, 139, 140, 159, 172, 213
Spain 46, 52, 145, 158
Spencer, Sir John 156, 158-60
Sports 189-90
Stade 142, 147
Staper, Richard 155-6
Staple Inn 224
Steelyard 40, 47, 48, 49, 60, 96, 116, 142
Stettin-Pomerania, Philip Julius, Duke of 190, 205-6
Stocks Market 42
Stokker, Sir William 13
Stow, John 17, 22, 23, 88, 103, 104, 107, 111, 127, 152, 153, 156, 157, 163, 164, 167, 174, 188, 190, 191, 198, 207-16, 222
Strand, The 15, 108, 218
Strand Inn 109
Sugar refining 146-7
Sutton Valence 154
Swan, The 199, 201, 204
Sweat, The 12, 13, 14, 69-70, 80, 141, 178
Sweden 143
Switzerland 127
Symmes, William 39

Tallis, Thomas 223
Tate, Sir Richard 103

Taxation 133
Temple, The 224
Temple Bar 125
Tetzel, Gabriel 9
Thames, River 10, 15, 78, 140
Thames St 16, 21, 210, 213, 220-1
Theatre, The 198, 199, 200, 204
Threadneedle St 31, 157
Throwstone, John 210
Thurston, Sir John 54
Thwaites, Sir Thomas 89
Tilney, Sir Edmund 201, 203
Tombs, destruction of 103-4, 130
Torregiano, Pietro 25, 57, 58
Toulouse 52, 147
Tournai 51
Tower of London 11, 15, 18, 24, 43, 55, 125, 188, 224
Tower Hill 16, 114, 153, 159, 162, 214
Tower St 16
Trevisano, Andrea 10, 17, 20, 26, 28, 29, 37, 75
Tuke, Sir Brian 70
Tull, John 144
Tunstall, Cuthbert 96
Turkey Company 144
Tyball, John 97
Tyburn 76, 100
Tynbygh, William 99
Tyndale, William 96, 97, 98, 102, 128

Underwood, Philip 87
Utrecht 52
Utrecht, Treaty of 48

Venice 10, 17, 20, 46, 52, 53, 55, 56, 71, 143, 144, 145, 156
Vergil, Polydore 96
Verzelini, Jacob 212
Vincent, Dr John 98
Vintners' Company 68
Vintry, The 173, 210
Virginia Company 144
Vlissingen 40, 147

Waits, City 192, 194, 195
Walbrook 210, 213
Waldstein, Baron 197
Walker, Humphrey 57
Walsingham, Sir Francis 216, 217

Wapping 215
Warde, John 13
Ware 149
Warner, John and Robert 90
Watermen 49, 74, 149, 213
Watling St 16, 209
Webbe, William 197
Wedel, Lupold von 194, 195, 196, 197
Weights and measures 35
West Indies 145, 146
Westminster 15, 24, 25, 52, 170, 172, 176, 217
Westminster Abbey 24-5, 57, 67, 85, 101, 177, 222, 224
Westminster Hall 120, 224
Westminster, Palace of 25, 43, 44, 224
Wherries 198-9
Whetstone, George 170
White, Sir Thomas 124, 125, 154-5
Whitebakers' Company 36
Whitechapel 15, 198, 214
White Friars 84, 101, 213
Whitefriars 106, 172
Whitehall Palace 207, 217, 224
Whittington, Richard 65, 67
Wilson, Dr Thomas 114
Winchelsea 147
Winchester 115
Wiresellers' Company 32, 34
Witt, Johannes de 204
Wolgast 206
Wolsey, Thomas 56, 69-70, 71-2, 75, 76, 85, 99, 108
Women, in society 27-8, 30, 65, 67, 92, 153, 160, 173, 174, 190, 191, 194, 200, 206
Wood St 42, 113
Wood, Thomas 17, 90
Worcester 149
Worcester Inn 109
Worde, Wynkyn de 52
Worms 96
Wriothesley, Charles 94, 130
Wyatt, Sir Thomas 125
Wycliffe, John 94

Yonge, John 57
York 11, 49, 149, 151
York Place 108, 224
York, Cicely, Duchess of 87

Zante 52, 156